The New Park
Fawn Grove Railroad:
Interchanging with
the Stewartstown Railroad

A Pictorial History

Robert L. Williams

with Scott L. Mingus

Publisher

SCOTT MINGUS ENTERPRISES
1383 Sterling Drive
York, PA 17404
e-mail: scottmingus@yahoo.com

Printed by Amazon Kindle Direct Publishing

ISBN: 9798345011799

First Edition

PRINTED AND BOUND IN THE UNITED STATES OF AMERICA

Front cover: Railroad stations at Fawn Grove and Stewartstown, Pennsylvania. (Robert L. Williams Collection)

Title page and back cover: One of the steam locomotives of the New Park & Fawn Grove Railroad. (Courtesy of the Stewartstown Area Historical Society. This and the other several dozen images in this book from that organization's extensive collection of artifacts, documents, and photographs are used with written permission under license.)

This book is dedicated to all the farmers, businessmen, and community leaders for their vision, insight, and wisdom to construct the New Park & Fawn Grove Railroad / Stewartstown Railroad without any outside assistance.

Special Thanks:

Douglas Winemiller, president of the Stewartstown Area Historical Society (www.stewhist.org)

Kurt Bell
Eric J. Bickleman
Neal DeVoe
Greg Halpin
Jody Anderson Leighty
Donald Linebaugh
James E. McClure
Russell Mellinger, Sr.
Ken Myers
Dale Orwig
Martin K. Van Horn
William Ward

We also acknowledge the efforts of Doug Winemiller, Eric Bickleman, and archivist Kurt Bell to save the original records of the Stewartstown Railroad at the depot building in 2010. Those records were indispensable for this book.

FOREWORD

The New Park & Fawn Grove Railroad was a 9.2-mile short line in southern Pennsylvania just north of the Mason-Dixon Line that separated the commonwealth from Maryland. It typifies the brief life-cycle of so many small regional railroads that existed near the turn of the 20th century.

For generations, the farmers and businessmen of southern York County had used freight wagons to haul their produce and goods from their places of origin to the markets in nearby villages and towns. As railroads became more widely available and tracks began to reach these rather remote locations, freight cars offered a way to move higher quantities in a faster manner. Investors were often the same people who would most benefit from the development of the railroad infrastructure.

In 1905-1906, many farmers and businessmen and prominent women of the region pledged money through a subscription process to finance the construction of the New Park & Fawn Grove Railroad to connect to the existing 7.4-mile Stewartstown Railroad (the latter had started operations in 1885 with local funding). The investors did not rely on outside capital or technical assistance but rather pooled their resources to turn their collective vision into a reality.

The need for these short-haul regional railroads began to wane in the 1920s and '30s as gasoline-powered trucks became more prevalent. They offered lower prices, more flexibility in delivery options with the road networks, and more frequent service. The officials of the Stewartstown Railroad, which by then owned and controlled the New Park & Fawn Grove Railroad Company, finally decided to shut down the latter's operations in 1936 and sell or repurpose the assets.

With the passage of nine decades since the NP&FG RR ceased operations, few living York Countians have any memory of seeing that once bustling line in operation. All that is left to modern railfans are the company's records (many of which are in the collection of the Stewartstown Area Historical Society), scattered photographs and postcards, and a few physical reminders such as abandoned or reused buildings and structures. The Stewartstown Railroad continues as a popular excursion enterprise with regularly scheduled themed train rides for the public to enjoy.

In this book, railroad collector and frequent author Robert L. Williams has assembled many of the extant records and images. The Lutherville, Maryland, resident worked closely with the Stewartstown Area Historical Society and local railroad experts to present this general history of the New Park & Fawn Grove Railroad and the adjoining larger Stewartstown Railroad. He and I have collaborated on a few previous railroad books, so when he asked me to publish this work, knowing of my interest in the 19th-century railroads of York County, I was happy to oblige.

All information presented herein was taken or derived from local primary sources and period newspaper accounts that we believe to be accurate. The photographs are used with the written permission of the owners or are from author Robert L. Williams' personal collection. He drew the track plans and site plans from existing railroad documents.

Sit back, peruse the text and photos, and allow your mind to wander back to the heyday of the small-town railroads of America, an era when the tracks spurred the growth of industry, provided new or rejuvenated outlets for agricultural products, connected distant families and friends, widened business travel opportunities, and inspired vacation and recreational travel.

We sincerely thank you for purchasing this book and hope you enjoy this nostalgic trip.

Scott L. Mingus, Manchester Township, York County, Pa.

TABLE OF CONTENTS

The New Park & Fawn Grove Railroad

The Stewartstown Railroad

Employees wore many hats on the Stewartstown Railroad. Charles W. Heaton, normally an engineer, was the acting conductor for the train on July 3, 1935. He punched and stamped this one-way passenger ticket on that day. The conductor's punch mark invalidated the ticket and showed who collected it.
(Robert L. Williams photograph; ticket is in the collection of Scott Mingus)

THE NEW PARK AND FAWN GROVE RAILROAD

CHRONOLOGICAL HISTORY 1905 TO 1936

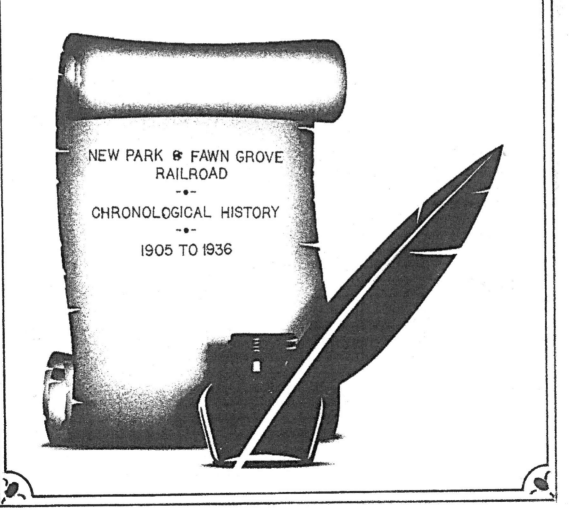

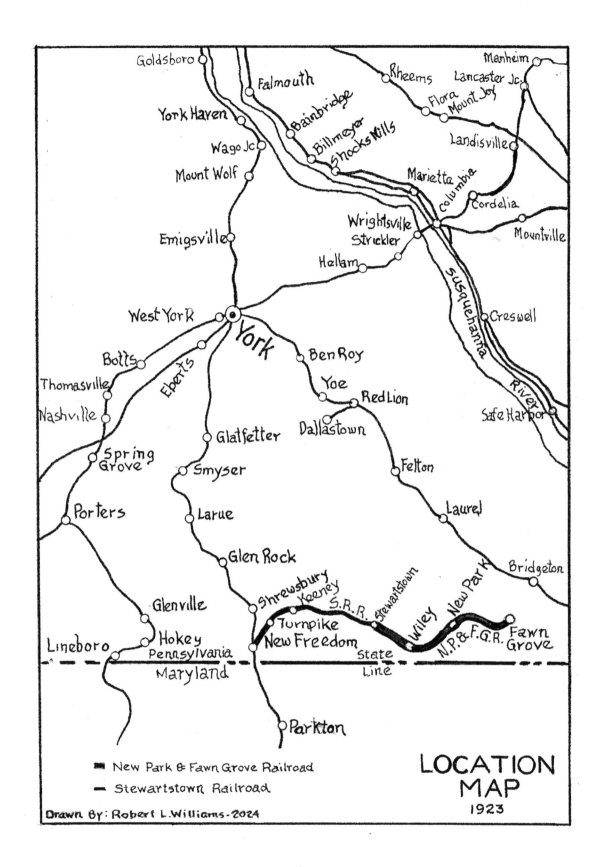

LOCATION
MAP
1923

■■ New Park & Fawn Grove Railroad
— Stewartstown Railroad

Drawn By: Robert L. Williams - 2024

JOHN H. ANDERSON

The first elected president of the New Park & Fawn Grove Railroad

1905–1915

(Photograph from the *Baltimore Sun*, August 6, 1906)

NEW PARK & FAWN GROVE RAILROAD

Chronological History
1905 to 1936

Apr. 4, 1868	The New Park & Fawn Grove Railroad made this statement in its 1913 Report to the Interstate Commerce Commission located in Washington, D.C., after being asked the following question: 110.) Under the laws of what Government, State, or Territory was the respondent organized? "State of Pennsylvania, Act of April 4, 1868 and its supplements. (I.C.C.)
Jan. 19, 1905	An organizational meeting was held at the school house in New Park. J. C. Wiley was elected president and J. A. Gailey, secretary. The president was directed to form a committee composing of five residents from New Park and five from Fawn Grove who would meet with the officials of the Stewartstown Railroad at Stewartstown on Saturday, January 21. The purpose was to encourage and request that the Stewartstown Railroad extend its charter and expand to Fawn Grove. The 57 people in attendance were unanimous in their support for the proposed railroad. (D.M.N.)
Jan. 27, 1905	Prospects are bright for the extension of the railroad from Stewartstown to New Park, a distance of 6 miles, may be run as far as Fawn Grove. (A&I)
Jan. 31,1905	Committee members met at New Park and reported that they were not encouraged but that Stewartstown Railroad officials were considering their request. Many offers were made for free right-of-way. (D.M.N.)
Feb. 01, 1905	Stock in the New Park & Fawn Grove Railroad is being offered by subscription. (D.M.N.)
Feb. 09, 1905	Committee report on the February 4 meeting with Stewartstown Railroad officials: it was decided to withdraw the request to Stewartstown to construct and operate the line. Instead, the New Park & Fawn Grove Railroad will construct and maintain the line asking that Stewartstown Railroad operate it. The nine miles are expected to cost about $50,000. (D.M.N.)
Feb. 1905	A list of land owners who made available their land for the construction of the New Park & Fawn Grove Railroad.

1.) J. C. Leib & Co. – 40 ft. (mill)	23.) Maurice Davis – 40 ft.
2.) Miss Emma Fulton – 40 ft.	24.) John H. Anderson – 40 ft.
3.) Wm. G. Trout – 40 ft.	25.) John W. Marsteller – 40 ft.

4.) J. Benson Gable – 40 ft.

5.) Miss J. Gable, E. A. Gable,
   and Mrs. Thoburn – 40 ft.

6.) Tompkins – 40 ft.

7.) Jos. W. Anderson – 40 ft.

8.) Jos. W. Anderson – 40 ft

9.) Mrs. Margaret Hammon – 40 ft.

10.) J. Mitchell Jordan – 40 ft.

11.) Lida Ebaugh – 40 ft.

12.) Aquilla M. Bartol – 40 ft.

13.) J. Clark Strawbridge – 40 ft.

14.) John S. Gemmill – 40 ft.

15.) Jacob Yost – 40 ft.

16.) John S. Gemmill – 40 ft.

17.) John H. Beard – 40 ft.

18.) Hannah B. Wiley – 40 ft.

19.) Daniel Harman – 40 ft.

20.) John E. Stansbury – 40 ft.

21.) Strawbridge Bros. – 40 ft.

22.) John B. Jenkins – 40 ft.

26.) Jos. A. Gailey – 40 ft.

27.) John H. Anderson – 40 ft.

28.) Samuel Harman – 40 ft.

29.) Doris A. Shirley – 40 ft.

30.) John H. Anderson – 40 ft.

31.) W. C. & Rachel Van Hart – 40 ft.

32.) Chas. B. Bartol – 40 ft.

33.) R. C. Liggit – 40 ft.

34.) I. T. Hostler – 40 ft.

35.) George M. Kisiner – 40 ft.

36.) E. S. Irwin & sister – 40 ft.

37.) Daniel A. McElwain – 40 ft.

38.) J. A. Merriman – 40 ft.

39.) Wm. L. Duncan – 40 ft.

40.) Henry T. Brown – 40 ft.

41.) Wm. L. Duncan – 40 ft.

42.) Mary A. Almoney – 40 ft.

43.) Wm. L. Duncan – 40 ft.

44.) Henry T. Brown – 40 ft.

Feb. 23, 1905	Permanent officers were elected at the meeting for the New Park & Fawn Grove Railroad:

President – John H. Anderson

Directors – H. S. Merryman. B. F. Morris, W. R. Webb, H. C. McElvain, A. W. Webb, N. A. Manifold, M. E. Smith, J. Wiley Norris, R. S. McDonald, Maurice Davis, S. G. Lowe, R. W. Anderson, J. C. Wiley, Joseph W. Anderson, M. W. Bahn, A. M. Strawbridge, and J. A. Gailey. (MMN)

Feb. 25, 1905   The building of a railroad from Stewartstown to Fawn Grove, nine miles assured. The line will be along the Mason-Dixon Line and will be partly in Maryland and partly in Pennsylvania. There will be no bridges to build and only a few small culverts. The Stewartstown Railroad, with which it will connect over whose line it will reach the Northern Central at New Freedom, is interested in the project, and it is thought that the line will be in operation during the coming summer. (DA)

Mar. 4, 1905   Going Ahead with the New Railroad – A letter from York dated February 24, says: "Merchants and farmers of Fawn Township met in Stewartstown last night and organized a company to build a railroad from Fawn to Stewartstown as an extension of the Stewartstown and New Freedom

Railroad. About $20,000 was subscribed toward the project. The proposed line will be called the New Park & Fawn Grove Railroad. It will be nine miles long and it will be operated by the Stewartstown Railroad Company. The company organized to build the railroad will be capitalized at $90,000.00." (U)

Mar. 07, 1905	MORE MONEY SUBSCRIBED – Enthusiastic Meeting Held by Railroad Projectors at Norrisville

Another enthusiastic meeting of the promoters of the New Park & Fawn Grove Railroad was held at Norrisville Md., just across the line yesterday. J.W. Strawbridge of Norrisville was chairman. About one hundred prominent citizens were present and took part in the meeting. The subscription was run up to $32,000, with immediate prospects of about $5,000 more. No more public meetings will be held for some time, but the committee will be active in getting the monied people to subscribe. (YD)

Mar. 20, 1905	Meeting attendees reported that 771 shares worth $38,550 had been subscribed. No construction was to be undertaken until the full $50,000 has been subscribed. (D.M.N.)
Mar. 30, 1905	NEW RAILROAD WORK – New Survey for New Park & Fawn Grove Railroad Will Be Next Week Under Direction of Sheriff Manifold.

The New Park & Fawn Grove extension of the Stewartstown Railroad will be built this summer. The committees in charge of the collection of the funds have secured the $40,000 that was required to start the work. A new survey will be started next week under the supervision of Sheriff Samuel Manifold. It is planned to have the road in operation in time to transport the crops out of that section of the road this coming fall. Contracts for the road bed will not be made until $50,000 has been raised.

The subscriptions now become binding on the subscribers. Fifteen dollars per share will be payable on demand and $5 per month per share until the subscriptions are all paid. (YD)

Apr. 15, 1905	The Subscription Committee reported that 831 shares or $41,550 have been sold. H. S. Merryman will look into the matter of a charter. (D.M.N.)
Apr. 26, 1905	APPLIED FOR CHARTER – Papers Forwarded by New Railroad Company

The application for the charter for the New Park & Fawn Grove Railroad was forwarded to the governor [Samuel W. Pennypacker] yesterday, and the charter is expected to be granted within the next few days. As soon as this is accomplished, right of way will be secured and this will be followed by actual work on the building of the new railroad. The projectors are still meeting with encouragement in the way of subscriptions to the stock. (YD)

May 1905	The New Park & Fawn Grove Railroad acquired Locomotive No. 1, a D-8a type, 4-4-0 (former PRR No.4017 constructed in 1888). (F.R. of R.R.)
May 11, 1905	The New Park & Fawn Grove Railroad was incorporated under the laws of Pennsylvania. Principal office located in New Park. (MMN) (I.C.C.)
May 12, 1905	The prospects for building the New Park & Fawn Grove Railroad are very bright. The line will run from Stewartstown to Fawn Grove, a distance of nine miles. There is already $43,000 of the necessary $60,000 subscribed, and the work will be commenced as soon as the subscription reaches $50,000. Hopes are entertained that sometime in the near future the line can be continued to Delta, which would require the building of six more miles of track. The section of Harford and York counties is prosperous, but only the railroad can fully develop its many resources. The citizens are to be commended for their liberal contributions and deserve every necessary encouragement to help complete the line. (AI)
July 1, 1905	New Line to be finished by Christmas
	If all goes well with the construction of the New Park & Fawn Grove Railroad, the people of that section will enjoy a ride over the new road no later than next Christmas day. Most of the right-of-way has been secured, and the company expects to have little trouble with the work. Several of the farmers who have land along the proposed route are holding out for big prices, but the company expects to adjust these matters satisfactorily by the time the work of construction begins. The directors of the company will hold their next meeting on Wednesday, July 5, when they will be ready to receive the bids for construction. (U)
Jul. 06, 1905	CONTRACT AWARDED
Jul. 14, 1905	REFUSED RIGHT OF WAY
	Condemnation Proceedings Will Be Instituted by the New Park & Fawn Grove Railroad Company
	Papers are being prepared for condemnation proceedings which will be instituted against five property owners who have refused to give the New Park & Fawn Grove Railroad Company the right of way over their land. These are Mrs. Margaret Hammond, 850 feet, J. Mitchell Jordan, 3010 feet: Mrs. Lydia Ebaugh, 716 6/10 feet: Jacob Yost, 534 feet, and Daniel

McElwain, 2488 feet, making a total of 7604 feet, or about a mile and half.

Yesterday Contractor John H. Dobbling commenced the work of grading the New Park & Fawn Grove Railroad and he expected to have it completed by November 20. Mr. Dobbling has a force of nearly 100 men at work. Sixteen teams are in use and the contractor intends to permit some of the farmers to assist with their teams and do the grading at the least difficult places. The contractor camp is pitched near Stewartstown, where he has equipment for the comfort of his men and quarters for his horses and mules. Nearly all of the workmen are negroes. (YD)

Aug 05, 1905   The extension in the near future of the Stewartstown branch of the Northern Central Railroad to Fawn Grove seems to be assured. This will be distinctively a farmer's railroad as they will furnish the bulk of the necessary capital and will tap what is generally recognized as one of the finest farming sections in the East. The Stewartstown branch has contracted to operate the road at a cost which will be based on their own experience will be less than $1,000 per mile. The early sequel to this road will be its further extension of 4 to 5 miles to the Maryland & Pennsylvania Railroad at Pylesville, thus giving a valuable outlet for our slate and a cheaper inlet for our coal. (A&I)

Aug. 11, 1905   It is said that a movement is on foot to purchase the Stewartstown Railroad and that the purpose of the prospective buyers is to extend the line by the way of the New Park & Fawn Grove Railroad across the Susquehanna to Oxford [in Chester County, Pa.]. (A&I)

Aug. 12, 1905   Mr. William Trout, who lately purchased a large farm near Stewartstown, has let the contract for the building of a half-mile track thereon. He proposes to engage in the breeding of light harness horses. The New Park & Fawn Grove Railroad, now being built, passes through Mr. Trout's farm. (U)

Aug. 15, 1905   LANDOWNER REFUSES CONSENT

Samuel McElvane is said to be the only landowner who now refuses right of way for the New Park & Fawn Grove Railroad, all the others having come to terms with the managers of the enterprise. It is probable that the condemnation proceedings will be directed against Mr. McElvane, as intended for some time. Mr. McElvane owns a strip of land that lies along the proposed route a distance of about half a mile. (YD)

Sept. 01, 1905   The Norrisville Farmer's Club held its annual picnic on Thursday of last week. The meeting was in conjunction with the directors of the New Park

& Fawn Grove Railroad, and speeches were made, both on farming and railroading, the two enterprises in this section being identical. When this road is completed, it will bear the unique distinction of being financed entirely by the rural interests through the vicinity that it passes. (A&I)

Nov. 07, 1905   SCARCITY OF LABORERS – Delay in Work on New Park & Fawn Railroad

Because of the scarcity of laborers, work on the grading and construction of the New Park & Fawn Grove Railroad in the lower end of the county is not progressing as rapidly as desired by John Dobbling, contractor, Sheriff S. M. Manifold, engineer, and the directors of the company having the improvements made. Although an effort has been made to have the road in operation shortly after Thanksgiving it is now a certainty that it will be after the first of the year before it will be ready for use.

The grading of the roadbed has been completed as far as Strawbridge's store, near the Center Presbyterian Church, leaving about three and one half to be done yet. But little rock has been encountered so far and not much is expected to be struck the rest of the route. The remainder of the grading will be much lighter work than what has already been done and it is now considered that the improvements can be finished at a figure which may be a trifling less than what was originally estimated.

Several slight changes have been made in the original plans of the road, as some additional concessions have been made by property owners through whose lands the road will be built, so that as many curves and road crossings as possible can be eliminated.

The only bridges on the road have been erected by the York Bridge Company. The one, a 60-foot span, has been built at an overhead crossing on the farm of John Manifold. The other, which is a ten-foot structure, has been constructed as a guard for the passage of cattle on the farm of Mrs. Hannah B. Wiley.

About one mile of rails has already been laid. This portion of the improvements, it is said, will consume a comparatively brief period for its completion. It is the purpose of the directors of the company to place the road in operation as soon as it is built. (TYD)

Nov. 24, 1905   Complaints are being made of a large number of thefts operating along the line of the New Park & Fawn Grove Railroad; farmers are missing all kinds of edibles, and Mr. J. A. Gailey, a merchant of New Park, recently had 70 pounds of butter stolen. (AI)

Nov. 25, 1905   Railroad Offices Elected – The directors of the New Park & Fawn Grove Railroad have elected the following officers: General Manager – Frank B.

Morris, Superintendent – John C. Wiley, and Auditor – Joseph A. Gailey. About 4 miles of roadway have been completed and tracks have been laid for one mile and a half. This road is being built almost entirely with local capital, it being the property of the farmers whose lands it will benefit. (AI)

Dec. 04, 1905

RAILROAD TO BE EXTENDED – New Park & Fawn Grove Line to be extended on to Delta

There is a strong probability that as soon as the New Park & Fawn Grove Railroad is completed and placed in operation an extension of the road will be made from New Park to Delta, a distance of about seven miles, giving railroad connections in that potato-growing belt of the lower end of the county between New Freedom and Delta.

It is stated with some authority that the road, which would be operated in a manner similar to that of the New Park & Fawn Grove, will entail a cost of about $60,000, which capitalists say would be a good investment, especially for the farmers of that section.

Engineers, who have gone over the prospective route, say that there would be no streams to cross, thereby causing no bridges to be built. It is also said that the route could be laid out as to necessitate but few large cuts, making the grading cost a sum that would be comparatively small. The project is considered so feasible that an attempt will be made to have it carried to a successful culmination.

The work on the New Park & Fawn Grove Road is progressing slowly. About 2 and a half miles of track is laid, while the grading is completed to the Strawbridge property, about a mile from New Park. (YD)

Jan. 5, 1906

The New Park & Fawn Grove branch of the Stewartstown Railroad is rapidly progressing, every effort having been made to expedite track lying before winter closes in. Seven of the nine miles have already been graded, and the track has been laid for nearly three miles. The residents along the route are greatly interested in the benefits the road is expected to bring. (AI)

Jan. 05, 1906

The Stewartstown Railroad gave a banquet for the New Park & Fawn Grove Railroad officers and employees at the Leader House on Monday afternoon. It was a turkey dinner followed by a ride over the 3-mile portion of the New Park & Fawn Grove Railroad that has been completed. Grading has nearly been completed to New Park. (SN)

Feb. 1906

Freight service operations began on the New Park & Fawn Grove Railroad between Fawn Grove and Stewartstown. (D.M.N.)

Feb. 2, 1906 — The stockholders of the New Park & Fawn Grove Railroad Company have re-elected the old directors for the ensuing year. The stockholders were taken for a ride over the road to New Park; general satisfaction was expressed by everyone. (A&I)

Feb. 21, 1906 — REGULAR TRAINS ON NEW PARK-FAWN GROVE ROAD START RUNNING TODAY — YORK COUNTY NEW RAILROAD THROUGH A PROSPEROUS WHEAT BELT WILL BE OFFICIALLY OPENED THIS MORNING — OFFICIALS OF CONNECTING ROADS ADJUSTING "RAILROAD RATES"

Beginning this morning, a regular train service will be started on the New Park & Fawn Grove Railroad from Stewartstown to New Park. The service will be maintained every other day for the next two weeks, or until complete arrangements can be made with the management of the Stewartstown and Northern Central railroads over tariffs when a daily service will be put on.

The railroad has been completed into New Park and the roadbed has been ballasted to that place so that trains can run. The first shipment, according to a clerk at Gailey's store, will be of wheat, of which there is a great deal in that community.

The tariff committees of the New Park & Fawn Grove Railroad and the Stewartstown Railroad after discussing tariffs for the line for two weeks will meet today at Stewartstown and finally settle the question of rates to be charged by both roads. As soon as the tariffs are fixed between the two local roads, a committee representing the two roads will meet the tariff authorities of the Northern Central Railroad. As those rates are about agreed upon, it will be small, it is said.

The New Park & Fawn Grove Railroad was built entirely by local capital and was pushed to completion by the leading men of Fawn Township and Hopewell, and prominent citizens across the line in Maryland. The road opens up a great country.

The train service which will be put on this morning will mean one train a day, leaving Stewartstown at 9:30 in the morning and arriving at New Park about 10 o'clock. (G)

Feb. 22, 1906 — MUCH CEREMONY ATTENDED OPENING OF NEW RAILROAD

The first regular train over the New Park & Fawn Grove Railroad in accordance with the outline as printed in the Gazette yesterday was run from Stewartstown to New Park yesterday. The train consisted of two loaded cars of lumber, two empty cars for wheat, and one empty box car in which some of the officials rode over the road.

The train on arriving at New Park was greeted by the populace, the schools were adjourned and everybody gave three cheers for the success of the venture.

President Anderson said last evening that no passenger coach would be used for ten or fifteen days or until the "Y" switch could be laid at New Park. After that time there will be one passenger train a day until the line is completed to Fawn Grove when a splendid service will be put on, allowing the public to get in and out of Fawn Grove on the same day.

Sheriff S. M. Manifold, President Anderson, and other officials of the road made the maiden trip yesterday. (DA)

Feb. 23, 1906	On Wednesday this week, freight service commenced on the New Park & Fawn Grove Railroad between Stewartstown and New Park. Freight trains will be operated every other day by the Stewartstown Railroad. (SN)
Feb. 25, 1906	It appears to be practically settled that the electric railway between Stewartstown and Fawn Grove will be built before the end of the present year. It will extend along the Mason-Dixon Line in Pennsylvania and partly in Maryland and will traverse a rich agricultural section. The length of the road will be 9 miles. The connection will be made with the Northern Central at New Freedom utilizing the Stewartstown Railroad. (U)
Apr. 13, 1906	It is said that moment is on foot to purchase the Stewartstown Railroad and that the purpose of the prospective buyers is to extend the line by way of the New Park & Fawn Grove Railroad, across the Susquehanna River to Oxford. (A&I)
Apr. 27, 1906	Track reaches Fawn Grove. (D.M.N.)
Apr. 30, 1906	Mr. [John H.] Dobbling, the contractor for the New Park & Fawn Grove Railroad, is rushing the grading toward completion at Fawn Grove. By April 27 grade had reached the borough line and would be completed within another month. Everyone is well pleased with the service being provided over their railroad at New Park and shipments of phosphate have arrived already. (SN)
May 11, 1906	A traffic agreement contract between the New Park & Fawn Grove Railroad and the Stewartstown Railroad companies has been agreed upon. (SN)
June 1, 1906	The grading of the New Park & Fawn Grove Railroad was completed from Stewartstown to Fawn Grove. (F.R. of R.R.)
June 8, 1906	Grading on the New Park & Fawn Grove Railroad has been completed; however, a shortage of iron spikes has delayed track laying. (SN)

June 22, 1906	It is reported that an "extensive" engine house will be built at Fawn Grove. A warehouse is already under construction, as is a cannery. (SN)
July 05, 1906	New Park & Fawn Grove Railroad's first train schedule was published in the *Stewartstown News*. (SN). See Appendix No.4
	The Stewartstown Railroad Company will conduct the operations of the New Park & Fawn Grove Railroad. The crew will consist of the following: A. T. Cox – engineer, Smith Jones – fireman, Ollie Morris – conductor, and George Channell – brakeman. (SN)
	THE GRAND OPENING WILL BE HELD AT FAWN GROVE ON THURSDAY, AUGUST 9.
	An immense crowd is expected and extra trains will operate leaving Stewartstown at 8:00 a.m., 9:47, 12:15 p.m., 4:30, and 6:30. Returning trains will leave Fawn Grove at 7:05 a.m., 9:00, 11:20, 3:35 p.m., and 5:40. The round-trip fare will be 25 cents. (SN)
July 24, 1906	The New Park & Fawn Grove Railroad carried nearly 500 passengers to Fawn Grove Saturday to attend the Sunday school picnic held by the Methodist Protestant Sunday school. (YD)
July 28, 1906	**THE FORMAL OPENING** – The formal opening of the New Park & Fawn Grove Railroad will take place on Thursday, August 9, when an elaborate celebration will be held at New Park. Several well-known gentlemen will make addresses. This new line will open up a rich farming section, and already the people are beginning to appreciate its benefits. (U)
Aug. 09, 1906	**THE NEW PARK & FAWN GROVE RAILROAD GRAND OPENING** – See Appendix No. 5 (AI)
Aug. 10, 1906	PICNIC AT FAWN GROVE TO CELEBRATE OPENING OF RAILROAD
	Countryside Learns How Industry Follows Railroad Line — Many Prominent Speakers There.
	The opening of the railroad to Fawn Grove from Stewartstown and other points was celebrated yesterday at Fawn Grove. Four thousand people attended. Extra trains were running from New Freedom to Fawn Grove and were all crowded.
	Mr. John H. Anderson called the meeting to order and the officers for the day included:

President – John C. Wiley
Secretary – Joseph C. Gailey
Vice President – H. W. Kapp

Harry Hughes, S. O. Malin, Samuel Smith, W. H. McCall, J. Wiley Norris, John B. Gemmill, C. W. Shaw, Chas. A. Hawkins, Thomas McKenzie, Samuel Irvin, Clark Liggit, S. A. Williams.

Mr. Milton E. Smith, of Norrisville, delivered the address of welcome. Rev. Silas B. Tredway, of Fawn Grove, opened the exercise with prayer. (BS)

Nov. 11, 1906	Stewartstown Railroad authorized the sale of Engine No.3 to the New Park & Fawn Grove Railroad (their No.1). (SRDMN)
Dec. 22, 1906	J. A. Gailey is erecting a passenger and freight station at Fawn Grove for the New Park & Fawn Grove Railroad Company. The building will be a three-story frame structure.
	The New Park & Fawn Grove Railroad has purchased a locomotive and an interest in a passenger coach so that hereafter its patrons will not have to change cars en route from New Freedom to New Park and Fawn Grove. The railroad is prosperous and is doing a big business. (YD)
Dec. 28, 1906	The New Park & Fawn Grove Railroad paid J. H. Kisiner five dollars for working on the construction of the water tank in Fawn Grove. (F.R. of R.R.)
1906	LIST OF EMPLOYEES WHO WORKED FOR THE NEW PARK & FAWN GROVE RAILROAD IN 1906:

TRACK LAYING

William A. Whitekettle – Foreman	H. N. Dirk – Foreman
Charles Jones	J. A. Breneman
R. A. Miller	J. C. Wiley
E. Wise	

LABORERS

W. C. Channell	W. J. Wise
C. C. Kinard	Lewis Harman
W. A. Scott	Frank Trout
Wm. E. Almoney	A. Neal
J. E. Mayes	R. B. Mathews
H. M. Anderson	F. P. Strawberry
H. T. McCallister	G. P. Day
E. H. Jones	J. W. Thompkins
E. A. Wayne	C. W. Alloways
George T. Mathews	Robert Myers

(R.R.R.)

1907	Train Crew: J. Smith Jones – Engineer, George Channell – Fireman, A. H. Morris – Conductor and J. H. Allen – Brakeman. (F.R. of R.R.)
Jan. 11, 1907	New Park & Fawn Grove Railroad paid for services provided by the following individuals for December 1906:

J. Smith Jones – Locomotive engineer	$50.00
George Channell – Track foreman	$34.50
Arlington Morris – Conductor	$32.50
J. H. Allen – Brakeman	$30.70
H. T. Brown – Agent at Fawn Grove	$10.00
J. A. Gailey – Agent at New Park	$10.00
Total:	$167.50 (F.R. of R.R.)

Feb. 01, 1907	The annual meeting of the New Park & Fawn Grove Railroad was held. The Committee on Construction reported that cost was kept so low because not one cent was spent on graft or corruption. It was reported that outside capitalists were looking at the New Park & Fawn Grove Railroad and the Stewartstown Railroad with "longing eyes" but that leading stockholders proposed to keep the railroad in local hands. A proposed extension of the line from Fawn Grove to Delta was not taken up since it is up to the residents of that area to carry that project on. (SN)
Feb. 07, 1907	The New Park & Fawn Grove Railroad paid J. H. Kisiner nineteen dollars and eleven cents for the iron pipes and fittings for the pumping station and water tank at Fawn Grove. (F.R. of R.R.)
Mar. 21, 1907	The New Park & Fawn Grove Railroad paid W. T. Strawbridge fifteen cents an hour for the construction of the water tank at Fawn Grove. For the month of February, Mr. Strawbridge worked 147 hours totaling $22.05. (F.R. of R.R.)
Mar. 21, 1907	New Park & Fawn Grove Railroad paid for services rendered by the following individuals: (F.R. of R.R.)

Dr. Vallie Hawkins – supplied lumber for engine house	$32.52
Peerless Slate Co. – slate for engine house, 20 sq. ft.	$78.00
Richard Roberts & Son – smoke stack for engine house	$30.00
	$140.00

Mar. 24, 1907	New Park & Fawn Grove Railroad paid O. Hansberger $4 for working on the construction of the engine house. (F.R. of R.R.)
Apr. 10, 1907	New Park & Fawn Grove Railroad paid H. C. McElwain and John Kisiner $23.43 each for the construction of the engine house. (F.R. of R.R.)
Apr. 10, 1907	New Park & Fawn Grove Railroad paid George W. Channell, Fireman,

$1.35 a day for 26 days totaling $35.10. (F.R. of R.R.)

May 1, 1907   Report on the exact number of statute miles between stations on the New Park & Fawn Grove Railroad:

Station	Mile Post	
Stewartstown	Mile Post 0	0+00
Manifold	Mile Post 0.90	47+52
Anderson	Mile Post 1.7	89+76
Maple Hill	Mile Post 2.3	121+44
Gimmel	Mile Post 3.0	158+40
Wiley	Mile Post 4.0	211+20
Strawbridge	Mile Post 4.9	258+72
New Park	Mile Post 6.0	316+80
Kisiner	Mile Post 8.0	422+40
Fawn Grove	Mile Post 9.1	480+10 (E.N. of R.R.)

Oct. 30, 1907   New Park & Fawn Grove Railroad rents Coach Car No. 2883 from the Pennsylvania Railroad for two business days (Aug. 14 and Aug. 15) for $14.38. (F.R. of R.R.)

Apr. 3, 1908   New Park & Fawn Grove Railroad paid J. T. M. Smith seventy cents for a Fire Insurance Assessment. (F.R. of R.R.)

Apr. 10, 1908 $40,000 in 4½ percent bonds have been sold to cover the cost of construction of the New Park & Fawn Grove Railroad. Stock sold amounted to $49,050. There were not enough bonds available to satisfy the demand for them. (SN)

Apr. 12, 1908   New Park & Fawn Grove Railroad paid the Fawn Grove Lumber Company $57.10 for the lumber used in the construction of the sand house, shop, battery house, and the piers for the pumping station at the water tank. (F.R. of R.R.)

Apr. 13, 1908   New Park & Fawn Grove Railroad paid B. F. Morris S170 for a plot of ground in Fawn Grove. (F.R. of R.R.)

Apr. 12, 1908   New Park & Fawn Grove Railroad paid Fred Pepo $17.50 for seven days of masonry work on the ash pit at Fawn Grove. (F.R. of R.R.)

Oct. 2, 1908 $40,000 BOND ISSUED

Mortgage on the New Park & Fawn Grove Railroad Recorded

A mortgage on the New Park and Fawn Grove Railroad was executed yesterday and entered for record in the office of Recorder [Daniel] Conrad to secure an issue of $40,000 bonds, drawing four-and-a-half percent interest, payable semi-annually. The mortgage is held by the Guardian Trust Company, trustee. The purpose of the bond issue is to take up the floating indebtedness of the company.

The New Park & Fawn Grove Railroad is in a flourishing condition and has spent much money on the improvement of the roadbed. The road is more than nine miles long. (YD)

Mar. 04, 1909	20 inches of snow closed the Stewartstown Railroad all day; however, several gangs of snow shovelers were able to open the line the next day. The New Park & Fawn Grove Railroad was closed until Saturday and it took all available men to dig out cuts on that line. (SN)
Apr. 14, 1909	SURVEY FOR NEW RAILROAD
	City Engineer [Robert B.] McKinnon has a party of surveyors at work surveying the extension of the New Park & Fawn Grove Railroad from Fawn Grove to Delta, seven miles. In the party are Messrs. Hanze, Downs, and Sechrist, from this city, and Messrs. John Anderson, president of the New Park & Fawn Grove Railroad; J. A. Gailey, of Fawn Grove, and W. Scott Whiteford, of Delta, who are interested in the project. The route follows a beautiful ridge from Fawn Grove to Delta, and it said the grade will be quite easy and that no bridges will be required. (G)
May 12, 1909	New Park & Fawn Grove Railroad paid Edison Manifold $10 for his duties as the station agent at Fawn Grove. (F.R. of R.R.)
May 12, 1909	New Park & Fawn Grove Railroad paid Joseph Williams, engineer, a salary of $50 for April. (F.R. of R.R.)
July 6, 1909	Milton W. Bahn, general manager of the Stewartstown and New Park & Fawn Grove Railroad, died here tonight, age 70 years. He was one of York County's most influential citizens being affiliated with all movements and institutions which tended to make Southern York County one of the most prosperous farming districts in the state. By assisting in the building of the Stewartstown Railroad, Mr. Bahn aided in opening up the richest farming district. Mr. Bahn served for several years as chief burgess and postmaster of New Freedom. (U)
Aug. 25, 1909	Fifteen carloads of hay, cabbage, and potatoes were shipped over the New Park & Fawn Grove Railroad last Saturday. (YD)
Sept. 8, 1909	New Park and Fawn Railroad installed a new switch at Wiley Station for Mr. Raymond G. Baird. (E.N. of R.R.) *Editor's note*: The hamlet of Wiley is at the intersection of Draco and Marstellar roads just north of the Mason-Dixon Line.

1910   LIST OF EMPLOYEES THAT WORK FOR THE NEW PARK & FAWN GROVE
         RAIL FROM 1906 TO 1910:

STATION AGENTS

J. O. Fitzpatrick – Fawn Grove   W. E. Wiley – Wiley
Joseph A. Gailey – New Park   Wm. E. Manifold – Fawn Grove
H. T. Brown – Fawn Grove

STATION ATTENDANTS

Wm. B. Hawkins – Fawn Grove   Joe Glessic – Stewartstown
John S. Gemmill – Fawn Grove

MAIL MESSENGERS

Wm. B. Hawkins – Fawn Grove   Joe Glessic – Stewartstown
John S. Gemmill – Fawn Grove (hauling mail)
Harry R. Brooks – Fawn Grove

ENGINEERS

Jasper Williams   J. Smith Jones
George Channell – Extra Engineer

CONDUCTORS

Arlington H. "Ollie" Morris

TRAINMEN

J. C. Wiley   John Barton
John T. Shanberger

FIREMEN

Samuel C. Pomraning   John T. Shanberger
John Barton   George Channell

BRAKEMEN

Frank McLain   John Barton
William Keppler   John T. Shanberger
Samuel C. Pomraning   John H. Allen
William Edgar Almoney
Milton T. Morris – Extra Brakemen

FOREMEN

Samuel C. Pomraning   E. F. Mandie
H. N. Dirk   George Channell

TRACKMEN

E. Evert Morris	John C. Hostler
George Gibney	A. McCallister
William Keppler	J. F. McLane

CARPENTERS

William T. Gibney	W. D. Brown
Charles M. Almoney	Arlington H. Morris
(R.R.R.)	

Jan. 29, 1910

MEAN TO EXTEND RAILROAD – (Special to *The Gazette*)

Delta, Jan. 28 – The New Park & Fawn Grove Railroad must be extended to this place. The Delta Board of Trade has issued a call to every businessman, be he farmer, merchant, banker, doctor, lawyer, or whatnot, laborer or capitalist, rich or poor, to attend a public meeting at the K. G. E. [Knights of the Golden Eagle] Hall, this place, Wednesday next, February 2 at 2 p.m. The object is to have the road built in the coming summer. (G)

Feb .9, 1910

New Park & Fawn Grove Railroad purchased from the Peach Bottom Slate Company 2-and-a-half square feet of No.2 slate for the shop rooftop for $10. (F.R. of R.R.)

June 11, 1910

Stewartstown Railroad makes its first offer to buy out the New Park & Fawn Grove Railroad for 12.50 a share for the New Park & Fawn Grove railroad stock or exchange 4 shares for 1 Stewartstown Railroad share. (SRDMN)

June 12, 1910

Raymond G. Baird paid the New Park & Fawn Grove Railroad $123.15 for moving the switch at Wiley Station. (F.R. of R.R.)

W. T. Strawbridge repaired the Wiley Station platform. (F.R. of R. R.)

Jul. 16, 1910

Anderson Station Siding – 97 feet long – installed – shared cost, railroad portion $42.50, and the owner of the private business portion is $42.50.

Manifold Station Siding – 82 feet long – installed – shared cost, railroad portion $37.85, and the owner of the private business portion is $37.85. (F.R. of R.R.)

Aug. 13, 1910

New Park & Fawn Grove Railroad declines to sell out – will pay $10 per month towards joint agency at Stewartstown. (SRDMN)

Aug. 23, 1910

SEEK BETTER MARKETS – New Park & Fawn Grove Railroad to Be Extended to Make Baltimore Connection

The New Park & Fawn Grove Railroad Company has been granted a charter by the state department at Harrisburg for the extension of its line to the property of Edward James, near the Maryland state line, a distance of five miles. The capital is fixed at $90,000. At a later date, the company will secure a charter in Maryland for the line to be built three miles longer, so that a connection may be made with the Maryland & Pennsylvania railroad in Maryland, at a point south of Delta.

With the extensions in operation, the company will have a direct connection with Baltimore. It is expected that the first extension, as authorized by [Pa.] Governor [Edwin S.] Stuart, will be started shortly. When the plans of the promoters of the project are materialized, the farmers of lower York County will be able to reach the markets of the larger cities with their products, thereby enabling them to secure better prices for them. The present road of the company runs through one of the most fertile spots in Southern Pennsylvania. (YD)

Aug. 27, 1910	R. B. McKinnon received payment of $30 for the proposed profile and specifications for the extension of the New Park & Fawn Grove Railroad to connect with the Maryland & Pennsylvania Railroad. (F.R. of R.R.)
Aug. 31, 1910	New Park & Fawn Grove Railroad paid R. B. McKinnon $30 for making plans and profiles for the extension to Delta, Pa. (F.R. of R.R.)
Sept. 01, 1910	EXTENSION FOR YORK COUNTY RAILROAD

A charter has been granted to the New Park & Fawn Grove Railroad Company, of Pennsylvania, to extend its present lines to Maryland, and later the company intends to form a connection with the Maryland & Pennsylvania Railroad. This will give the farmers of the section traversed by the New Park & Fawn Grove Railroad an outlet for their products through Baltimore that, it is thought, will materially benefit the section. A charter will have to be secured from the Maryland Legislature to make the connections with the Maryland & Pennsylvania Railroad, but it is thought that will be readily granted.

Work on the first extension, to the Maryland line, will start at once. The farmers of lower York County are pleased with the new venture. The present route runs through one of the most fertile spots in Southern Pennsylvania. (BS)

Sept. 12, 1910	New Park & Fawn Grove Railroad paid W. T. Strawbridge $4.80 for repairing the platform at Wiley Station. (F.R. of R. R.)
Sept. 17, 1910	The New Park & Fawn Grove Railroad needs the help of the Norrisville people to build a section of state road between Hughes Hill and Wiley

Station. (R.R.R.)

Sept. 19, 1910	Stewartstown Executive Committee suggests that a new depot be built on Pennsylvania Avenue if the New Park & Fawn Grove Railroad does not extend its line to connect with another railroad. (SRDMN)
Sept. 30, 1910	New Park & Fawn Grove Railroad paid J. C. Wiley $2 for boarding the train crew at Stewartstown during the Stewartstown Fair. (F.R. of R.R.)
Oct. 20, 1910	New Park & Fawn Grove Railroad paid the Stewartstown Railroad $20 for August and September proportion of the agent salary and expenses and use of the facilities at the station in Stewartstown. (F.R. of R.R.)
Dec. 9, 1910	REGRETS THAT RAILROAD STATION WAS NOT ERECTED

Some weeks ago the New Park & Fawn Grove Railroad lodged a complaint with the Pennsylvania state railroad commission against the Stewartstown Railroad with reference to the manner of the interchange of passengers at Stewartstown, and asks the commission to use its good offices to bring about an arrangement which would relieve the New Park & Fawn Grove Railroad of burdens and delays which the offices of the latter road deem disadvantageous to it and inconvenient and annoying to its passengers travel over both roads.

It was suggested that the erection of a station at Pennsylvania Avenue in Stewartstown would remove all causes of complaint and would greatly facilitate travel and prevent much delay in the transition of the mails.

The officers of the Stewartstown Railroad, it seems, refused to heed the efforts of the state commission to bring about an amicable arrangement in the matter, and deeming the case one in which they could make no recommendation, the commission has declined to proceed to a hearing upon the merits.

This appears from the following letter to the New Park & Fawn Grove Railroad from the secretary of the state railroad commission:

"In the matter of the complaint of the New Park & Fawn Grove railroad vs. the Stewartstown railroad company, I am directed by the commission to advise you that ever since the inception of this trouble the commission has sought by mediation to bring the complainant and respondent together on some amicable basis but without avail.

"As the matter is understood, the complainant seeks to have the respondent unite with it in establishing and maintaining a joint station at Pennsylvania avenue, which the respondent is apparently unwilling to do."

"While the commission is authorized to recommend the establishment of stations by common carriers, its powers do not extend to requiring that two such carriers shall join in any such station. Such being the situation the commission does not see how it is possible for it to proceed further in the matter so long as one of the parties expresses and unwellness to join in such enterprise with the other."

"It is very regrettable, said the gentleman interested in the matter yesterday, that an amicable arrangement has not reached, for the charter of the New Park & Fawn Grove railroad was recently extended southeastwardly from Fawn Grove to the Maryland line to a point from which connection can readily be made with the Maryland & Pennsylvania railroad. If this extension is made, it will no doubt divert much traffic from this city."

"These two railroads, it should hope, will now get together and reach an adjustment of their apparent differences in a spirit of neighborliness and then work in full concord and harmony." (G)

Jan. 11, 1911	New Park & Fawn Grove Railroad paid J. A. Gailey $105 for half the installation cost of a switch installed in New Park. (F.R. of R.R.)
Feb. 08, 1911	New Park & Fawn Grove Railroad paid W. E. Jones, New Park, $35 for the materials and labor for the construction of the waiting room and platform at Kisiner Station. (F.R. of R.R.)
Feb. 14, 1911	Water tank construction was started by the J. M. Stritehoff & Bros. (F.R. of R.R.)
Mar. 11, 1911	New Park & Fawn Grove Railroad paid W. E. Manifold & Company $8.96 for coal furnished for the passenger car. (F.R. of R.R.)
Apr. 12, 1911	New Park & Fawn Grove Railroad paid Leslie Trout, Stewartstown, Pa., $11.54 for furnishing stone ballast. (F.R. of R.R.)
Apr. 18, 1911	New Park & Fawn Grove Railroad paid George Lau $102.75 to record 39 right-of-way deeds and 6 property deeds. (F.R. of R.R.)
May 13, 1911	The New Park & Fawn Grove Railroad purchased from the Buda Company one No. 14W Buda Bridge Motor Car for $425. Order No.5186, Shop No.1496, and Engine No.2277. 4'8½" gauge and comes with a toolbox and two extra spark plugs. (F.R. of R.R.)
June 2, 1911	The New Park & Fawn Grove Railroad has put a gasoline truck in service on its line. (SN)
June 2, 1911	N.P.&F.G.R.R. will pay trainmen for extra trips 1/3 of their day wages for each extra road trip.

N.P.&F.G.R.R. will pay the engineer and fireman each $1 per month for washing out the locomotive boiler to be done 1st and 15th of each month.

No strong drink for all trainmen while on or off duty; violation of this rule means immediate discharge. (R.R.R.)

July 11, 1911	W. E. Jones received a payment of $35 from the New Park & Fawn Grove Railroad for the construction of the waiting room and platform at Kisiner Station. (E.N. of R.R.)
Aug. 19, 1911	PROPERTY TRANSFERS

James M. Hendrix to New Park & Fawn Grove Railroad Company, property in Stewartstown.

Isabel Fulton to New Park & Fawn Grove Railroad Company, property in Stewartstown.

Thomas B. Griffith, et. ux., to New Park & Fawn Grove Railroad Company, property in Stewartstown.

William Sechrist, et. ux., to New Park & Fawn Grove Railroad Company, property in Stewartstown.

William L. Duncan, et. ux., to New Park & Fawn Grove Railroad Company, property in Fawn Grove.

Lillie A. Tompkins to New Park & Fawn Grove Railroad Company, a tract of land in Hopewell Township. (G)

Sept. 12, 1911	Fawn Grove Lumber Company Ltd. – President and owner J. W. Kisiner won the contract to furnish the materials and workmanship for the construction of the engine house in Fawn Grove for $898. (F.R. of R.R.)
Dec. 07, 1911	New Park & Fawn Grove Railroad paid $14.15 to J. H. Kisiner for operating the pumping station at Fawn Grove for three days. (F.R. of R.R.)
Dec. 09, 1911	Stewartstown Railroad agreed to run one train on Sunday in order to handle the growing milk business if necessary. Consideration is being given to the purchase of a gas motor passenger car jointly with the New Park & Fawn Grove Railroad. (SRDMN)
Apr. 05, 1912	New Park & Fawn Grove Railroad paid Frank Toomey, Inc. of Philadelphia $933 to supply the machinery and tools for the shop in Fawn Grove. (F.R. of R.R.)
May 11, 1912	The New Park & Fawn Grove Railroad Company has just erected a frame engine house, 64 by 24 feet 650 feet east of the square, and close to the machine shop. All will be ready in a short time when laying the tracks into

the new engine house. When that is completed, anything can be done to a locomotive except to turn it. (DA)

V. A. Mathews completed the "Y" in Fawn Grove. (F.R. of R.R.)

May 18, 1912	New Park & Fawn Grove Railroad paid B. F. Morris $16.60 for hauling stone and sand for the foundation of the machine shop in Fawn Grove. (F.R. of R.R.)
June 12, 1912	New Park & Fawn Grove Railroad paid Harry Hughes of Fawn Grove $4.50 for 30 ties at 15 cents per tie. (F.R. of R.R.)
Aug. 01, 1912	New Park & Fawn Grove Railroad, as per the agreement with the Stewartstown Railroad, paid for the cost of the work completed on the "Y" track located in Stewartstown. The half-cost was $513.56. (F.R of R.R.)
Sept. 27, 1912	The heavy freight traffic on the Stewartstown and New Park & Fawn Grove railroads still keeps up. The Stewartstown crew seems to be on the road all the time, from very early in the morning until bedtime. (TYD)
Oct. 5, 1912	NEW RAILROAD FOR THE COUNTY – It is reported that the new management of the Lancaster, Oxford and Southern Railroad will extend its system to Singerly, this county, a distance of 15 miles, where connection with the Baltimore & Ohio Railroad will be made. A western extension is also to be built from Peach Bottom, on the York County side of the river, to Fawn Grove, a distance of 12 miles, to connect with the New Park & Fawn Grove Railroad. The latter road connects with the Northern Central R.R. at New Freedom. (CW)
Oct. 26, 1912	RECORD FREIGHT TRAIN – On New Park & Fawn Grove Railroad – Consisted of 14 Cars.
	New Park, Oct. 25 – The longest freight train on the New Park & Fawn Grove Railroad passed through here on Tuesday. It was made up of 13 freight cars and one passenger car and was drawn by "Old Susie," an engine that has been in service for more than a quarter of a century. Engineer Joe Williams takes pride in having hauled this record freight train. Business on the New Park & Fawn Grove Railroad has been picking up considerably during the last year. It serves as the outlet for the farm products of one of the best sections of the county, and it is only beginning to develop a territory that will make a good feeder for any railroad. The freight is getting heavier every year but the past 12 months have no equal in the history of the road. (YD)
Nov. 1, 1912	The New Park & Fawn Grove Railroad paid $6.90 or 30 hours at .23 cents an hour to W. T. Strawbridge for working on the machine shop. (F.R. of

	R.R.)
Nov. 8, 1912	The New Park & Fawn Grove Railroad paid Frank Buchanan 0.45 cents for each first-class chestnut tie and 0.30 cents for each second-class chestnut tie. The total amount was $18. (F.R. of R.R.)
Dec. 12, 1912	John W. Barton resigned his position as fireman with the New Park & Fawn Grove Railroad Company and accepted a similar position with the Stewartstown Railroad, to take effect Jan. 1, 1913. (YD)
Jan. 1, 1913	The New Park and Fawn Grove Railroad paid Anderson Bros. of New Park $13.55 for furnishing the cement for the Wiley Station. (F.R. of R.R.)
Jan. 28, 1913	The New Park & Fawn Grove Railroad paid Samuel C. Pomraning of Fawn Grove $1.40 for 10 hours of work using a team of horses to grade the station lot at Fawn Grove. (F.R. of R.R.)
Feb. 4, 1913	Charles H. Macnab of Cardiff, Md., completed the survey of the "Y" track and the station grounds located at Fawn Grove and Wiley. (R.R.R.)
Feb. 7, 1913	The New Park & Fawn Grove Railroad paid the Buda Company of Harvey, Illinois, $5.90 for repairs to the No.14 bridge gang motor car. (F.R. of R.R.)
Feb. 13, 1913	J. N. Marsteller completed the wiring for electricity in the Fawn Grove passenger and freight station. (F.R. of R.R.)
Mar. 12, 1913	New Park & Fawn Grove Railroad paid C. F. Orr of Fawn Grove $12.95 for blacksmithing work. (F.R. of R.R.)
Mar. 25, 1913	New Park & Fawn Grove Railroad paid Wm. F. Baughman of Whiteford, Md., $17 for 1000 feet of dry chestnut boards for the construction of a small station at Strawbridge. (F.R. of R.R.)
Apr. 9, 1913	New Park & Fawn Grove Railroad paid W. T. Strawbridge $85.54 for 364 hours of carpenter work on the station building at Wiley. (F.R. of R.R.)
Apr. 23, 1913	New Park & Fawn Grove Railroad paid Stewartstown Lumber & Manufacturing Co. $271.02 for the materials used in the construction of the Wiley Station. (F.R. of R.R.)
May 19, 1913	New Park & Fawn Grove Railroad paid Wm. F. Baughman $17 for furnishing the lumber for the construction of the Strawbridge Station. (F.R. of R.R.)
May 24, 1913	A. M. Strawbridge recorded a deed for the right-of-way and station grounds for $3. (F.R. of R.R.)
May 28, 1913	New Park & Fawn Grove Railroad paid J. C. Wiley $25 for supervising the erection of the Wiley Station. (F.R. of R.R.)

July 1913	The station agent at Wiley Station is Lester W. Brillhart. (R.R.R.)
	Martin Althouse is working on the ground around New Park. (F.R. of R.R.)
July 1, 1913	J. W. Wabrooks furnished the paint for the Fawn Grove passenger and freight station. (R.R.R.)
July 9, 1913	Rented the offices at New Park for $30 every 6 months. (F.R. of R.R.)
July 16, 1913	Fawn Grove Lumber Manufacturing Company won the contract to build the station at Fawn Grove for $868.36. (F.R. of R.R.)
Aug. 12, 1913	New Park & Fawn Grove Railroad ordered one complete Lorenz Switch from the Pennsylvania Steel Company for $15.39. (F.R. of R.R.)
	The station agent at Fawn Grove is Avon W. Hess. (R.R.R.)
Sept. 1913	New Park & Fawn Grove Railroad paid J. N. Marsteller, the proprietor of the Fawn Grove Electrical Light Work, $8.50 for the materials and wiring used in the new station at Fawn Grove. (F.R. of R.R.)
Sept. 3, 1913	New Park & Fawn Grove Railroad paid Buda Company of Harvey, Illinois, $61.50 for the repairs of motor car no.14. (F.R. of R.R.)
Sept. 7, 1913	New Park & Fawn Grove Railroad paid $14.13 to M. F. Manifold for working on the turntable and engine house. (F.R. of R.R.)
Oct. 2, 1913	Northern Central Railroad — Orangeville Station shipped to the New Park & Fawn Grove Railroad two engine springs for $6.91. (F.R. of R.R.)
Nov. 25, 1913	Eugene McDermott, who has been employed on the New Park & Fawn Grove Railroad as a conductor for the past two years, has resigned and accepted a position as a brakeman on the Pennsylvania Railroad from Harrisburg to Philadelphia. John Shenberger, who has been a brakeman on the New Park & Fawn Grove Railroad, is filling the position of conductor for the present, and Grant Kauffman as a brakeman. (YD)
Dec. 3, 1913	The York Eastern Telephone Company charged the New Park & Fawn Grove Railroad $22.50 for three months of telephone service for the following locations: Wiley Station, Fawn Grove Station, and 4 telephones along the railroad right-of-way. (F.R. of R.R.)
Dec. 13, 1913	FREIGHT CAR DERAILED — TIED UP TRAFFIC ON THE NEW PARK AND FAWN GROVE RAILROAD FOR 24 HOURS;
	Fawn Grove, Dec. 15 – A freight wreck in Shirley's Cut Saturday afternoon tied up the New Park & Fawn Grove Railroad for 24 hours. A freight car on the train leaving here at 3:25 p.m. jumped the track. The mail and passengers were conveyed on the engine to Stewartstown, and the

passengers and freight cars remained in the cut until Sunday evening, when the workmen, after a day's labor, succeeded in replacing the car on the track. The Stewartstown car was used in the evening and brought the mail and passengers to New Park, where they were met by automobiles and brought to this place. (SHS)

Dec. 31, 1913   LIST OF EMPLOYEES THAT WORKED FOR THE NEW PARK & FAWN GROVE RAIL FOR THE YEAR ENDING IN 1913:

John H. Anderson – President
W. H. Fulton – Payroll, Superintendent, Treasurer
A. G. Bowman – Supervisor
C. W. Shaw – Auditor, General Manager
Jacob Rider – Engineer, Laborer
John Barton – Fireman, Laborer
Lawrence Shaw – Brakeman, Bridge Work, Laborer
C. E. Yost – Laborer
Howard Waltemeyer – Laborer
George Gibbs – Brakeman, Bridge Work, Laborer
H. E. Anstine – Agent-Freight, Laborer
S. F. Shaffer – Laborer

H. W. Rehmeyer – Agent, Laborer	Lewis Rosenberry – Laborer
Frank McConnell – Laborer	Glen Brown – Laborer
J. E. Glessick – Laborer	William Duncan – Laborer
D. F. McKinley – Blacksmith	Frank McLane – Laborer
Ralph Evans – Mail Carrier	John Barton – Fireman, Laborer
Thomas Cox – Carpenter, Laborer	Nelson Waltemyer – Laborer
Arthur Fix – Laborer	L. B. Shaw – Brakeman, Laborer
Thomas B. Fulton – Payroll	S. G. Boss – Laborer
George B. Hale – Laborer	J. A. Gailey – Agent
Chas. McLeary – Bridge Work	N. A. Manifold – Agent
Ora Fix – Bridge Work	Orem Kurtz – Blacksmith
Bentz Hendrix – Bridge Work	Alec Rosenberry – Laborer
John Wilkerson – Bridge Work	Oliver Duncan – Laborer
Curtis Stambaugh – Bridge Work	M. Almoney – Laborer
Fay Shaw – Auditor, Bridge Work	Chas. McElwain – Laborer
William Norris – Bridge Work	J. R. McClain – Laborer
George B. Hale – Bridge Work	V. Amberman – Train Work
E. L. Eckenrode – Blacksmith	George Schminkey – Laborer
O. S. Bell – Treasurer	Geo. Gibbs – Brakeman, Laborer
Elmer Evans – Mail Carrier	F. Fletcher – Provided R.R. ties
J. Dixon – Agent, Clerk	F. Swift – Provided R.R. ties

C. A. Diehl – Agent, Laborer F. Buchanan – Provided R.R. ties
Charles Heaton – Laborer J. W. Tredway – Provided R.R. ties
John S. Brown – Carpenter, Wiley Sta. B. F. Morris – Laborer – Grading
Lester W. Brillhart – Agent, Wiley Sta.
J. C. Wiley – General Manager, work on improvement at New Park
Station, filed deed for the station grounds at Wiley.
Winfield B. McElwain – Furnish lumber for Eng. House, Shop, Turn Table
J. N. Marsteller – Furnish stone for the Eng. House, Shop, Turn Table
Anderson Brothers – Furnish supplies for Eng. House, Shop, Turn Table
W. T. Strawbridge – Carpentry work on Eng. House, Shop, Turn Table
Y. A. Mathews – Masonry work for Eng. House, Shop, and Turn Table
W. E. Jones – furnish the materials for the construction of Kisiner Station

S. C. Pomraning – Track Foreman J. A. Gailey – Provided R.R. ties
W. T. Strawbridge – Carpenter R. C. Liggit – Hauling ballast
C. H. MacNabb – Surveyor Asa J. Vansant – Carpenter
C. M. Almoney – Carpenter W. E. Jones – Repair freight cars
R. W. McMahon – Agent E. N. Morris – Water for locomotives
J. S. Strawbridge – Legal services J. F. Wolf – Provided switch timbers
C. E. Orr – Blacksmith
(R.R.R.)

1914	Yesterday morning, when the New Park & Fawn Grove train was coming through Howard Anderson's large farm, a big flock of turkeys was encountered. The turkeys instead of getting out of the way, simply ran ahead of the train and stayed on the track. The engineer stopped the train and the turkeys were driven off. (SHS)
Jan. 5, 1914	New Park & Fawn Grove Railroad paid George F. Mutter's & Sons of York, Pa., $11.78 to furnish the materials and install the smoke stack in the locomotive house in Fawn Grove. (F.R. of R.R.)
Jan. 19, 1914	Stewartstown Railroad declined the proposal set forth by the New Park & Fawn Grove Railroad to run their train and crew over the Stewartstown Railroad from Stewartstown to New Freedom for $10 per day. (SRDMN)
Feb. 18, 1914	RAILROAD NOTES – Negotiations are underway whereby the Stewartstown Railroad Company is to become the purchaser of the New Park & Fawn Grove Railroad Company, and it is understood that there is only a difference in the price holding up the deal. The Maryland & Pennsylvania Railroad also has eyes on the New Park and Fawn Grove Railroad and if the plans materialized with the purchasing of the road an extension would be built to Delta, a distance of nine miles. (G)

Feb. 19, 1914	No mail was received here Monday evening, which was due to the train of the New Park & Fawn Grove Railroad being unable to make its usual evening run on account of snow drifts. The train made the usual run on Tuesday morning. (YD)
Apr. 16, 1914	Recorded the deed for the right-of-way and station ground for $3.25. (F.R. of R.R.)
May 1, 1914	An order has been placed by the New Park & Fawn Grove Railroad with the Baldwin Locomotive Works of Philadelphia for a new locomotive. The order calls for the delivery of the engine by June 20. (DHT)
May 11, 1914	The New Park & Fawn Grove Railroad paid J. W. Brooks of Fawn Grove $11.89 for the paint material and the painting of the No.5 wooden coach car. (F.R. of R.R.)
June 10, 1914	STEWARTSTOWN, June 10 – The new engine purchased by the New Park & Fawn Grove Railroad arrived on Monday. It is a six-driver engine and was built by the Baldwin Locomotives Works of Philadelphia. (YD)
June 30, 1914	The New Park & Fawn Grove Railroad paid J. A. Gailey $60 for rent of the station and conference room located in his building at New Park from July 1, 1913, to June 30, 1914. (F.R. of R.R.)
July 1, 1914	New Park & Fawn Grove Railroad paid the electric bill from the Fawn Grove Electric Company for April, May, and June for the amount of $3.00. (F.R. of R.R.)
July 31, 1914	New Park & Fawn Grove Railroad paid the Buda Company $6.66 for the repair of its No.14 water-cooled motor car. (F.R. of R.R.)
Aug.14 & 15, 1914	New Park & Fawn Grove Railroad paid the Pennsylvania Railroad $20 for the rental of passenger coaches 1208, 3486, and 2859 for use of the Farmer's Annual Picnic and County Fair. (F.R. of R.R.)
Oct. 17, 1914	New Park & Fawn Grove Railroad paid Richard W. McMahon $5 to represent the railroad before the Interstate Commerce Commission. (F.R. of R.R.)
Dec. 28, 1914	Stewartstown Railroad erected a new station in Stewartstown for $3,717.73. The New Park & Fawn Grove Railroad leased space in the new station. (F.R. of R.R.)
Feb. 23, 1915	B. F. Morris sold a stove for $5 to the railroad for the Fawn Grove station. (F.R. of R.R.)
May 18, 1915	New Park & Fawn Grove Railroad purchased from the Fairbanks Morris Company a No.1 standard section hand car No.94396 for $27. (F.R. of

R.R.)

May 31, 1915

LOWER END WRECK

FREIGHT TRAIN SMASHUP ON NEW PARK & FAWN GROVE RAILROAD DUE TO SPREADING RAILS

Stewartstown, May 31 – One of the biggest wrecks in its history occurred on Friday evening on the New Park & Fawn Grove Railroad, in Howard Anderson's field, about two miles southeast of town. The train consisted of the engine, one coach and five freight cars. The cause of the wreck is said to have been spreading rails. Three freight cars and the front truck of the coach left the track and ties for a distance of four car lengths were torn up as well as the ground at the side of the roadbed. The trucks are buried almost their depth in the dirt. The trucks were torn from two of the freight cars, and the cars toppled over against a fence and a tree by the tracks. Luckily no persons were hurt. On account of the limited facilities of the road, the wreck will not be cleared up for several days. However, train service is maintained, the New Park & Fawn Grove train running up to the wreck and the Stewartstown train meeting it there and transferring passengers and mail. (YD)

Jul. 16, 1915

JOHN H. ANDERSON DEAD — Was President of the New Park & Fawn Grove Railroad and a Prominent Lower End Farmer.

John Henry Anderson, one of the most prominent farmers and businessmen of York County, died shortly before 7 o'clock last evening at his home in Fawn Township, near New Park. He was 79 years old and for some time had been suffering from jaundice.

Mr. Anderson was a son of Mr. and Mrs. Joseph Reed Anderson and was born on the old homestead near Fawn Grove, Sept. 9, 1835. He was educated in the public schools of Fawn township and afterward engaged in farming, which became one of his main occupations. His success with scientific methods of agriculture attracted wide attention. He had long been a figure in business enterprises of Lower York County. Numbered among the founders of the First National Bank of Delta, he was a director of the institution until his death.

Mr. Anderson was an active worker in the Center Presbyterian church, in which his father was an elder for many years, and served as a trustee. In 1867 he married Miss Elizabeth Wilson, daughter of Mr. and Mrs. David Wilson. She died in March 1911. Both the Wilson and Manifold families, with which Mrs. Anderson was connected, have long been well known in Pennsylvania.

When the New Park & Fawn Grove Railroad Company was incorporated in February 1905, Mr. Anderson, one of the organizers, was chosen president. He held this position until his death.

He leaves three sons, Joseph Clay Anderson, Stewartstown; D. Ross Anderson, New Park, and Harry M. Anderson, in charge of his father's farming interests; and three brothers and sisters: Joseph W. Anderson, Stewartstown; Reed W. Anderson, New Park; Mrs. D. A. Wilson, and Mrs. John M. Brown, Gatchellville, and Mrs. Zena Dougherty, New Park.

The funeral will be held next Monday morning at 9:30 from the house, with further services and burial at Center Church. (YD)

Aug. 11, 1915	New Park & Fawn Grove Railroad purchased 4 standard No.39 "Casey RR" lanterns from the Keystone Lantern Company for $2.05. (F.R. of R.R)
Oct. 31, 1915	New Park & Fawn Grove Railroad paid the Cumberland & Pennsylvania Railroad $18.25 for freight car repairs. (F.R. of R.R.)
1916	Interstate Commerce Commission Report

!.) **TRACK MILEAGE**:

Main Line Track	9.234
Yard Track & Sidings	1.141
Total for all Tracks	10.375

2.) **TELEGRAPH AND TELEPHONE SYSTEM**:

None

Note: Telephones are located in each of the following stations: Stewartstown, Wiley, New Park, and Fawn Grove

3.) **TRACK RAILS**:

Bessemer Steel and weighing 50 and 56 pounds per linear yard. Cross ties of mixed wood 7"x7"x8'6"

4) **BRIDGES, TRESTLES, & CULVERTS**:

Bridge No.1 – (Station 64+15)
    Three Spans – Built: 1905
    Substructure – Concrete abutments
    Superstructure: Deck plate girder – 69 Feet Long
    Built by the York Bridge Company on the land of John Manifold

Bridge No.2 – (Station 197+21)
    Substructure – Concrete Abutments – Built: 1905
    Superstructure, I Beams – 20 feet long

Built on the land of Mrs. Hannah B. Wiley

Pile and Frame Trestle:
 One trestle – 10 feet long
 Mixer of masonry and timber

5.) SWITCHES:

 Main Track – 9 sets of switches
 Yard Track – 1 set of switches

6.) GRADE CROSSINGS:

 Grade crossings with posted signs – 14

7.) STATION AND OFFICE BUILDINGS:

Anderson, Pa. – Passenger Shelter – built 1910
 One story, 8'x10', frame with platform
Gemmill, Pa. – Passenger Shelter – built 1914
 One story, 8'x10', frame with platform
Wiley, Pa. – Passenger Station – built 1913
 One story, 21'x41', frame with platform
 One frame toilet
Strawbridge, Pa. – Passenger Shelter – built 1913
 One story, 8'x10', frame with Platform
New Park, Pa. – Frame Platform – built 1907
 Ticket office and conference room leased
Kisiner, Pa. – Passenger Shelter – built 1911
 One story, 10'x10', frame – Frame Platform
Fawn Grove, Pa. – Passenger Station – built 1913
 One story, 23'x51', frame – Frame Platform
 Toilet – Frame
 Section House – built 1908
 One story – 10'x18', frame
 Water Tank – 10'x10' Diameter, frame, built 1911
  5,900-gallon capacity.
 Well – built 1907
 Pump House – Frame, one story, 14'x15', built in 1907
 Engine House – Frame, one story, 25'x65', with pit –
  built 1912
 Machine Shop – Purchased secondhand with land in 1908 –
  Frame, one story, 25'x41' – rebuilt 1912
 Engine House – Frame, 19'x21' – built 1907
 Boiler House – Frame, one story, irregular shape – built 1913

Ash Pit – Masonry – built 1908

8.) FUELING STATIONS:

Coal Wharf – Timber – Station 472+55
Coal Wharf – Timber – Station 487+36

9.) ROADWAY MACHINERY:

One Motor Car
Two Push Cars

10. STEAM LOCOMOTIVE:

Mixed Service – No.2 – Baldwin – Purchased new in 1914
Type 2-6-0 – cyls. 16"x24" – Total weight – 49 tons

11.) PASSENGER TRAIN CARS:

Joint Ownership – Stewartstown Railroad and the New Park &
Fawn Grove Railroad – Car No.5 – (1914) – wood underframe –
wood body

12. WORK EQUIPMENT:

One Work Train Car – Gondola type – No. 1 – (1906) – capacity
40,000 pounds – wood underframe – wood body

13. WORK SECTION:

Stewartstown, Pa. – 0+00 to Station 15+50 (1)
Station 15+50 to Station 307+00 (2)
Station 307+00 to Station 326+00 (3)
Station 326+00 to Station 372+00 (4)
Station 372+00 to Station 462+00 (5)
Station 462+00 to Station 487+10 (6)

The above information was provided by Valuation Docket No. 255 – completed by the
Interstate Commerce Commission June 30, 1916 – Information approved by Louis Hood.

Jan. 16, 1916	The stockholders elected Reed W. Anderson as president of the New Park & Fawn Grove Railroad. (R.R.R.)
Jun. 15, 1916	Charley Shenberger of Fawn Grove was involved in an accident where he injured his foot. (R.R.R.)
Jul. 1, 1916	New Park & Fawn Grove Railroad paid William M. Barton, Jr. $2 for his services with the right-of-way committee that was looking into the right-of-way needed to go from Fawn Grove to Delta. Pa. (F.R. of R.R)

Jul. 19, 1916 — Stewartstown Railroad billed the New Park & Fawn Grove Railroad $10 for services rendered by the station agent. (F.R. of R.R.)

Nov. 1916 — The New Park 7 Fawn Grove Railroad Locomotive No. 1 – D-8a – type – 4-4-0 – ex PRR No.4017 constructed in 1888 was sold $475 (F.R. of R.R.)

Nov. 16, 1916 — The New Park & Fawn Grove Railroad paid A. J. Vance $2.50 for working on the engine house and hauling passengers to New Park. (F.R. of R.R.)

1917 — List of Public Grade Crossings on the New Park & Fawn Grove Railroad.

> 1.) Church Street – 1350 feet east of the Stewartstown RR Station
> 2.) Trout's Crossing – 2640 feet east of the Stewartstown Station
> 3.) Gable's Crossing – 3960 feet east of the Stewartstown Station
> 4.) Barshinger's Crossing – 850 feet east of Anderson Station
> 5. Winemiller's Crossing – 3960 feet east of Anderson Station
> 6.) State Road Crossing – at Gemmill Station
> 7.) Public Road Crossing – at Wiley Station – siding removed
> 8.) State Road Crossing – at Strawbridge Station
> 9.) Badder's Crossing – at Strawbridge Station
> 10.) Davis's Crossing (State Road) – 1500 feet west of New Park
> 11.) Harman's Crossing (State Road) – 1500 feet east of New Park
> 12.) Kisiner's Crossing – at Kisiner Station
> 13.) Main Street Crossing – at Fawn Grove Station – 1 siding track
> 14.) Morris Ave. Crossing – at Fawn Grove Station – 2 siding tracks
> (I.C.C.)

Apr. 24, 1917 — CARS THROUGH ENGINE HOUSE

Fawn Grove, April 24 – There was a smashup on the New Park & Fawn Grove Railroad last Saturday. Two box cars, loaded with fertilizer, crashed through the new engine house, tearing out each end. The engine shifted these two cars into the switch that has the new engine house as a terminal. Finding the brakes would not hold, John Shenberger, the brakeman, jumped from the cars, just as they crashed through the doors of the engine house, finally running off the end of the track and tearing out the rear end of the track and tearing out the rear and smashing the small motor truck stored there. The loss is estimated at about $500. (YD)

Jul. 17, 1917 — CHARGED WITH RAISING GRADE OF RAILROAD

To have raised the grade of the New Park & Fawn Grove Railroad where it crosses the state road in Hopewell Township is the charge against the lower end transportation company. Numerous complaints brought about an investigation by the state highway department with the result that it was found no permit for the change of grade had been granted by the state. Thomas Green, superintendent of the highway department's York office, and C. W. Erisman, assistant engineer, went to the scene yesterday and took several photographs of the location in question. (YG)

Dec. 31, 1918

Officers: President – Reed W. Anderson
            Vice President and General Manager – John C. Wiley
            Secretary, Auditor, Gen. Passenger & Freight Agent – J. A. Gailey
            Treasurer – A. M. Strawbridge
            General Superintendent – B. F. Morris
            Attorney – W. F. Bay Stewart

Annual Report states the following:

Net Earnings	$21,236.19
Expenses	$15,110.76
Net Profit	$ 6,125.43 (R.R.R.)

Jan. 1, 1919

NEW PARK & FAWN GROVE RAILROAD – RULES AND REGULATIONS:

1.) **CHILDREN** – Children under the age of five years of age when accompanied by parent or guardian, free; each child five years of age and under twelve, one half of the adult fare (half a cent to be counted as one cent); each child twelve years of age and over, full adult fare. To reduce a whole ticket to a half ticket, the contract and each coupon must be faced "half" or ½ by stamping or writing with ink. Children's fares in this traffic will apply to fares in coaches only. Minimum fare 10 cents.

2.) **CORPSES** – Corpses must be accompanied by a competent person in charge who shall hold necessary transportation, and in addition present proper Health Authority Certificate and a full class one-way ticket (unlimited, limited or continuous train), regardless of age, for transportation of the corpse. Tickets covering transportation of a corpse should have the word "Corpse" stamped or plainly written in ink contract and each coupon. The minimum charge for moment of a corpse will be $1.00.

The through movement of corpses will be subject to the rules of the Local Health Board of the cities or towns through which same may be carried, and when transfer is necessary between stations, provision for same must be made by person in charge.

3.) **FARES** – Fares shown herein apply for passengers in coach only, for passengers traveling in Standard Sleeping and Parlor Cars higher than Coach Fares will be charged.

4.) **STOP-OVERS** – Not allowed

5.) **TIME LIMITS** – The fares made effective by this traffic apply only for tickets limited to continuous passage, commencing not later than one day after the day of sale, in coaches only.

6.) **TRAIN SERVICE** – Agents will be careful to sell tickets only when trains are advertised to start at the standing point to receive passengers, and at the destination to discharge passengers.

7.) **BAGGAGE** – 150 pounds of baggage will be checked free on each whole ticket and 75 pounds on each half ticket.

8.) **EXCESS BAGGAGE** – On baggage weighing over 150 pounds on each whole ticket and 75 pounds on each half ticket, a charge will be made for excess weight from point on selling line to company participating in this traffic at the Excess Baggage rate per 100 pounds. The minimum will be 18 cents per 100 pounds and the minimum collection for any shipment will be 25 cents (SRR).

ONE-WAY FARES ON THE NEW PARK & FAWN GROVE RAILROAD

Anderson, Pa. to New Freedom, Pa. – $0.34
Fawn Grove, Pa. to New Freedom, Pa. – $0.60
Gemmill's, Pa. to New Freedom, Pa. – $0.39
Kisiner, Pa. to New Freedom, Pa. – $0.57
New Park, Pa. to New Freedom, Pa. – $0.50
Strawbridge, Pa. to New Freedom, Pa. – $0.46
Wiley, Pa. to New Freedom, Pa. – $0.42 (R.R.R.)

Aug. 6, 1919	Special stockholder meeting was held and it authorized Federal control of the line. (D.M.N.)
Oct. 28, 1919	The New Park & Fawn Grove Railroad submitted an equipment report to the Interstate Commerce Commission:

1.) Locomotive No. 1 was sold for scrap in November 1916.
2.) Locomotive No. 2 is in service – purchased 2-6-0 from the Baldwin Locomotive Works in 1914.
3.) Half interest in Passenger and Baggage Car No.5 with the Stewartstown Railroad.
4.) Flat Work Car
5.) Two Hand Push Cars purchased from E. H. Wilson Company in 1906 for $22 each. (I.C.C.)

Jan. 1, 1920	American Railway Express Company extended its contract with the New Park & Fawn Grove Railroad for one full year ending December 31, 1920. (F. R. of R.R.)

Feb. 12, 1920	**STEWARTSTOWN WATER RESERVOIR EMPTIED** Leak in Main Allows Supply in Town Tank to Escape Before Discovery is Made Stewartstown, Feb. 11 – The main of the Stewartstown Water Company, on Church Street, froze and burst, where it is crossed by the tracks of the New Park & Fawn Grove Railroad, and before the leak was discovered the water in the tank has been emptied. This borough has emerged from the period of isolation, and conditions are nearly normal. The New Park & Fawn Grove Railroad got the road opened up yesterday. The milk deliveries were resumed on Tuesday, by Harry G. Hall, who receives his milk supply from the Sanitary Milk Company at York. (YDR)
May 5, 1920	The water tank of the New Park & Fawn Grove Railroad Company collapsed the last of the week and fell on the track, the train having to back out. (YD)
Dec. 10, 1920	**RUNAWAY TRAIN WITH CAB ABLAZE** With the passengers and conductor unaware that the deserted engine was aflame, with the throttle wide open, residents along the New Park & Fawn Grove Railroad witnessed a thrilling runaway of a passenger train. As the train was approaching Stewartstown, fireman Lewis Rosenberry began shoveling coal in the firebox. An explosion, the cause of which has not been ascertained, hurled him back on the coal. In an instant the cab was aflame and he and the engineer, Charles Heaton, were compelled to jump. At Stewartstown, the engine is changed to take the train to New Freedom. Jacob Rider, the engineer of the waiting train, was attracted by the flames, which spread out 10 feet from the cab of the approaching engine, and just in time got his engine underway to avoid a collision. William Rider, son of the engineer Rider, was with his father. He ran back to the Stewartstown Station, and as the blazing engine with passenger cars roared through at about 20 miles per hour, he leaped and landed on the rear steps of the last car. The brakes were applied and the train stopped. (DA)
Apr. 1, 1921	**N.P. & F.G. OFFICERS** New Park, April 1 – Reed W. Anderson was re-elected as president of the New Park & Fawn Grove Railroad at the annual meeting of the stockholders. The following directors were chosen: J. A. Gailey, J. W. Norris, H. M. Anderson, Maurice Davis, R. H. McDonald, Milton E. Smith,

H. S. Merryman, W. H. Webb, J. B. Jenkins, S. C. Love, B. F. Morris, H. C. McElwain, A. W. Webb, E. W. Norris, and J. O. Fitzpatrick. (YD)

Aug. 18, 1921 Canners from Baltimore have been traveling over the Stewartstown Railroad en route to New Park and Fawn Grove, where they will spend several weeks assisting in canning the corn and tomato crops of those vicinities. Two coaches went to New Park on Tuesday and two to Fawn Grove yesterday. (YD)

Nov. 2, 1921 SHOT RABBITS FROM TRAIN

While the train over the New Park & Fawn Grove Railroad from Fawn Grove to Stewartstown was making its first run this morning and in motion, four rabbits were shot by workmen on the train; three being killed by Engineer Charles Heaton and one by Fireman Herman Few.

The same thing happened last season on the Stewartstown and New Park & Fawn Grove Railroad trains.

A party composed of Paul Bailey, Alfred Miles, Norman McClain, and Gerry McClain shot twenty rabbits, each getting the limit before 9:30 a.m. Mr. Bailey also shot a squirrel. (YDR)

1922 NEW PARK & FAWN GROVE RAILROAD WAGE RATES:

Agents:

  New Park – $40 per month
  Fawn Grove – $40 per month

Train Crews:

  Freight Engineer – $3.45 a day
  Freight Fireman – $3.25 a day
  Freight Conductor – $3.45 a day
  Freight Brakeman – $3.15 a day
  Trackman – $0.35 per hour (F.R. of R.R.)

1922 Interstate Commerce Commission inventory of the New Park & Fawn Grove Railroad:

  A.) 2 Steam Locomotives,1 Passenger Car, and 1 Work Equipment.
  B.) Joint use of the station in Stewartstown.
  C.) Two small steel bridges.
  D.) Bessemer Steel: 50-pound rail and 56 pounds per linear foot.
  E.) N.P. & F.G. R.R. consists of 46 acres and 17 parcels of land that make up the railroad. (iCC)

N.P.&F.G.R.R. Annual Meeting was held and it was reported that $1,500 netted from operations. (D.M.N.)

Jan. 18, 1922	Frank Mantz, route agent of the American Railway Express Company, located in York, visited several of the stations on the Stewartstown Railroad and the New Park & Fawn Grove Railroad yesterday in the interest of the company. (YD)

Jan. 21, 1922 — Joseph A. Gailey, general manager of the New Park & Fawn Grove Railroad, was on a business trip to York yesterday.

The large hay crop harvested the past summer and stored in barns until the present has begun to move forward to markets from points on the Stewartstown and New Park & Fawn Grove railroads. During the past few weeks, a large number of carloads of hay have been shipped.

The greater amount of it goes to the Baltimore markets. Since a 10 percent reduction of freight rates has been put into effect on certain farm products, the hay is moving more rapidly. The markets are empty and the hay reaches a quick buyer and is readily disposed of. (YD)

Jan. 31, 1922 — The New Park & Fawn Grove Railroad is in a worse condition than the Stewartstown Railroad. The train was on its regular return trip from Stewartstown to Fawn Grove Saturday evening but has not got to its destination yet. Near Anderson Station a large drift was encountered and the train was hung up. The passenger car was uncoupled from the engine and then an attempt was made to break through the drift. The engineer succeeded in getting the engine through several drifts farther on but when he wanted to return to get the passenger car he was unable to get back to it. After making several attempts, the engine got into the snow so deep that it could not be moved backward or forward. The supply of coal and water on board became exhausted and the train had to be abandoned in the snow drifts. A large gang of snow shovelers was secured from the surrounding neighborhood, who are now shoveling out the train. Fuel and water are being transported to the locomotive on sleds so as to keep the boilers from freezing up. The coach which was left standing is now in a snow drift so deep that only a small smoke pipe leading from the heating apparatus is visible and it will have to be shoveled out also.

At present, all freight, mail, and express for points on the road are being held at Stewartstown. No mail is being received except that which can be brought in by horseback or on sleds. There is no passenger service whatsoever. The company will endeavor to have the road in operation within several days. (YD)

Feb. 27, 1922

DERAIL – While making the return trip in the evening from Stewartstown to Fawn Grove, the train on the New Park & Fawn Grove Railroad was derailed at Barlett's Crossing. A car load of lath [wooden slats] became derailed. The locomotive and the remainder of the train which was ahead of the derailed car were uncoupled and moved to Fawn Grove. Large jacks were secured and moved to the scene Saturday morning at which time the car was replaced on the rails again. There were slight damages to the car. The track was not damaged badly and was soon repaired. (YD)

Mar. 9, 1922

MERGER STILL PENDING

New Park, March 9 – No definite action was taken at a meeting of the stockholders of the New Park & Fawn Grove Railroad Tuesday on the proposed sale to the Stewartstown Railroad. Another meeting of the company will be held on April 11. (YD)

Mar. 22, 1922

During the past few days several carloads of cattle were forwarded from points on the Stewartstown and New Park & Fawn Grove railroads, Wilson Rehmeyer purchased three cars for H. B. Gingrich, representative of the Consolidated Dressed Beef Company, of Philadelphia. The cattle were sent to the West Philadelphia stockyards. (YD)

Apr. 10, 1922

STOCKHOLDERS' MEETING

A meeting of the stockholders of the Stewartstown Railroad Company will be held on April 11, 1922, at 10 o'clock in the morning at its office in Stewartstown, York County, Penna., for the purpose of voting upon the adoption or rejection of an agreement for the purchase by the Stewartstown Railroad Company of the franchises and all the property, real, personal and mixed, of the New Park & Fawn Grove Railroad, and for the merger and consolidation of the New Park & Fawn Grove Railroad into and with the Stewartstown Railroad Company, forming one corporation to be known as the Stewartstown Railroad Company.

STEWARTSTOWN RAILROAD CO.,

By Joseph W. Anderson, President

Attest: H. E. Anstine, Secretary,
W. B. Gemmill, Attorney. (YDR)

Apr. 19, 1922

TURNPIKE

Turnpike, April 19 – Lawrence Shaw, a brakeman on the Stewartstown Railroad, is off duty this week account serving on the jury during court at York. Brakeman [Glen] Brown, of the New Park & Fawn Grove Railroad, is filling Mr. Shaw's position during his absence. (YD)

Jul. 21, 1922	RAILROAD – Derailed Car Delays Traffic on New Park & Fawn Grove Line

Railroad, July 21 – While making the morning run from Fawn Grove to Stewartstown yesterday, the train on the New Park and Fawn Grove Railroad was delayed almost the entire day account of a wreck.

The locomotive and three loaded freight cars were derailed a short distance east of Anderson's station. The track was damaged to a great extent and required much fixing to get it into shape again. The derailed locomotive and cars had to be replaced on the rails with hand power jacks which also required the afternoon, when the train was able to make a run to New Freedom. The New Park & Fawn Grove train made no connections with the Stewartstown train for New Freedom during the day. Because of having several carloads of freight, of which same was marketing for Baltimore, the New Park & Fawn Grove train made a special trip to New Freedom with the loaded cars. (YD)

Oct. 30, 1922 — The noon train on the Stewartstown Railroad was annulled Saturday account of making repairs to the locomotive. The locomotive of the New Park & Fawn Grove Railroad was used to make the morning and evening runs from Stewartstown to New Freedom. (YD)

Jan. 1, 1923 — The Stewartstown Railroad Company leases the New Park & Fawn Grove Railroad Company and merges both operations, whereby the Stewartstown Railroad is in control. The New Park & Fawn Grove Railroad locomotive No.2 was renumbered No.5 by the Stewartstown Railroad. (R.R.R.)

Jan. 25, 1923 — NOTICE

There will be a meeting of the stockholders of the New Park & Fawn Grove Railroad Company in its office at New Park, Pa., on Saturday, March 31st next, between the hours of 1 and 2 o'clock in the afternoon, for the purpose of voting on a resolution to sell all its corporate property, real, personal and mixed, to the Stewartstown Railroad Company, at and for the consideration mentioned in said resolution.

New Park & Fawn Grove Railroad Company
Harry M. Anderson, Secretary (SN)

March 1923 — The New Park & Fawn Grove Railroad and the Stewartstown Railroad purchased the Brill-White Rail Bus and was fondly given the nickname "Snookie" (EJB)

Mar. 15, 1923 — Two new stops have been added – Jordan Crossing and Jos. Manifold's. If this service is not patronized, it will be withdrawn. (SN)

Mar. 22, 1923	The first single line schedule appears in the newspaper. (SN)
Apr. 4, 1923	MOTOR CAR ARRIVES – New Passenger Schedule on Stewartstown Railroad Will Start Tomorrow – Three Round Trips Daily.
	Stewartstown, April 4 – The motor car of the Stewartstown Railroad, which will carry passengers between New Freedom and Fawn Grove, arrived here yesterday at 2:30 p.m. and unless something unforeseen prevents it will begin its service tomorrow. Three round trips will be made each day. Freight trains will be hauled by steam engine as heretofore. The new car was made by the John G. Brill Company, Philadelphia, at a cost of approximately $14,000. Its weight is about 20,000 pounds. It is fractioning more than 35 feet in length and will have a seating capacity of 43. The car can maintain a speed of from 30 to 35 miles an hour. (YD)
Apr. 5, 1923	Our two local railroads are united in one line. After long negotiations and lots of red tape, the merger is finally complete. A new schedule of trains went into effect last Monday. The new motor bus was delayed in in arriving at Stewartstown but arrived on Tuesday, and will be put into operation as soon as the instructor arrives. Three round trips will be operated each weekday from New Park (make that Fawn Grove) to New Freedom with George B. Hale as motorman and Charles McElwain as conductor. The freight schedule now calls for two round trips each weekday and at present the train is being operated by the Fawn Grove crew since it must start at that point. Most of the Stewartstown men took other employment: brakeman Lawrence Shaw is working at the lumber company and engineer George Gibbs is working for carpenter Ben Busler. (SN)
Oct. 1, 1924	RAILROAD DEAL APPROVED
	Harrisburg, Oct. 1 – The public service commission today announced its approval of the acquisition by the Stewartstown Railroad Company of the capital stock and property of the New Park & Fawn Grove Railroad Company. Both railroads operate in York County. (TT)
June 23, 1925	The New Park & Fawn Grove Railroad offered the Stewartstown Railroad to lease the railroad and all of its property providing it is approved by the Interstate Commerce Commission. (R.R.R.)
July 1925	During the month, the railroad quit advertising its passenger schedule as it had done almost every week since it opened. (SN)
Jul. 2, 1925	A new schedule has been announced. The noon rail bus trip has been discontinued. Passengers may ride from Fawn Grove to Stewartstown on

the regular freight train leaving Fawn Grove at 10:55 a.m. or on the mixed train leaving Stewartstown at 12:25 p.m. The noon bus had carried few passengers on the lower end. (SN)

Oct. 1, 1925 — W. E. Manifold, the NP&FG station agent, turned over $1,810.84 to the Stewartstown Railroad auditor. (F.R. of R.R.)

May 10, 1927 — Stewartstown Railroad notes a decline in traffic on the New Park & Fawn Grove Railroad. Area residents are to be notified by a circular. A meeting will also be held to drum up business. (SRDMN)

1928 — New Park & Fawn Grove Railroad made the following stops: Fawn Grove, Kisiner, New Park, Strawbridge, Wiley, Gemmill, Maple Hill, Anderson, Manifold and Stewartstown. (R.R.R.)

1929 — It was reported that a truck line, Southern Freight Company, was preparing to haul milk and general freight between York and Fawn Grove. (SRDMN)

May 14, 1934 — Notice of Abandonment was posted in the newspaper by the Stewartstown Railroad Company and the New Park & Fawn Grove Railroad Company to abandon nine miles of track from Stewartstown, Pa. to Fawn Grove, Pa. (G&D)

Jun. 30, 1934 — GIVEN PERMISSION TOI ABANDON RAILROAD – I.C.C. Authorizes Disuse of Link Between Fawn Grove and Stewartstown – NO LONGER PROFITABLE

Stewartstown, June 29 – The New Park & Fawn Grove Railroad Company and the Stewartstown Railroad Company were authorized by the Interstate Commerce Commission today to abandon their railroad line from Fawn Grove to Stewartstown, according to a dispatch from Washington, D.C. The road is nine miles long and was built primarily to facilitate the marketing of farm produce. During recent years the greater portion of the farm produce has been transported by motor vehicles over a hard surface highway paralleling the line and as a result its revenues have declined to the point where a loss has been sustained. (SN)

Jul. 14, 1934 — The New Park & Fawn Grove Railroad deeded their property over to the following individuals:

> Harry E. Burns, Fawn Grove, for $550
> Benj. F. Morris for $50
> Wm. Sechrist, Stewartstown, for $94
> Thomas B. Griffith, property sold to the furniture factory in Stewartstown

	Isabella Fulton, Stewartstown, for $200 Jas. M. Hendrix for $400 J. Harry Bear, Hopewell Township, for $200 Margaret Marsteller, Fawn Grove Township, for $100 (F.R. of R.R.)
Oct. 1, 1934	Operation of the New Park & Fawn Grove Railroad discontinued by the Stewartstown Railroad. The New Park & Fawn Grove Railroad operated independently between 1906 and 1923 until the Stewartstown Railroad leased it (R.R.R.) (SRDMN)
Nov. 20, 1934	Stewartstown Railroad offered to sell Engine No.5 (former New Park & Fawn Grove Railroad Engine No. 2). (SRDMN)
May 14, 1935	New Park & Fawn Grove Railroad property to be liquidated by the Stewartstown Railroad. (SRDMN)
May 22, 1935	Harry E. Burns purchases land from the Stewartstown Railroad in Fawn Grove known as the old railroad shops of the N.P&F.G.R.R. for $250. (SR.R.R.)
June 3, 1935	Stewartstown Railroad leases the old machine shop of the New Park & Fawn Grove Railroad to John W. Kisiner for $7 per month. (S.R.R.R.) Stewartstown Railroad leases the old Fawn Grove Station of the N.P.&F.G.R.R. to Kenneth S. Manifold at $4 per month to be paid quarterly. (SR.R.R.) See Appendix No.41
1936	Maryland & Pennsylvania Railroad repaired Eng. No.5 (former locomotive of the New Park & Fawn Grove Railroad). (R.R.R.)
Nov. 29, 1939	Stewartstown Railroad Engine No. 5 (former N.P. &. F.G.R.R. Eng. No.2) was placed out of service. (R.R.R.) (SRDMN)
May 1941	Maryland & Pennsylvania railroad estimated that it would cost $3,500 to repair Eng. No.5. (SRDMN)
1947	Stewartstown Railroad scrapped Locomotive Eng. No.5. (R.R.R.)
Jun. 26, 1947	New Park & Fawn Grove land at Wiley Station is sold for $1,700. The balance of the New Park & Fawn Grove Railroad land is transferred to the Stewartstown Railroad allowing for final liquidation of the New Park & Fawn Grove Railroad. (SRDMN)

Nov. 9, 1977   Fond memories of the New Park & Fawn Grove Railroad by Charles Heaton (engineer for the N.P.&F.G.R.R. and the Stewartstown Railroad):

1.) The water tank in Fawn Grove was located near the station across the track.
2.) The coach car was painted a PRR red. In the interior, the seats were red.
3.) Joe Williams lived in Delta, Pa., and worked for N.P.&F.G.R.R. as a machinist.
4.) List of stations: Fawn Grove, Kisiner, New Park, Centre Church, Strawbridge, Wiley, Gemmill, Jordan's (Maple Hill), Howard Anderson, and Stewartstown.
5.) Railroad re-alignment occurred at Anderson Fruit Packing House (now Barton) where the track was shifted to the other side of the road to eliminate 2 of the 3 grade crossings.
6.) The N.P.&F.G.R.R. tracks were removed in 1935.
7.) Gas Motor stopped running when the mail contract with the Stewartstown Railroad was canceled.
8.) N.P.&F.G.R.R. Engine No.2 was constructed by Baldwin Locomotive Works.
9.) Fawn Grove Station Agents: Elwood Scott and Alvin [Avon W.] Hess. Stewartstown Agent: Harry Anstine for many years.
10.) Conductor: Ollie Morris
11.) B. F. Morris was one of several presidents and general managers of the N.P.&F.G.R.R.
12.) No Train Orders were used: We had specific times when we could make moves and operate safely. (SHS)

Sources:

Documents and books:
(DMN) – Directors Meeting Notes of the N.P. & F.G.R.R., New Park, Pa.
(F.R. of R.R.) – Financial Records of the railroad of N.P. & F.G.
(E.N. of R.R.) – Engineering Notes of the railroad of N.P. & F.G.
(MMN) Stewartstown RR Directors Meeting Minute Notes
(R.R.R.) – Railroad Records of the N.P. & F.G.
(SRDMN) – Stewartstown Railroad Director's Meeting Notes
(S.R.R.R.) – Stewartstown Railroad Records, Stewartstown, Pa.
(S.H.S.) – Stewartstown Area Historical Society, Stewartstown, Pa.
(ICC) – Interstate Commerce Commission, Washington, D.C.
(EJB) – Eric J. Bickleman, *The Story of the Stewartstown Railroad, 1885–1996* (Baltimore, 1995)

Period Newspapers:
(BS) – *Baltimore Sun*, Baltimore, Md.
(DA) – *Democratic Advocate*, Westminster, Md.
(G) – *Gazette*, York, Pa.
(SN) – *Stewartstown News*, Stewartstown, Pa.
(YD) – *York Dispatch*, York, Pa.
(GD) – *Gazette & Daily*, York, Pa.
(AI) – *Aegis and Intelligencer*, Bel Air, Md.
(YDR) – *York Daily Record*, York, Pa.
(TYD) – *The York Daily*, York, Pa.
(YG) – *York Gazette*, York, Pa.
(DHT) – *Delta Herald Times*, Delta, Pa.
(CW) – *Cecil Whig*, Elkton, Md.
(TT) – *The Times-Tribune*, Scranton, Pa.

THE NEW PARK AND FAWN GROVE RAILROAD

PHOTOGRAPHS

ROUTE MAP OF STATIONS, SHELTERS, AND FLAG STOPS
ON THE NEW PARK & FAWN GROVE RAILROAD

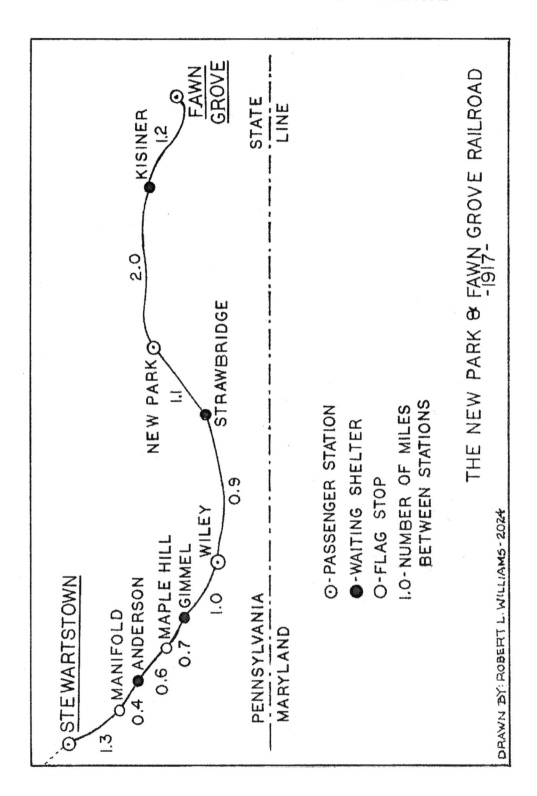

The first Board of Directors of the New Park & Fawn Grove Railroad. In the center of the first row is John Henry Anderson, the first elected president.

From the collection of John Hope Anderson – 1907

Several of the property owners who contributed the right-of-way to the New Park & Fawn Grove Railroad.

From the collection of John Hope Anderson – ca.1910

A 1912 gathering of John and Elizabeth Anderson's family. On the far left stands John Henry Anderson, the president of the New Park & Fawn Grove Railroad.

From the collection of John Hope Anderson – 1912

Trustees at the Centre Presbyterian Church. In the first row to the far right is John Henry Anderson, the president of the New Park & Fawn Grove Railroad.

From the collection of John Hope Anderson – ca.1910

Construction of the New Park & Fawn Grove Railroad: cutting through a hill to establish a level profile in 1905.

From the collection of Neal DeVoe

Construction of the New Park & Fawn Grove Railroad: establishing a profile by using fill dirt (profile not seen in this 1905 photograph).

From the collection of Neal DeVoe

Front view of a souvenir fan given out by the New Park & Fawn Grove Railroad Company during the grand opening ceremony in Fawn Grove on August 9, 1906.

From the collection of the Stewartstown Area Historical Society

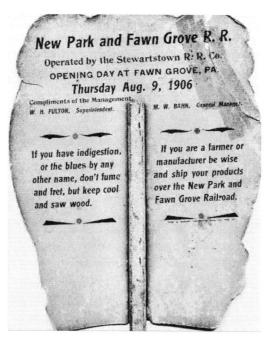

Back view of a souvenir fan given out by the New Park & Fawn Grove Railroad Company during the grand opening ceremony on August 9, 1906.

From the collection of the Stewartstown Area Historical Society

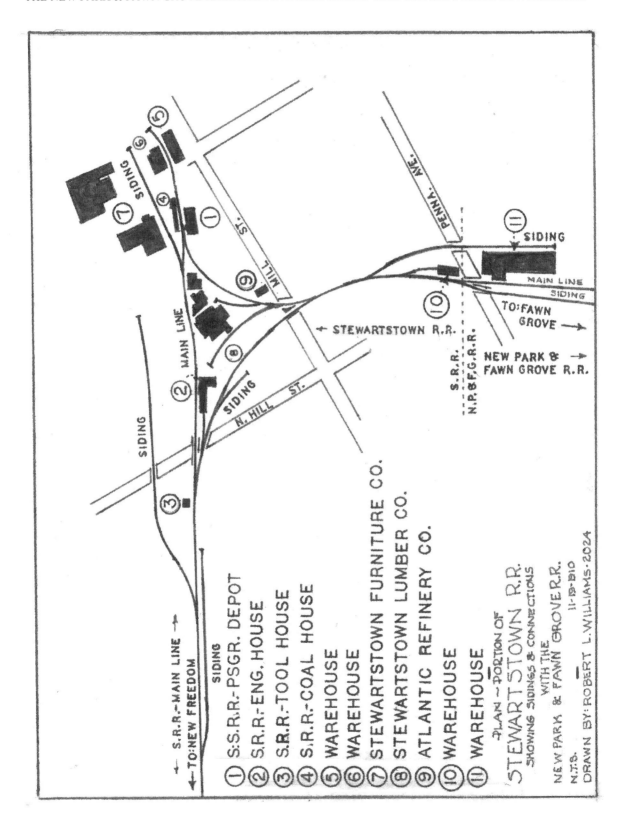

① S.S.R.R.-PSGR. DEPOT
② S.R.R.-ENG. HOUSE
③ S.R.R.-TOOL HOUSE
④ S.R.R.-COAL HOUSE
⑤ WAREHOUSE
⑥ WAREHOUSE
⑦ STEWARTSTOWN FURNITURE CO.
⑧ STEWARTSTOWN LUMBER CO.
⑨ ATLANTIC REFINERY CO.
⑩ WAREHOUSE
⑪ WAREHOUSE

PLAN → PORTION OF
STEWARTSTOWN R.R.
SHOWING SIDINGS & CONNECTIONS
WITH THE
NEW PARK & FAWN GROVE R.R.
N.T.S.   11-19-B10
DRAWN BY: ROBERT L. WILLIAMS · 2024

STEWARTSTOWN

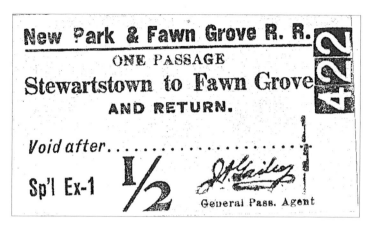

The railroad issued half-price tickets for special events and children under 12.

From the collection of Jody Anderson Leighty – ca.1910

A postcard of the first station that the Stewartstown Railroad built in Stewartstown in 1899. The New Park & Fawn Grove Railroad established an agreement with the Stewartstown Railroad in 1906 to have tickets sold at this station while dropping off and picking up passengers who were proceeding to all points along their line to Fawn Grove. Stewartstown R.R. Engine No.3 sits near the station.

From the collection of the Stewartstown Area Historical Society – ca. 1910

A southeast view of the first station built by the Stewartstown Railroad. Note that the building has been extended. It has been suggested that when the station was rented out to a private business, the company extended it to meet the renter's needs.

From the collection of the Stewartstown Area Historical Society – ca.1966

November 1911 freight bill from New Freedom to Baltimore on the NP&FG RR.

Courtesy of Greg Halpin.

Postcard view of the second station that the Stewartstown Railroad built in 1914.

From the collection of Robert L. Williams – 1918

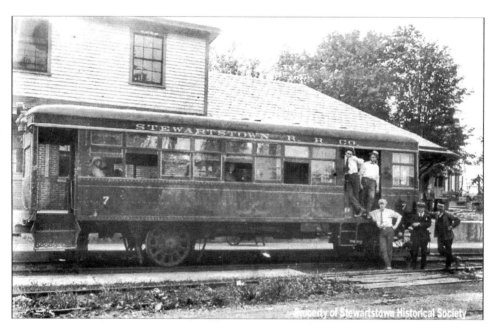

Gasoline Rail Car No. 7 with its crew sitting in front of the Stewartstown Railroad passenger station. The car made round trips from Fawn Grove to New Freedom daily except for weekends.

From the collection of Deane Mellander/Stewartstown Area Historical Society – ca.1923

The Board of Directors of the Stewartstown Railroad poses in front of the new Gasoline Rail Car No. 7 (purchased on March 13, 1923). Service was inaugurated on April 6, 1923.

From the collection of the Stewartstown Area Historical Society – ca.1923

Herman Few (1901–1983) went to work for the New Park & Fawn Grove Railroad at the age of 16 as a fireman. After 10 years of working for the railroad company, he resigned and pursued a second career as a stone mason.

York Daily Record photo dated April 25, 1972

The First National Bank of Fawn Grove opened in 1909. The New Park & Fawn Grove Railroad established an account there for all its monetary transactions. Prior to that, it used the First National Bank of Stewartstown, which opened in 1891.

From the collection of Neal DeVoe – ca.1910

New Park & Fawn Grove Railroad check dated June 6, 1906, to C. E. Strawbridge.

From the collection of the Stewartstown Area Historical Society

A postcard view of the first passenger station established in Fawn Grove in 1906. It was on the west side of Market Street at Mill Street. The small waiting room/ticket office was located in the front part of the mill building. Note the N.P.&F.G.R.R. Engine No.1 sitting on the main track with its coach car.

From the collection of the Stewartstown Area Historical Society – ca.1910

Builder's photograph of New Park & Fawn Grove Railroad Engine No.2, which was constructed in 1916 and sold to the railroad company on January 5, 1917.

From the collection of John Hope Anderson – ca.1917

A view of the N.P.&F.G.R.R. work train car (gondola) to the right of the photograph. The company purchased the car in 1906.

From the collection of Neal DeVoe – ca.1910

A drawing of a typical Buda Bridge Gang Motor Car. The Buda Company of Harvey, Illinois, sold a motor car to the New Park & Fawn Grove Railroad in 1907.

From the collection of the Stewartstown Area Historical Society – ca.1907

A track crew poses near Strawbridge in or about 1915.

From the collection of Mary Henderson / Stewartstown Area Historical Society

This N.P.&F.G.R.R. track foreman's report is dated February 1, 1913.

From the collection of the Stewartstown Area Historical Society

A P.R.R. placard that was posted on any freight car carrying flammable materials.

From the collection of the Stewartstown Area Historical Society – 1900

Often referred to as the "Market Car," this freight car was converted into a combination freight and caboose car. The Stewartstown Railroad owned it, but the New Park & Fawn Grove Railroad constantly used it because all freight car pickup started in Fawn Grove.

From the collection of Neal DeVoe – ca.1940

MANIFOLD

First-class passenger ticket from Wiley to Manifold (the latter was a flag stop).

From the collection of Ken Myers – ca.1914

Joseph W. Anderson built this impressive house on his farm in Manifold. Note the main line track of the New Park & Fawn Grove Railroad in the lower left-hand corner of the photograph. The home burned down in 1915.

From the collection of the Stewartstown Area Historical Society – ca.1910

A northeast view of the home of businessman/miller William E. Manifold. He built this house in the same location where the J. W. Anderson home had burned down earlier. The Manifold Flag Stop was located across the road from this dwelling.

From the collection of the Stewartstown Area Historical Society – ca.1920

Front view of the home of prominent businessman William E. Manifold.

From the collection of the Stewartstown Area Historical Society – ca.1920

ANDERSON

A one-way passenger ticket from Fawn Grove to Anderson. The latter was named for a prominent Stewartstown businessman, Howard W. Anderson (1878–1941), who owned a three-story fruit canning factory along State Route 24 about a mile south of Stewartstown in Hopewell Township. Lucious fruit from the nearby sprawling farm often won prizes or ribbons at the annual York Fair.

From the collection of Jody Anderson Leighty – ca.1920

Drawing of the Anderson Passenger Shelter that was constructed in 1910. The small wooden structure offered little amenity other than cursory protection from the rain while awaiting incoming trains.

From the collection of Robert L. Williams

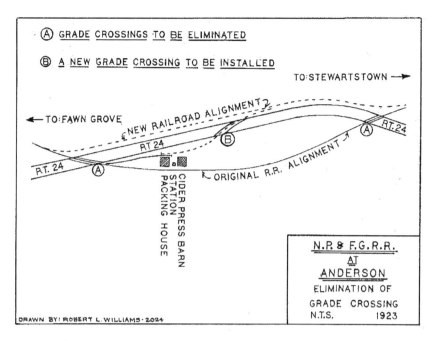

Drawing showing Anderson and the 1923 relocation of the New Park & Fawn Grove Railroad's main track from south of Route 24 to the north side.

From the collection of Robert L. Williams

Howard W. Anderson's fruit packing plant before the track relocation in 1923.

From the collection of Neal DeVoe – ca.1920

Howard W. Anderson's packing house supported his sprawling fruit farm.

From the collection of Neal DeVoe – ca.1927

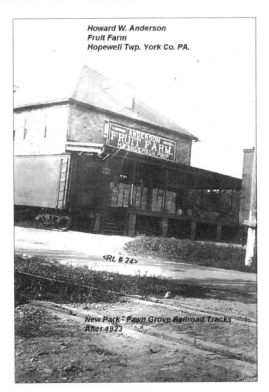

The packing house of Anderson's Fruit Farm. Note the freight box sitting on the siding to the left of the photograph.

From the collection of Neal DeVoe – ca.1930

MAPLE HILL

New Park & Fawn Grove R. R.
NEW PARK TO
MAPLE HILL
AND RETURN.

Void after................

Sp'l Ex-1

General Pass. Agent

499

Round-trip ticket from New Park to Maple Hill.

From the collection of Ken Myers – ca.1920

A drawing of a typical flag stop at Manifold and Maple Hill. A passenger would pull a red flag out of the box sitting next to the pole and insert it into a bracket on the pole. The engineer, seeing the distant red flag, knew to stop at this location to pick up a passenger.

From the collection of Robert L. Williams – ca.1918

GEMMILL

A one-way ticket from Stewartstown to Gemmill. Note that the conductor scratched out Strawbridge on the ticket and penciled in Gemmill.

From the collection of the Stewartstown Area Historical Society – ca.1920

Drawing of the Gemmill Passenger Shelter that was constructed in 1914.

From the collection of Robert L. Williams

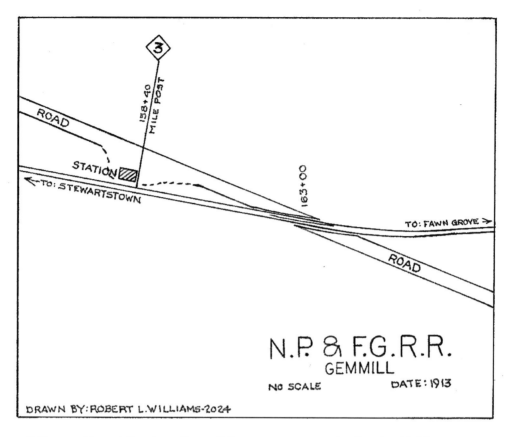

Site plan of Gemmill and the location of the passenger shelter in 1913.

From the collection of Robert L. Williams

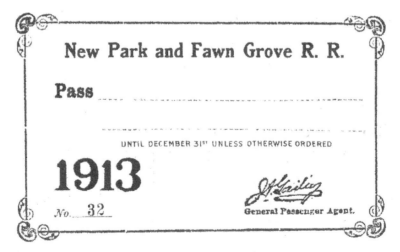

New Park & Fawn Grove Railroad general pass from 1913.

From the collection of Ken Myers

WILEY

One-way passenger ticket from New Freedom to Wiley – ca.1918

From the collection of Neal DeVoe

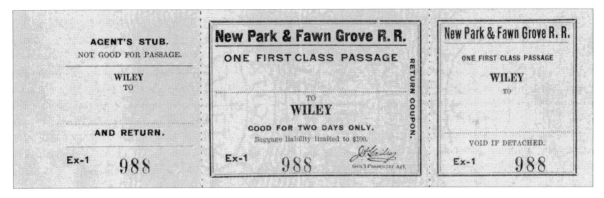

Unused first-class passenger ticket from Wiley Station.

Courtesy of Greg Halpin

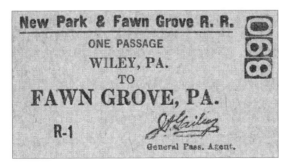

One-way passenger ticket from Wiley to Fawn Grove.

Courtesy of Greg Halpin

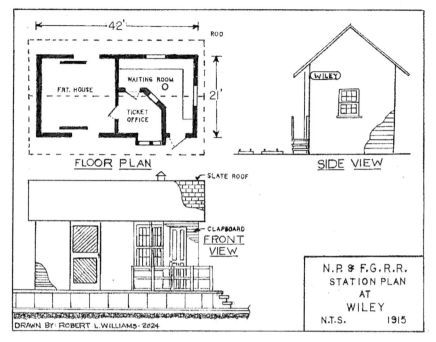

Station plan of Wiley Station in 1915.

From the collection of Robert L. Williams

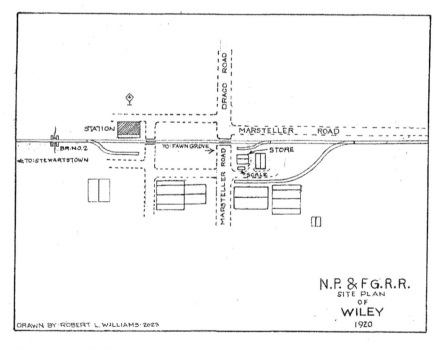

Site plan of Wiley, Pa., in 1920.

From the collection of Robert L. Williams

The hamlet of Wiley Station as seen in 1915.

From the collection of the Stewartstown Area Historical Society

Wiley Station in 1921. Eight-year-old John Hyson Wiley is shown with his dog. The canning house is to the left with the Wiley train station in the left center. A Ford Model T automobile is parked by the warehouse.

From the collection of the Stewartstown Area Historical Society

Wiley Station. Left: John Hyson Wiley; middle: Grandfather J. Harvey Anderson; and right: Burneta (Wiley) Hershner (sister). Wiley was born in 1913, so this image was likely taken before 1920.

From the collection of Neal DeVoe

Wiley Station. Hiram Davis is at the scales next to the local general store. The New Park & Fawn Grove Railroad often would use these scales to determine the weight and cost to haul the materials to be loaded on the freight car.

From the collection of the Stewartstown Area Historical Society

Wiley, Pa.: Just west of Wiley stands what is left of the piers of Bridge No.2. See Drawing No. 15. The bridge was constructed in 1905 as an undergrade cattle crossing on the land of Mrs. Hannah Ball (Lanius) Wiley, the widow of farmer John Wiley.

From the collection of Eric J. Bickleman – ca.1990

An early 20th-century postcard showing Centre Presbyterian Church, which is located just west of Strawbridge at 83 New Park Road.

From the collection of Robert L. Williams – ca.1920

Standing in the bell tower of Centre Presbyterian Church, the Reverend R. Lorenzo Clark (1849-1935) took this photo of a New Park & Fawn Grove Railroad train heading west from Strawbridge in 1908. Clark, a native of Hensel in Drumore Township, Lancaster County, wrote a book detailing the history of the church in 1903.

From the collection of Charles W. Boas/Stewartstown Area Historical Society

STRAWBRIDGE

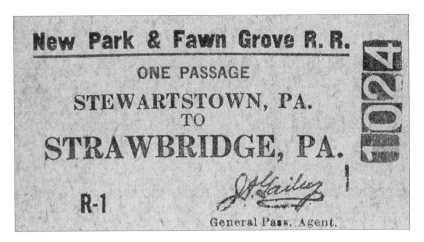

One-way passenger ticket from Stewartstown to Strawbridge – ca. 1918. This ticket was printed on a yellow tag stock.

From the collection of Greg Halpin

Drawing of the Strawbridge Passenger Shelter that was built in 1913.

From the collection of Robert L. Williams

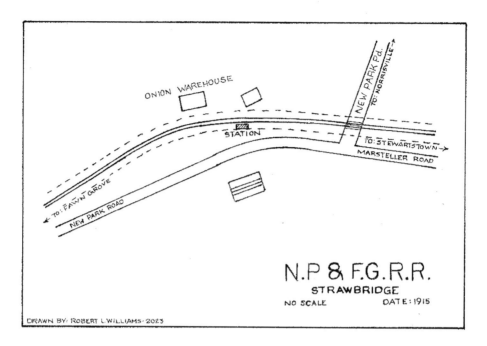

Site plan of Strawbridge in 1915. The stop was popular with local onion growers.

From the collection of Robert L. Williams

A northward view of the former onion warehouse that had served the Strawbridge community as a post office from 1840 to 1871. The post office was relocated in January 1872 to New Park by order of the U.S. postmaster general. (York *True Democrat*, December 26, 1871, and January 9, 1872)

From the collection of Neal DeVoe

A southward view of the former onion warehouse – ca.1990.

From the Stewartstown Area Historical Society

A westward view of the former onion warehouse – ca.1990.

From the Stewartstown Area Historical Society

Charlie Neal, a railroad trackman, poses near Strawbridge – ca.1910.

From the collection of Mary E. Henderson/ Stewartstown Area Historical Society

Station stamp for the New Park Station while under the operation of the Stewartstown Railroad for the New Park & Fawn Grove Railroad – October 25, 1907.

From the collection of the Stewartstown Area Historical Society

NEW PARK

Round-trip passenger ticket from Stewartstown to New Park.

From the collection of the Stewartstown Area Historical Society – ca.1915

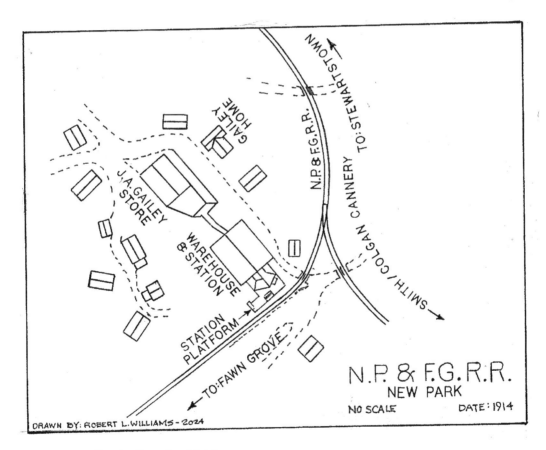

Site plan of New Park, Pa., in 1914.

From the collection of Robert L. Williams

General view of the New Park station and platform. Part of the first floor was used for the ticket office, waiting room, and freight warehouse while the second floor was used for the general offices and conference room of the New Park & Fawn Grove Railroad. All the space occupied by the railroad within the building was rented from the owner, businessman and railroad director Joseph Anderson Gailey (1863–1956).

From the collection of Robert H. Shaub/Stewartstown Area Historical Society

View of the station area owned by Joseph A. Gailey. The general store is in the center. Behind the store is Gailey's home.

From the collection of the Stewartstown Area Historical Society

N.P.&F.G.R.R. Engine No. 1 heading west from New Park toward Stewartstown. Standing in the foreground is John Henry Anderson, the president of the New Park & Fawn Grove Railroad.

From the collection of Cecil Morris/Stewartstown Area Historical Society

N.P.&F.G.R.R. Engine No. 1 heading eastward from New Park to Fawn Grove.

From the collection of the Stewartstown Area Historical Society

J. A. Gailey's general store and post office in New Park.

From the collection of the Stewartstown Area Historical Society

New Park School House where the first meeting was held concerning the formation of the proposed New Park & Fawn Grove Railroad on January 19, 1905.

From the collection of the Stewartstown Area Historical Society

The New Park Creamery, owned in the early 20th Century by J. A. Gailey, was located just east of the New Park Station. It had started operations in the 1890s, churning commercial quantities of butter. In the first half of 1897, the trackside facility averaged 700 pounds of saleable product a day. (*York Gazette*, June 9, 1897)

From the collection of the Stewartstown Area Historical Society

Aerial view of the James T. Smith/Lewis Colgan Cannery serviced by the New Park & Fawn Grove Railroad. The railroad constructed a new siding there in 1922. Smith and Colgan's largest product lines were canned sweet corn and canned tomatoes.

From the collection of Neal DeVoe – ca.1936

West of New Park looking back toward Wiley. Neal DeVoe built his home in the open area to the right of the photograph.

From the collection of Neal DeVoe – ca.1906

East of New Park: J. Clay Anderson and his brother D. Ross Anderson opened a feed store that also sold seeds and general farm supplies.

From the collection of Neal DeVoe

The Pennsylvania State Road Commission loaded heavy road-building equipment on a PRR flatbed railcar and had it shipped to New Park. Once offloaded from the railcar, construction could begin on the road between Wiley Station and Gatchellville.

From the collection of Nathalie Clugston/Stewartstown Area Historical Society – ca.1926

A construction crew works on a public road near New Park.

From the collection of Neal DeVoe – ca.1926

On the western edge of New Park, a cattle car sits on a siding opposite the McGinnis Farm.

From the collection of Jay McGinnis/Stewartstown Area Historical Society

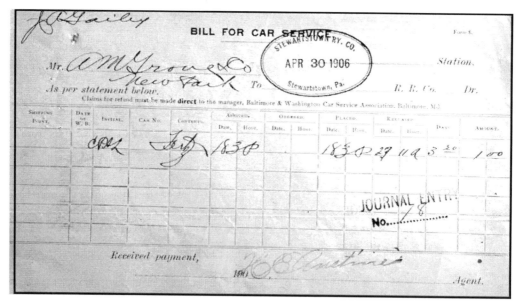

Stamped bill for car service for A. M. Grove at New Park, dated April 30, 1906.

From the collection of the Stewartstown Area Historical Society

KISINER

One-way passenger ticket from Stewartstown to Kisiner – ca.1918.

From the collection of the Stewartstown Area Historical Society

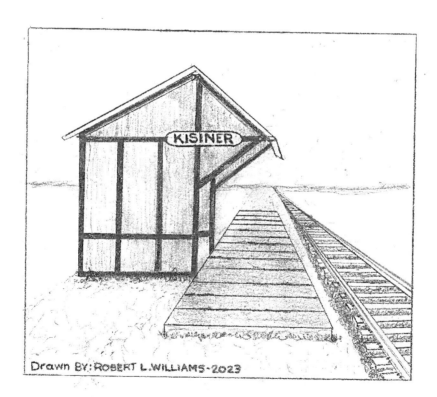

Drawing of the wooden passenger shelter in Kisiner that the railroad built in 1911.

From the collection of Robert L. Williams

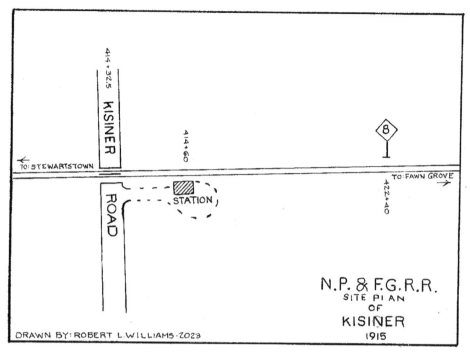

Site plan of the Kisiner station stop as it appeared in 1915.

From the collection of Robert L. Williams

A possible passenger waiting for a train opposite the McGinnis Farm?

From the collection of the Stewartstown Area Historical Society

FAWN GROVE

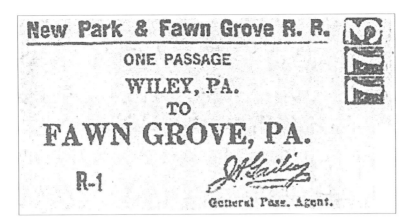

One-way passenger ticket from Wiley to Fawn Grove – ca. 1915.

From the collection of Neal DeVoe

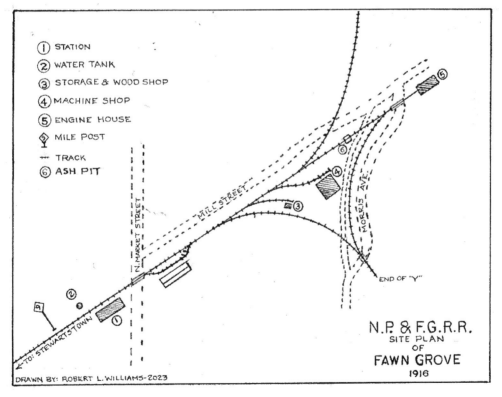

Site plan of the railroad facilities in Fawn Grove in 1916.

From the collection of Robert L. Williams

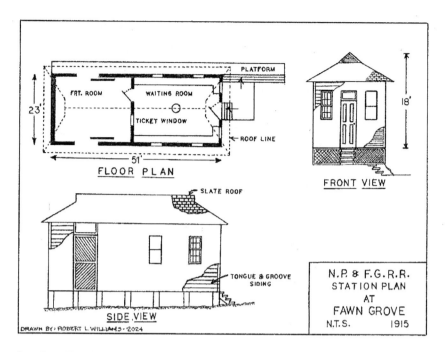

Fawn Grove Station Plan – 1915.

From the collection of Robert L. Williams

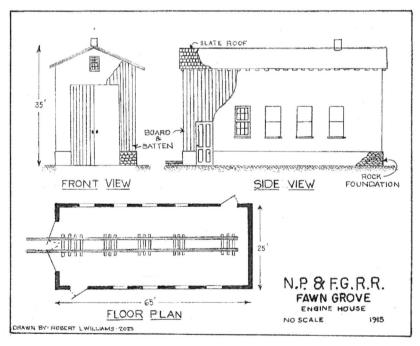

Fawn Grove Engine House Plan – 1915.

From the collection of Robert L. Williams

Stewartstown Railroad Engine No.3 with a passenger coach at Fawn Grove.

From the collection of Robert H. Shaub/Stewartstown Area Historical Society

A woman poses by the warehouse for the W.E. Manifold Mill at Fawn Grove. The N.P.&F.G.R.R. installed a new switch near here in 1909. John C. Wiley, the railroad's chief engineer, supervised the project. A small area inside the feed mill was used as a ticket office and waiting room until a larger and more spacious passenger station was built in 1913.

From the collection of the Stewartstown Area Historical Society – ca.1915

The Fawn Grove passenger station was built in 1913. Baldwin Engine No.2 awaits a westbound departure for Stewartstown. Photographed from left to right: John Hostler, mail carrier; Elwood Scott, ticket agent; B. F. Morris; Charles Heaton; William L. Duncan, conductor; Glen Brown, brakeman; Lewis Rosenberry, engineer; Lawrence Lyons; Herman Few, fireman.

From the collection of Wilson Hostler/Stewartstown Area Historical Society – ca.1920

Fawn Grove, Pa. — the intersection of Market and Mill streets. The New Park & Fawn Grove Railroad's passenger station is in the center-right.

From the collection of the Stewartstown Area Historical Society

Fawn Grove: Hauling ties for the New Park & Fawn Grove Railroad. The passenger station can be seen in the background.

From the collection of the Stewartstown Area Historical Society

Fawn Grove's Morris Park, which opened in 1927, was located on the north side of the New Park & Fawn Grove Railroad's terminus near the passenger station. The sprawling site featured exhibition halls, refreshment stands, and a large pavilion capable of holding 1,000 people for agricultural fairs, concerts, picnics, and political rallies.

From the collection of the Stewartstown Area Historical Society

A view looking westward at the end of the track. The photograph was taken from the second-story window of the engine house showing the machine shop, ash pit, storage & wood shop, and the "wye" track.

From the collection of Cecil Morris /Stewartstown Area Historical Society

The former New Park & Fawn Grove Railroad Engine House was located at 90 Mill Street in Fawn Grove, Pa.

From the collection of Neal DeVoe – ca.2003

New Park & Fawn Grove R.R. freight bills issued from the Fawn Grove passenger station. They are signed by station agent Avon Hess.

From the collection of the Stewartstown Area Historical Society – ca.1913–1915

THE NEW PARK AND FAWN GROVE RAILROAD

DRAWINGS

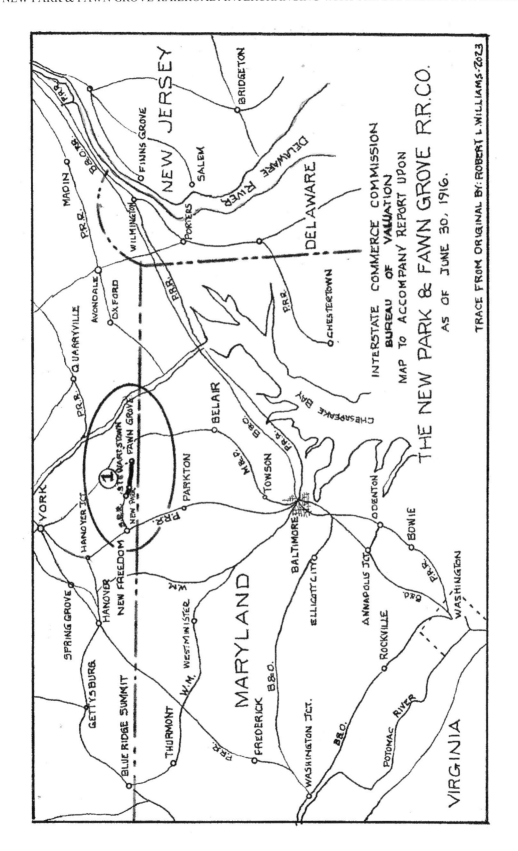

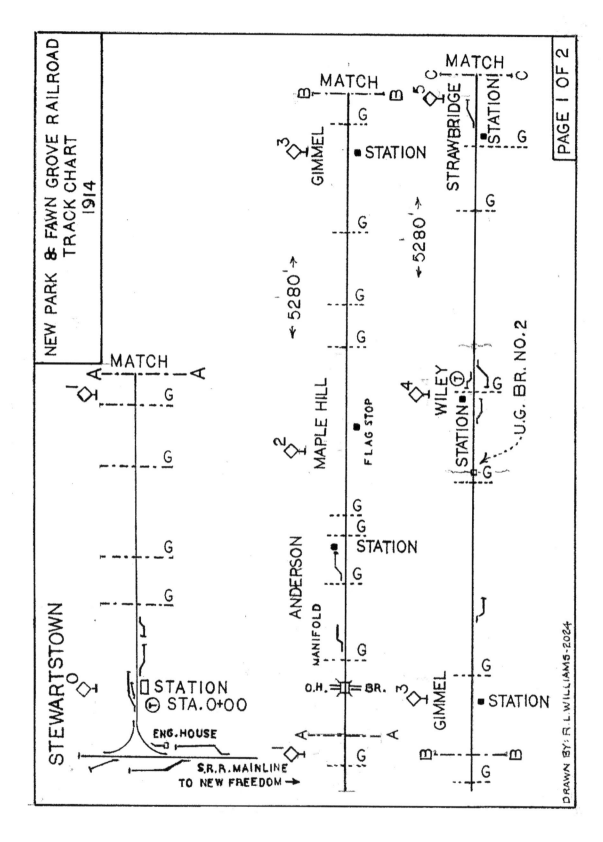

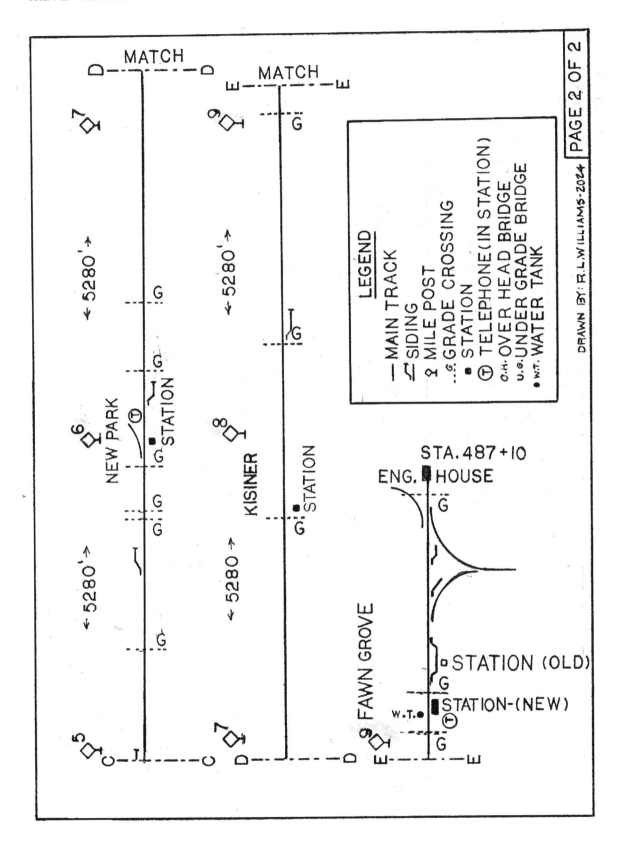

LEGEND

— MAIN TRACK
SIDING
MILE POST
GRADE CROSSING
STATION
TELEPHONE (IN STATION)
O.H. OVER HEAD BRIDGE
U.G. UNDER GRADE BRIDGE
W.T. WATER TANK

DRAWN BY: R.L.WILLIAMS-2024

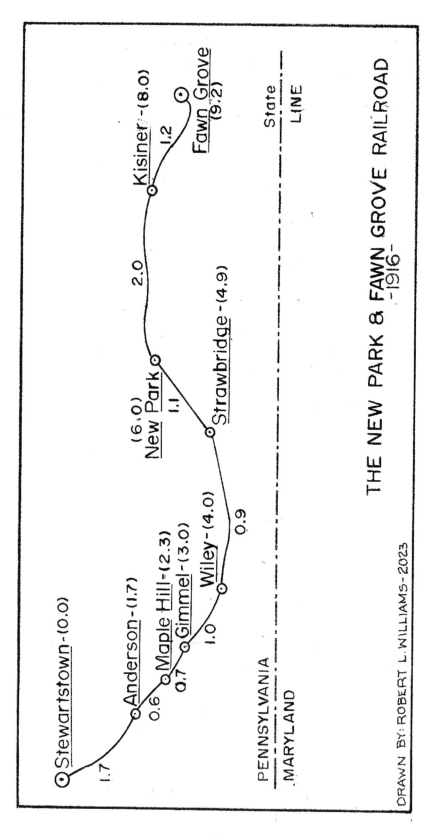

THE NEW PARK & FAWN GROVE RAILROAD
-1916-

DRAWN BY: ROBERT L. WILLIAMS - 2023

M.P.	POINT OF CURVE START	POINT OF TANGENT FINISH	DEGREE OF CURVE & DIRECTION
	NEW PARK & FAWN GROVE R.R.- CURVE DATA-1908		
0	12+75	19+17	6°C.L.
	24+88	27+59	4°C.R.
	40+67	45+33	6°C.L.
1	—	52+80	—
	51+46	55+56	2°C.R.
	59+61	64+71	2°C.L.
	82+00	87+78	6°C.R.
	89+81	ANDERSON	—
	90+90	93+52	6°C.L.
	—	—	R.
2	—	105+60	—
	108+00	110+00	2°C.R.
	113+14	117+33	4°C.L.
	129+17	132+00	2°C.L.
	158+40	GEMMILL	—
3	—	158+40	—
	163+00	166+37	4°C.L.
	181+09	183+00	6°C.L.
	192+54	199+22	2°C.R.
	211+20	WILEY	—
4	—	211+20	—
	220+55	121+95	1°C.L.
	238+41	239+10	2°C.L.
	247+08	260+23	10°C.L.
	258+72	STRAWBRIDGE	—
	263+25	265+00	4°C.R.
5	—	264+00	—

NEW PARK & FAWN GROVE R.R. – CURVE DATA – 1908

M.P.	POINT OF CURVE START	POINT OF TANGENT FINISH	DEGREE OF CURVE & DIRECTION
	277+29	278+36	2°C.R.
	295+00	298+30	3°C.L.
	300+13	303+00	5°C.R.
	312+76	315+74	10°C.R.
6	–	316+80	–
	316+80	NEW PARK	–
	347+00	348+15	6°C.R.
	365+83	371+81	6°C.L.
7	–	369+60	–
	376+26	381+58	6°C.R.
	409+80	413+81	5°C.R.
	414+65	KISINER	–
8	–	422+40	–
	422+49	426+44	6°C.R.
	450+96	455+79	6°C.L.
	466+23	474+00	6°C.L.
9	–	475+20	–
	474+00	479+10	6°C.R.
	480+58	FAWN GROVE	–
	ENG. HOUSE	487+10	–
	R=RIGHT	M.P.=MILE POST	
	L=LEFT		
	C=CURVE		
	DATA COMPILED	BY: ROBERT L. WILLIAMS	2

NEW PARK & FAWN GROVE R.R.
PROFILE DATA
1908

M.P.	STATION NAME	S.STA.(S)	S.STA.(F)	% OF GD. (+)	% OF GD. (−)
0	STEWARTSTOWN	−	−	−	−
	−	0+00	38+00	+0.25	−
1	−	52+80	−	−	−
	ANDERSON	89+76	−	−	−
	−	38+00	100+00	−	−1.58
	−	100+00	105+60	0.0	0.0
2	−	105+60	−	−	−
		105+60	127+00	+0.3	
	MAPLE HILL	121+44	−	−	−
	−	127+00	137+00	+0.10	−
	−	137+00	151+00		−0.8
	−	151+00	152+00	0.0	0.0
	GEMMILL	158+40	−	−	−
3	−	158+40	−	−	−
	−	152+00	182+00	+1.10	−
	−	182+00	184+00	0.0	0.0
	−	184+00	204+00	−	−2.0
	−	204+00	205+00	0.0	0.0
	−	205+00	217+00	+1.5	−
4	−	211+20	−	−	−
	WILEY	211+20	−	−	−
	−	217+00	220+00	0.0	0.0
	−	220+00	237+00	+0.65	−
	−	237+00	240+00	0.0	0.0
	−	240+00	268+00	+0.80	−
	STRAWBRIDGE	258+72	−	−	−

NEW PARK & FAWN GROVE R.R. PROFILE DATA 1908

2

M.P.	STATION NAME	S.STA.(S)	S.STA.(F)	% OF GD.(+)	% OF GD.(−)
5	–	264+00	–	–	–
	–	268+00	270+00	0.0	0.0
	–	270+00	290+00	–	−0.3
	–	290+00	319+00	+0.2	–
	NEW PARK	316+80	–	–	–
6	–	316+00	–	–	–
	–	319+00	340+00	+0.8	–
	–	340+00	340+40	0.0	0.0
	–	340+40	359+00	–	−1.00
	–	359+00	361+00	0.0	0.0
	–	361+00	375+00	+1.0	–
7	–	369+60	369+60	–	–
	–	375+00	377+00	0.0	0.0
	–	377+00	400+00	–	−1.36
	KISINER	414+60	–	–	–
	–	400+00	427+00	–	−0.2
8	–	422+40	–	–	–
	–	427+00	475+20	–	−1.56
9	–	475+20	–	–	–
	FAWN GROVE	480+48	–	–	–

NOTES:

PROFILE INFORMATION STOP AT 475+20
STEWARTSTOWN–900' ABOVE SEA LEVEL.
FAWN GROVE–750' ABOVE SEA LEVEL.
M.P.=MILE POST, S.STA(S)=SURVEY STATION START
(F)=FINISH, % OF GD(+)=PERCENT OF GRADE PLUS

R.L.W.-2024

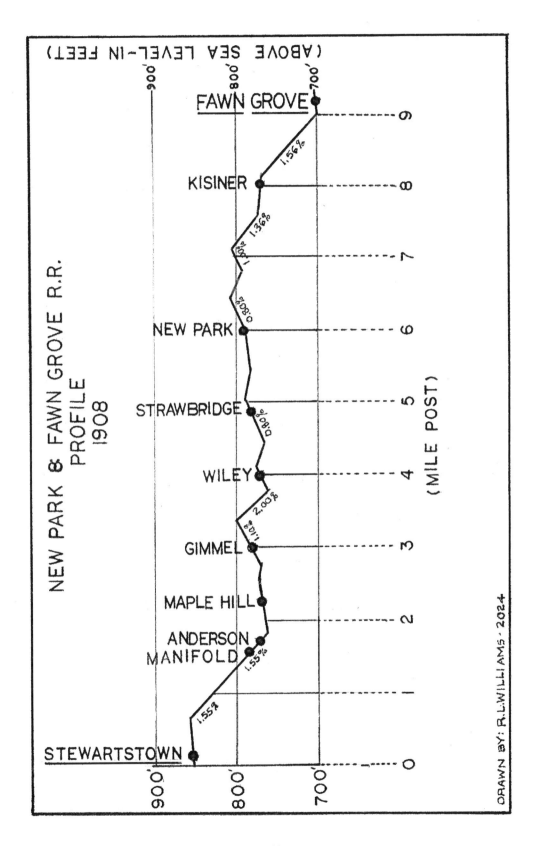

NEW PARK & FAWN GROVE RAILROAD
List of Owners & Structures
Fawn Grove to Stewartstown -1914

OWNER NAME	SURVEY STATION NUMBERS		WIDTH (in feet)	LENGTH (in feet)
Henry T. Brown	487+85	481+80	40'	605'
ENGINE HOUSE	487+85	487+20	25'	65'
Henry T. Brown	481+80	481+48	40'	32'
Henry T. Brown	Siding Agreement-No.11- 240 feet long – south side of Main Track			
GRADE CROSSING	481+80	481+48	40'	Morris Ave.
Wm. L. Duncan	481+48	478+52	40'	296'
MILL SIDING	--	--	--	--
GRADE CROSSING	--	--	--	N. Market St.
FAWN GROVE PSGR. STA.	480+73	480+23	23'	50'
WATER TANK	--	479+83	10 feet in Diameter – 5,900 gals.	
W. Almoney	478+52	477+22	40'	130'
W.L. Duncan	477+22	476+81	40'	41'
GRADE CROSSING	477+22	476+81	40'	W. Main St.
Henry T. Brown	476+81	469+42	40'	739'
MILE POST 9	--	475+20	--	--
Wm. L. Duncan	469+42	462+68	40'	674'
Harry S. Merryman	462+68	456+16	40'	652'
SECTION NO. 6	487+85	462+00	40'	2,585'
Dan'l E. McElwain	456+16	436+72	40'	1944'
Dan'l E. McElwin	Siding Agreement – No.10 – 120 feet long- southside of Main Track			
E.S. Irwin Sisters	436+72	436+47	40'	25'
GRADE CROSSING	436+72	436+47	40'	25'
Dan'l E. McElwain	436+47	431+00	40'	547'
E.S. Irwin & Sisters	431+00	423+64	40'	736'
Geo. Kisiner	423+64	414+20	40'	944'
George Kisiner	Siding Agreement – No.9 – 120 feet long – south side of Main Track			
MILE POST NO.8	--	422+40	--	--
KISINER STATION	414+65	414+55	10'	10'
GRADE CROSSING	414+45	414+20	40'	Kisiner Xing.
L.T. Hostler	414+20	403+68	40'	1052"
R.C. Liggett	403+68	390+63	40'	1305'
Charles R. Bartol	390+63	378+21	40'	1242'
Rachel Van Hart	378+21	361+97	40'	1624'
SECTION NO.5	462+00	372+00	40'	9,000'
MILE POST NO.7	--	369+60	--	--
John H. Anderson	361+97	346+70	40'	1527'
Dorcas A. Shirley	346+70	337+11	40'	959'
GRADE CROSSING	337+11	336+85	40'	26'
Sam'l Harman	336+85	328+69	40'	816'

NEW PARK & FAWN GROVE RAILROAD
List of Owners & Structures
Fawn Grove to Stewartstown -1914

OWNER NAME	SURVEY STATION NUMBERS		WIDTH (in feet)	LENGTH (in feet)
GRADE CROSSING	328+69	327+56	40'	Harman"s Xing.
SECTION NO.4	372+00	326+00	40'	4,600'
John H. Anderson	327+56	308+69	40'	1887'
John H. Anderson	Siding Agreement – No.8 – 400 feet long – southside of Main Track			
MILE POST NO.6	--	316+80	--	--
NEW PARK STATION	--	316+80	--	30' Platform
Joe Gailey	308+69	310+53	40'	184'
Joe Gailey	Siding Agreement – No.7 – 240 feet long – Southside of Main Track			
GRADE CROSSING	310=53	310+25	40'	28'
John W. Marsteller	310+25	307+43	40'	282'
SECTION NO.3	326+00	307+00	40'	1,900'
SECTION NO.2	15+50	307+00	40'	29,150'
John H. Anderson	307+43	298+40	40'	903'
GRADE CROSSING	299+20	298+40	40'	Davis Xing.
Maurice Davis	298+40	289+60	40'	880'
Maurice Davis	Siding Agreement – No.6 – 120 feet long – Northside of Main Track			
GRADE CROSSING	297+31	297+00	40'	31'
John M. Jenkins	289+60	277+82	40'	1178'
GRADE CROSSING	--	--	--	Baddre's Xing.
MILE POST NO.5	--	264+00	--	--
STRAWBRIDGE STA.	258+77	258+67	8'	10'
GRADE CROSSING	246+78	247+08	40'	State Rd. Xing.
Strawbridge Bro's	Siding Agreement – No.5 – 80 feet long – Northside of Main Track			
GRADE CROSSING	--	--	--	--
Strawbridge Bro's	277+82	240+03	40'	3770'
John E. Stansbury	240+03	231+85	40'	818'
Dan'l Harman	231+85	220+97	40'	1088'
Hannah B. Wiley	220+97	194+42	40'	2623'
MILE POST NO.4	--	211+20	--	--
WILEY STATION	211+41	211+00	21'	41'
BRIDGE NO.2	197+31	197+11	17'	25'
GRADE CROSSING	194+74	194+42	40'	Public Rd. Xing.
John H. Beard	194+42	179+70	40'	1472'
John S. Gemmill	179+70	161+79	40'	1791'
John S. Gemmill	Siding Agreement – No.3 – 80 feet long – Southside of Main Track			
GRADE CROSSING	161+79	161+21	40'	58'
Jacob Yost	161+79	156+45	40'	534'
MILE POST NO.3	--	158+40	--	--
GRADE CROSSING	--	158+45	--	State Rd. Xing

NEW PARK & FAWN GROVE RAILROAD
List of Owners & Structures
Fawn Grove to Stewartstown -1914

OWNER NAME	SURVEY STATION NUMBERS		WIDTH (in feet)	LENGTH (in feet)
GEMMILL STATION	158+45	158+35	8'	10'
J.S. Gemmill	156+45	152+09	40'	436'
J.C. Strawbridge	152+09	147+64	40'	445'
Aquilla M. Bartel	147+64	139+64	40'	800'
J.H. Ebaugh	139+64	131+36	40'	828'
J.M. Jordan	131+36	101+20	40'	3016'
GRADE CROSSING	--	126+41	--	Winemiller's Xing.
MAPLE HILL STATION	--	121+44	--	Flag Stop
MILE POST NO.2	--	105+60	--	--
GRADE CROSSING	101+20	101+00	40'	Barshhinger's Xing
Miss Margaret Harman	101+00	92+83	40'	817'
J.W. Anderson	92+83	51+04	40'	4179'
GRADE CROSSING	92+83	92+37	40'	46'
ANDERSON STATION	89+71	89+81	8'	10'
J.W. Anderson	Siding Agreement – No.2 – 120 feet long – southside of Main Track			
J.W. Anderson	Main Track and Siding was relocated to Northside of Public Road			
J.W. Anderson	Between Br. No.2 Manifold to Anderson in 1923			
GRADE CROSSING	--	--	--	--
MANIFOLD	--	--	--	Flag Stop
GRADE CROSSING	--	--	--	--
OVERHEAD BRIDGE NO.1	64+50	63+80	40'	70' Girder Br.
MILE POST NO.1	--	52+80	--	--
Thompkins	51+04	46+42	40'	462
Annie Gable	46+42	36+03	40'	1039'
GRADE CROSSING	--	39+60	--	Gable Xing.
J. Benson Gable	36+03	28+69	40'	734'
GRADE CROSSING	--	26+40	--	Trout Xing.
W.G. Trout	--	--	--	--
SECTION NO.1	00+00	15+50	40'	1,550'
Miss Emma Fulton	--	--	--	--
GRADE CROSSING	--	13+50	--	Church St. Xing
Lieb & Company	--	--	--	--
Stewartstown -Hill St.	00+00	00+00	--	--

Source: The New Park & Fawn Grove Railroad records housed at the Stewartstown Historical Society.

Complied by: Robert L. Williams

Abbreviations used: -- information not available,
Xing. - Crossing
Sta. - Station

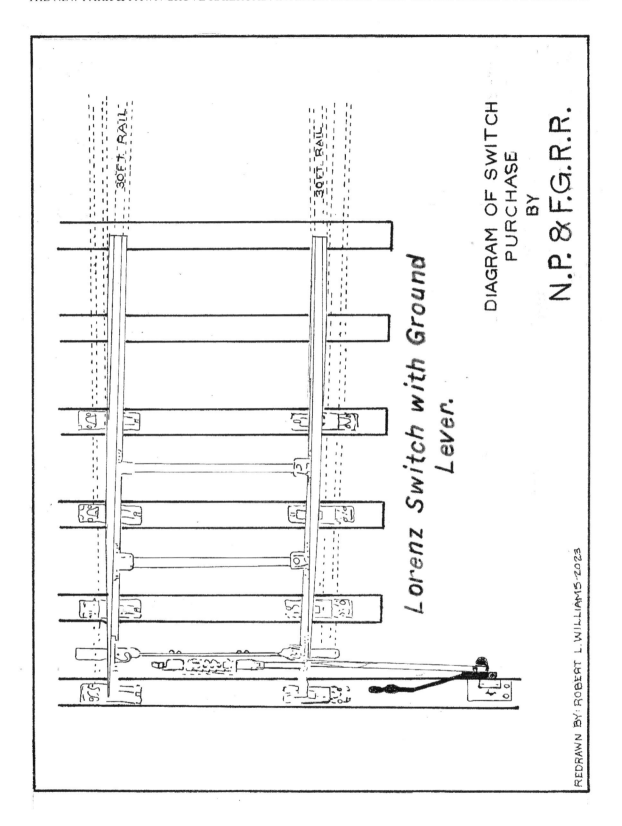

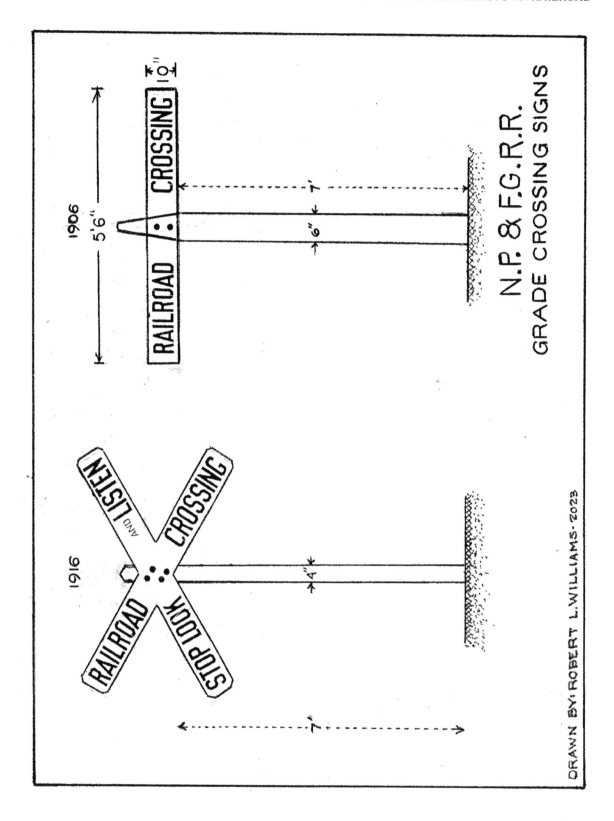

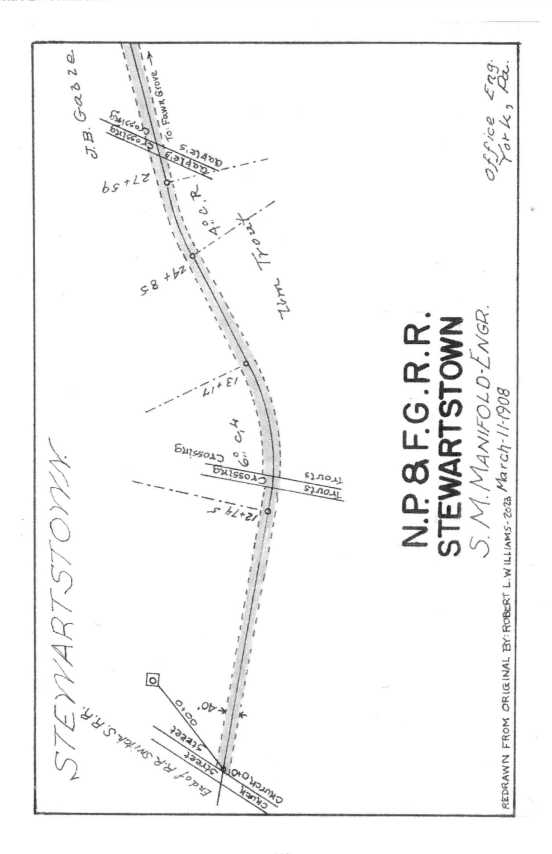

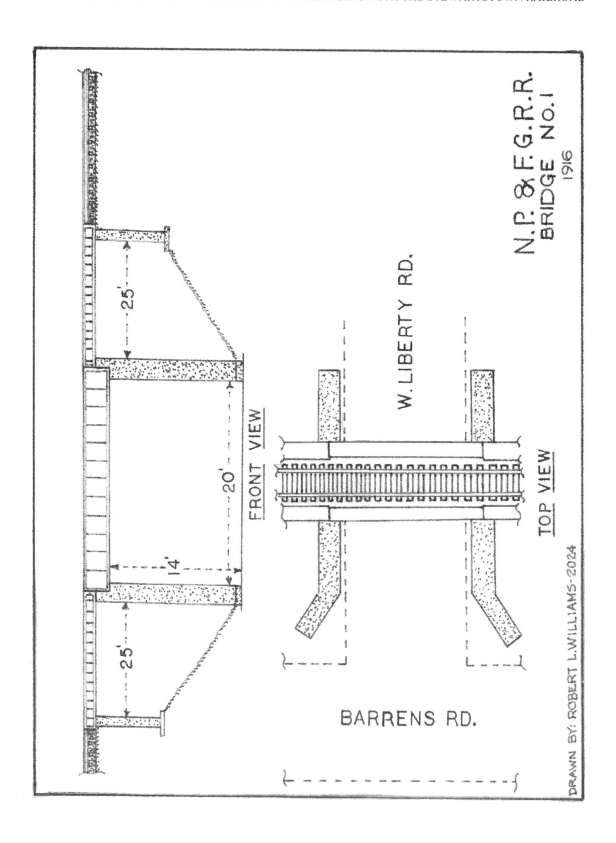

THE NEW PARK & FAWN GROVE RAILROAD: INTERCHANGING WITH THE STEWARTSTOWN RAILROAD

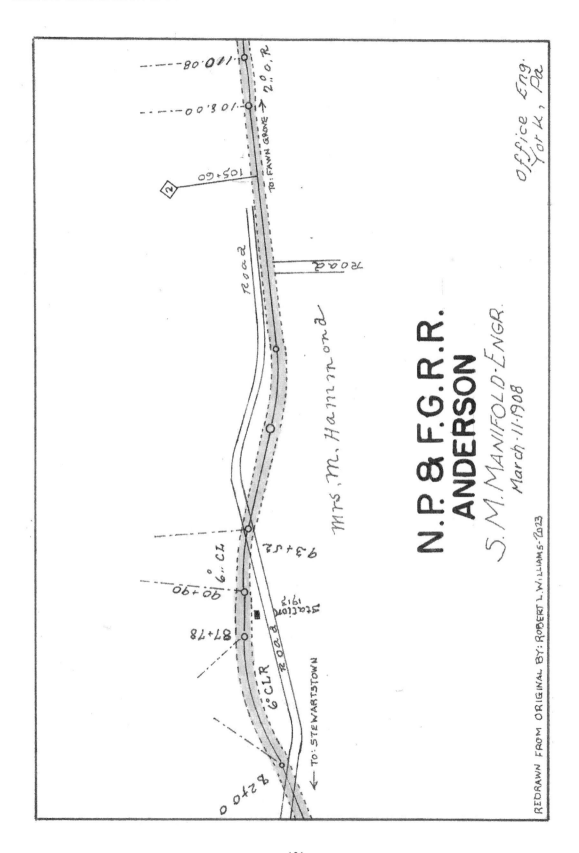

121

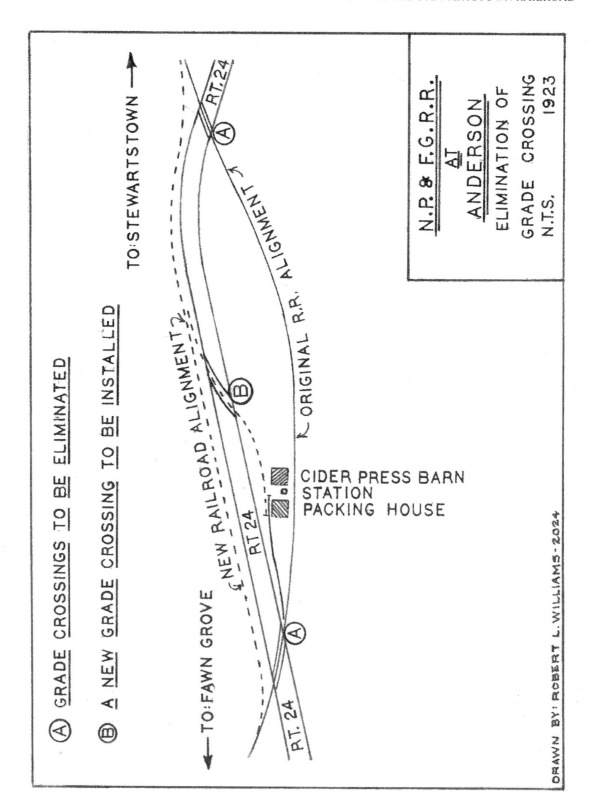

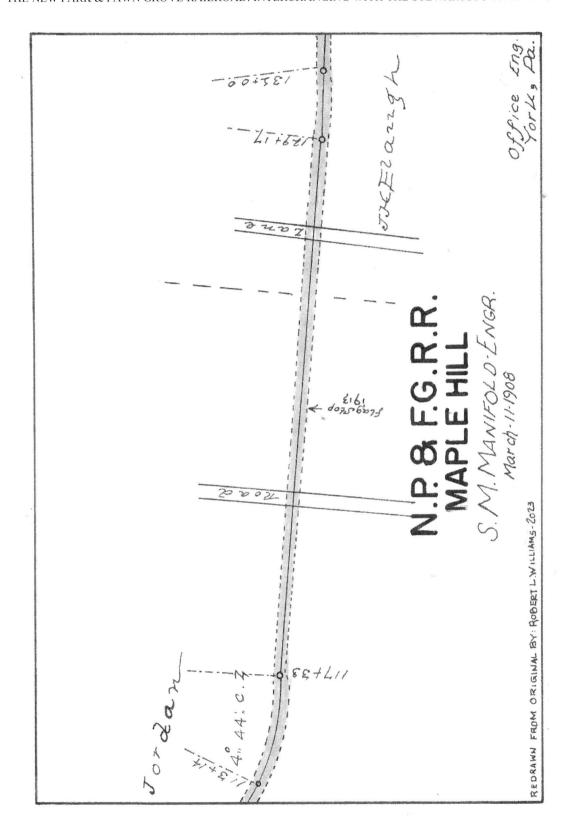

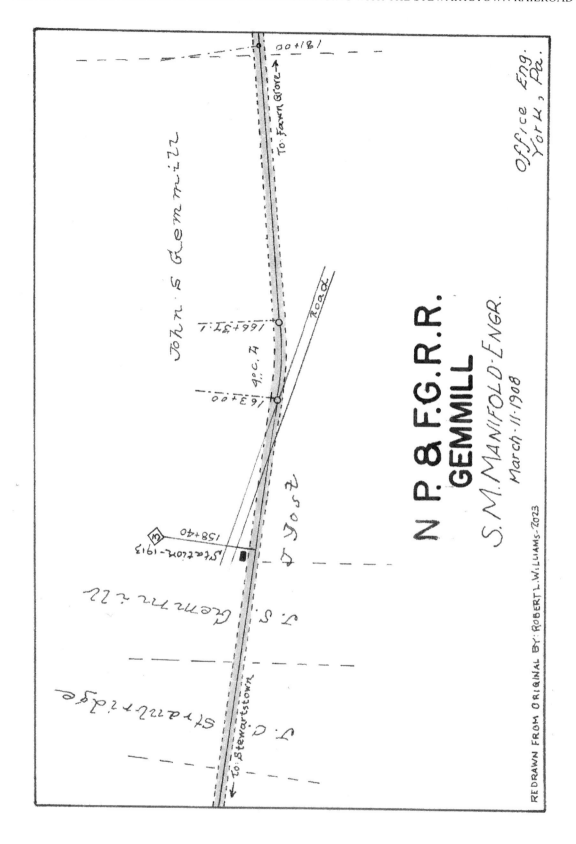

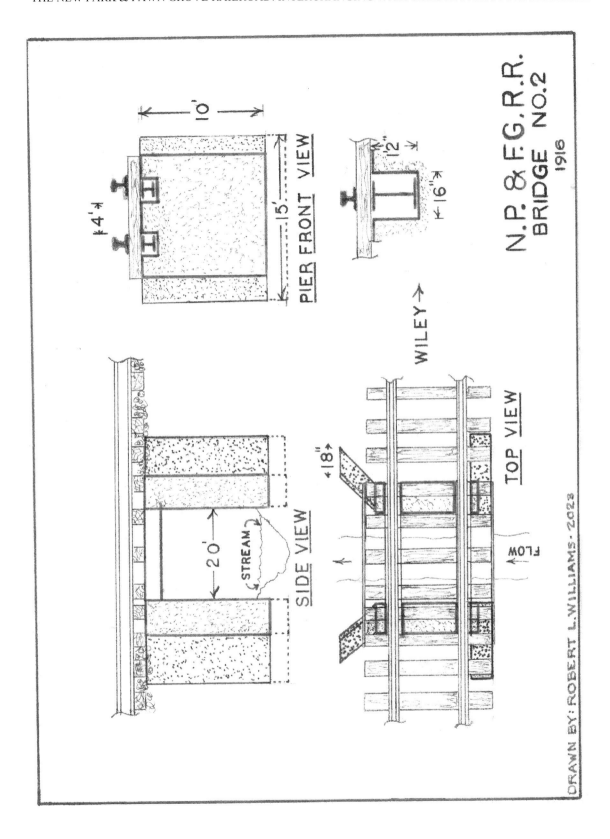

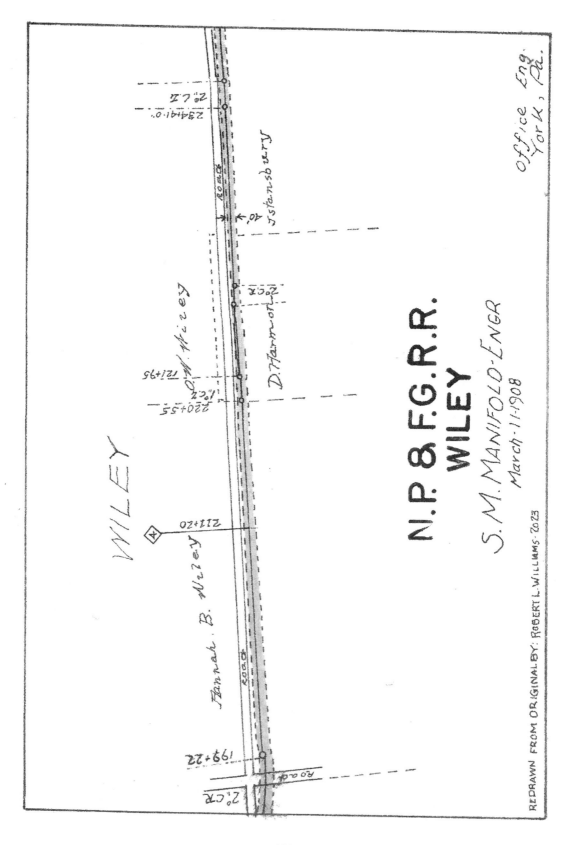

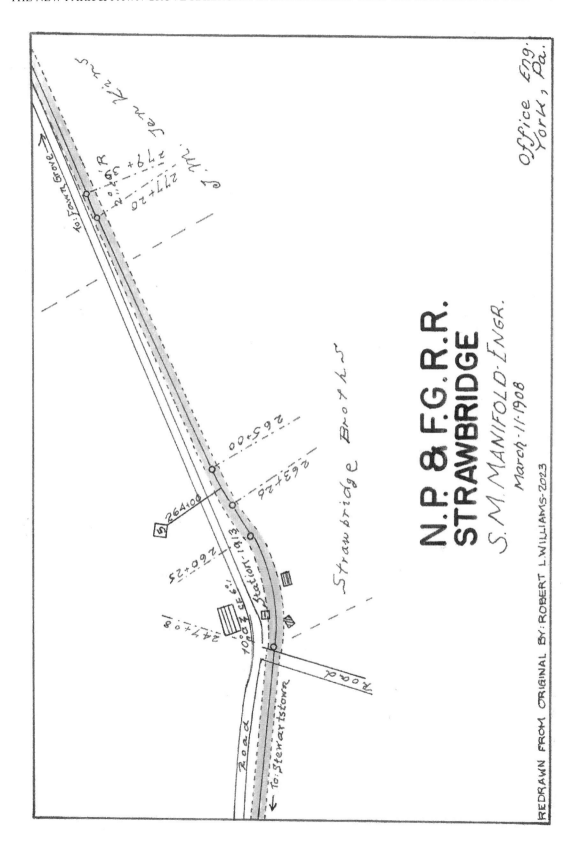

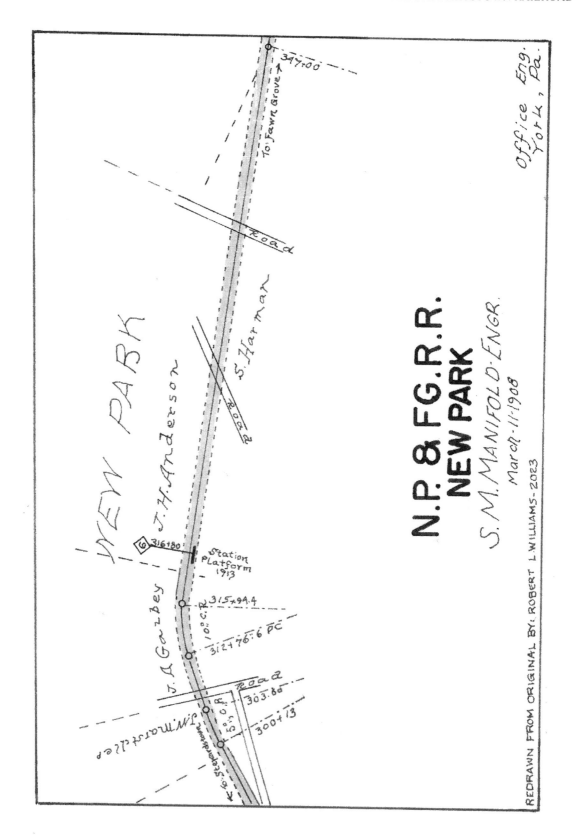

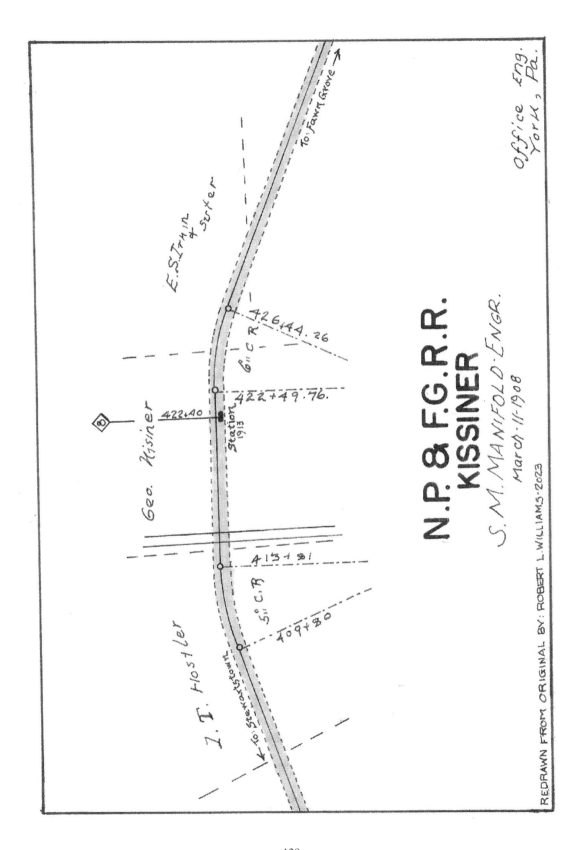

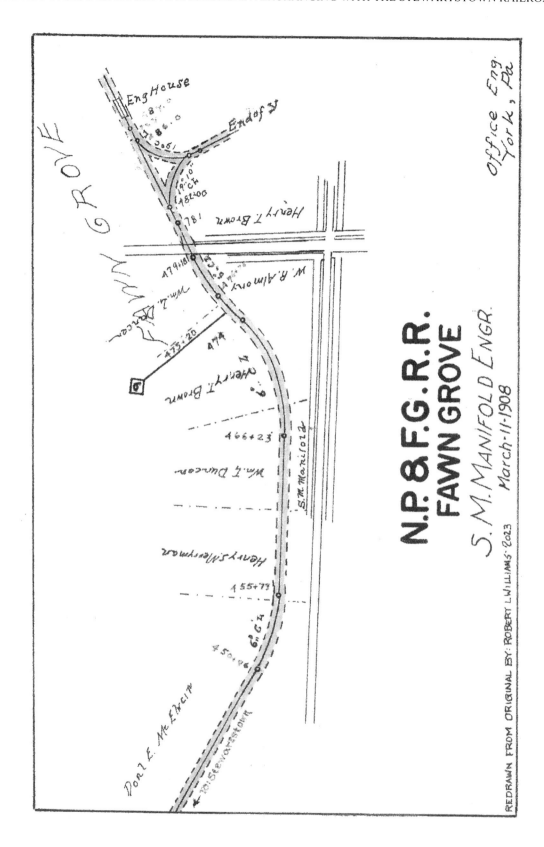

THE NEW PARK AND FAWN GROVE RAILROAD

APPENDIXES

TABLE OF CONTENTS
Appendices

	purchased – April 8, 1916
28	Purchase of a hand car from Fairbanks, Morse & Co. – May 18, 1916
29	James Fulton & Sons issued this bill to the N.P.&F.G.R.R. for merchandise purchased – December 10, 1914
30	Contract for the purchase of an engine from the Baldwin Locomotive Works – January 5, 1917
31	N.P.&F.G.R.R. auditor letter for the sale of Engine No. 2 – February 8, 1917
32	N.P.&F.G.R.R. resolution to authorizing the United States Government to take control of its railroad – August 6, 1919
33	N.P.&F.G.R.R. Train Schedule – June 13, 1921
34	Interstate Commerce Commission Evaluation Letter – June 21, 1922
35	Motion by the N.P.&F.G.R.R. to transfer all assets to the Stewartstown Railroad Company – January 8, 1923
36	List of contributors for the construction of a piece of road from Manifold's bridge to Anderson's siding – July 9, 1923
37	Letter from W. H. Anderson pertaining to contribution toward the movement of the railroad between Manifold's bridge and Anderson's siding – July 9, 1923
38	Stewartstown railroad accident report to the Board of Directors – September 25, 1923
38b	Documents related to the SRR's acquisition of the NP&FGRR - 1924
39	No Trespassing Sign – May 1, 1925
40	A Letter from the Stewartstown Railroad requesting Pennsylvania Railroad proxy for proposed leasing of the N.P.&F.G.R.R. – June 16, 1925
41	Letter from the Public Service Commission pertaining to changes made by the N.P.&F.G.R.R. at a grade crossing on their line – March 30, 1928
42	Stewartstown Railroad Timetable – April 28, 1928
43	Freight Bill issued at New Park – May 25, 1930
44	Station Agent Report, New Park, J. A. Gailey – February 20, 1933
45	Lease Agreement for the rental of the former N.P.&F.G.R.R. Fawn Grove Passenger and Freight Station – June 3, 1935

Sources:

All appendices reside in the archives of the Stewartstown Historical Society except where noted:
    Appendices Numbers 2, 5, and 41 – From the collection of Neal DeVoe
    Appendix 2b – From the collection of Robert L. Williams
    Appendices Numbers 4, 9, 25, and 32 – *Stewartstown News*, Stewartstown, Pa.
    Appendix No. 29 – From the collection of John Hope Anderson
    Appendix No. 33 – From the National Archives, Washington, D.C.
    Appendix No, 38b – Pennsylvania State Archives

Appendix No.1

New Park Pa

Jan 19 1905

The citizens of New Park &
Fawn Grove and vicinity
assembled at the School House
in New Park to talk about
getting a railroad.
John C. Wiley was elected
president and J H Gailey Secy
after a good deal of free and
open talk by several persons
expressing the great need
of a railroad and the absolute
necessity of having a railroad
to handle the large amount of
freight it now has and the
much larger amount that it
will produce with a railroad
in easy reach. It was moved and decided that
the president appoint a committee
of 10 Persons 5 from each district
to represent us with the committee
appointed by Stewartstown Railroad to
meet at Stewartstown next Saturday

Appendix No.2

Appendix No.2b

Know All Men by these Presents,

That, WHEREAS, "The New Park and Fawn Grove Railroad," a corporation formed under and in pursuance of the laws of the State of Pennsylvania, for the purpose of locating, constructing and operating a railroad from a point within the Borough of Stewartstown to a point within the Borough of Fawn Grove, York County, Pennsylvania, has located or is about to locate said railroad through,

over, and upon the lands, premises and property of the undersigned, ... *Hannah B. Wiley* ....

in the Township of *Hopewell* ... in the County of York and State of Pennsylvania, and for said purpose is desirous of obtaining the right of way in and through and upon said lands and premises.

Now, THEREFORE, the said *Hannah B. Wiley* .... for and in consideration of the location of the said railroad through and upon his lands, and of the ad-

vantages which may accrue to him therefrom, and also in consideration of the sum of .... *One* ....

dollar in hand paid, the receipt whereof is hereby acknowledged, ...*And further Hannah B Wiley reserves the right to attach a siding to the main track of the New Park & Fawn Grove railroad at any time she may request it The aforesaid railroad company to pay for as much of said switch as will clear the main track of said railroad. The said railroad company to construct and maintain five road crossing on said property of Hannah B Wiley The said Hannah B. Wiley agrees to Remove the tobacco shed for the sum of one hundred And twenty five dollars.*.........

the said ....*Hannah B Wiley*....doth hereby for himself, his heirs, executors or administrators, give, grant, sell and convey unto the said, "The New Park and Fawn Grove Railroad," its successors and assigns, for the uses and purposes of said railroad and the construction of works connected therewith, the absolute right of way through, over and upon his said lands, the whole distance of the said railroad through and over his lands as aforesaid, upon the line surveyed and designated by the engineer of the said "The New Park and Fawn Grove Railroad" to such extent as may

Hannah B. Wiley ....doth hereby for himself, his heirs, executors or administrators, give, grant, sell and convey unto the said, "The New Park and Fawn Grove Railroad," its successors and assigns, for the uses and purposes of said railroad and the construction of works connected therewith, the absolute right of way through, over and upon his said lands, the whole distance of the said railroad through and over his lands as aforesaid, upon the line surveyed and designated by the engineer of the said "The New Park and Fawn Grove Railroad," to such extent as may be necessary for the location, construction and opening to use of said Railroad not exceeding

...... *Forty* .... feet in width on and over said lands, with such additional width, however, as may be required at deep cuttings and embankments, one-half thereof on each side of the centre line of the main track of said railroad as laid down and established by said railroad on its located route; and the further liberty to make, maintain and use said railroad over, through and upon said lands with the usual roadbed, slopes, berms, ditches, spoil-banks and borrowpits; and also the right to take and use any water from springs or streams upon said lands, and to take and carry water by pipe or otherwise, over, through or under the said railroad, and establish water stations thereon.

And further, for the consideration aforesaid, the said ....
.... *Hannah B. Wiley* ....
for himself, his heirs, executors and administrators, doth by these presents remise, release, quit claim and forever discharge the said "The New Park and Fawn Grove Railroad," of and from any further payments for or on account of the use and occupancy of the said lands and premises, as well as for any and all damages which have accrued or which may hereafter accrue to him, his heirs and assigns, by reason of the location, construction, operating and using of the said railroad, through, over and upon the lands aforesaid.

IN WITNESS WHEREOF, the said ...*Hannah B. Wiley*...........

hath hereunto set his hand and seal this...... *12th* ....day of *June* ....
A. D. 1905. *witness*

H. S. Merryman   *Hannah B. Wiley* ... (SEAL)

STATE OF PENNSYLVANIA }
    YORK COUNTY,   } ss:

On this ....*12th*........ day of ...*June*............, A. D. 1905, personally came

before me, the undersigned, a ...*Justice of the Peace*......, in and for

said county, ...*Hannah B. Wiley*............who in due form of law acknowledged the above and foregoing release to be his act and deed, and desired the same might be recorded as such according to law.

WITNESS my hand and official seal the day and year aforesaid.

Aquilla M. Strawbridge
Justice of the Peace

Appendix No.3

J. A. GAILEY, SECRETARY, NEW 1   S. M. MANIFOLD, CHIEF ENGINEER, YORK

NEW PARK & FAWN GROVE RAILROAD CO.,

NEW PARK, PA., January 26, 1906.

To The

    President and Directors,

        The New Park and Fawn Grove R.R.,

           New Park, Pa.

Gentlemen:-   The following is a close approximate estimate of cost of construction of the six (6) miles of your Road between Stewartstown York County, Pa. and New Park, York County, Pa., which is now nearing completion.

Grading and culverts -----------------	$ 14,854.64
Track-Laying which will not exceed	
$450.00 per Mile --------------	2,700.00
15,840 ties at 45¢ each--------------	7,128.00
570 Tons rails, including unloading	
@ $25.00 per ton -------------	14,250.00
30,000 lbs. Spikes @ 2¢ per lb.-----	600.00
Splice Bars and Bolts -------------	500.00
Crossing Plank 4,000 @$15.- per M---	60.00
Bridging, including concrete--------	1,960.94
Engineering	900.00
TOTAL -----------------------------------	$42,953.58
Six (6) Individual Sidings @ $125.00 -----	750.00
TOTAL ---------------------------------	$43,703.58
Average cost per mile, not including individual	
sidings ---------------------------------------	$7,158.93
Average cost per mile, including individual	
sidings ---------------------------------------	$7,283.93

    Assuming the above figures to be correct and we know the quantities representing the items of grading and culverts to be, the construction of the three miles of your Road to Fawn Grove will be at least $1,000.00 per mile less than the above six (6) miles.

(2)

The cost of the construction of your Road to Fawn Grove will be as follows:

Six (6) miles to New Park ------------ $42,953.58

Three (3) miles to Fawn Grove -------- 18,476.79

Total, exclusive of Sidings, $61,430.37

Including 11 Sidings @ $125.- each---- 1,375.00

Total, exclusive Right-Of-Way $62,805.37

Our original estimate did not include Sidings, except three for Company use, nor did it contemplate steel bridges. We figured for wooden structures at Manifold's Overhead Crossing and Mrs. Hannah Wiley's Run, where we now have permanent structures of steel and concrete. The cost of your ties will probably exceed by about $2,000 our original estimate, add to this the additional cost over wooden bridges of $1200.00 for permanent concrete and steel structures, and $1000.00 for eight (8) private Sidings, aggregating $4200.00, which deducted from $62,805.37, the above estimate, leaves $58,605.37, hence you will see that the cost of building your Road is being kept close to our original estimate for same, i. e. $59,060.00.

Yours very truly,

Chief Engineer.

Appendix No.4

New Park and Fawn Grove Railroad.

Stewartstown Railroad Co Operating.

Time Table In Effect July 3, 1906. **Daily Except Sunday.**

No. 7 P.M.	No. 5 A.M.	No. 3 A.M.		No. 4 A.M.	No. 6 P.M.	No. 8 P.M.
3.35	11.30	7.00	Leave FAWN GROVE Arr.	10.12	3.10	7.15
3.50	11.35	7.20	KLINER	10.17	3.04	7.00
4.00	11.45	7.30	NEW PARK	10.07	2.44	6.50
			STRAWBRIDGE			
4.10	12.05	7.50	WILEY	9.47	2.24	6.30
			GEMMILL			
			ANDERSON			
			STEWARTSTOWN	9.37	2.14	6.28
			S. R. R.			
4.30	12.35	8.00	STEWARTSTOWN	9.37	2.14	6.28
4.57	12.47	8.35	NEW FREEDOM	9.10	1.47	6.00
			N. C. R.			
9.54	1.44		YORK	7.50	12.55	4.55
9.30	3.15		BALTIMORE Lve	7.30	11.44	4.00
P.M.	P.M.	A.M.	Arr	A.M.	P.M.	P.M.

Trains via ... run Wednesday only. Freight and Express business ... Grove, New Park, Wiley, and Stewartstown. Trains stop at Wiley ... when special, or on notice to conductor.

A. W. Barr, General Manager.

Appendix No.5

(Article Published in the AEGIS newspaper of Bel Air, MD)

BIG RAILROAD OPENING
AUGUST 9,1906

GRAND CELEBRATION OF THE COMPLETION AND OPENING OF THE NEW PARK & FAWN GROVE RAILROAD

Thousands of People Join in the Festal Occasion

Thursday, August 9, 1906 was a banner day for Fawn Grove, the occasion being the celebration of the completion and opening of the New Park & Fawn Grove Railroad. There was a great out-pouring of the people from far and near. They came by trains over the new railroad, and in vehicles from points within driving distance. The number present at some time during the day was estimated as high as 5,000, but probably 3,500 would be a more conservative estimate. Great preparations had been made by the people of Fawn Grove and other friends of the road to entertain and feed the vast concourse, and this they did most handsomely.

Extensive tables were constructed in the grove opposite the academy and near the railroad station. Provision had been made for feeding thousands of people. At the noon hour the good things were dealt out with a lavish hand, and there was plenty and to spare. The good dames and daughters of Fawn Grove and the surrounding country had done wonders in the culinary line, as the thousands who partook of their hospitality can testify.

This was the first, last, and perhaps the only "railroad opening" of the kind Fawn Grove will ever have, and the people did themselves proud with it. The day and the occasion will long be remembered.

The Felton cornet band was present for the day and furnished excellent music for the occasion.

The officers of the New Park and Fawn Grove railroad are: President, John H. Anderson, New Park; Secretary, J. A. Gailey, New Park; Treasurer; A. M. Strawbridge, New Park; Superintendent, B. F. Morris, Fawn Grove; General Manager, J. C. Wiley, Gatchelville.

Directors-J. C. Wiley, Simon G. Lowe, H. C. McElwain, R. W. Anderson, W. R. Webb, A. M. Strawbridge, Maurice Davis, B. F. Morris, H. S. McDonald, Milton E. Smith, H. S. Merryman, N. A. Manifold, J. A. Gailey, A. W. Webb, J. Wiley Norris, M. W. Bahn and J. W. Anderson.

Among those present and participating were several prominent officials of the Northern Central R. R., including H. W. Kapp, general superintendent; S. O. Malin, of the general offices, Baltimore; H. Hasson, Jr., district passenger agent, and Gilbert H. Copp, division freight agent, Assistant Trainmaster Orwig and Ticket Agent Harrington, this city.

John H. Anderson, president of the new railroad company, called the meeting to order at 11 o'clock, and John C. Wiley, of Gatchelville, was elected president; J. A. Gailey was chosen secretary and the following vice presidents were nominated and elected: H. W. Kapp, S. O. Malin, M. H. McCall, John B. Gemmill, Charles A. Hawkins, Samuel Irwin, S. A. Williams, Harry A. Hughes, Samuel H. Smith, J. W. Norris, C. W. Shaw, Thomas Mackenzie and Clark Liggitt.

A generous program of exercises had been prepared for the day. These exercises began about 11 o'clock, and continued, with an intermission for lunch, till about 4 o'clock. The program included addresses by the President Mr. John H. Anderson, Hon. John B. Gemmill, Hon. John W. Bittenger, Thomas Mackensie, Esq., Baltimore; Rev. Robert Reed Gailey, Missionary returned from China; Joseph R. Strawbridge, Esq., York; William B. Gemmill, Esq., York; Charles A. Hawkins, Esq., York..

Several other persons were called on for impromptu addresses, among whom were Miss Lida Mackenzie, Baltimore, Rev. T. H. Wright, Stevensyville, Md., Hon. E. D. Zeigler, York, and Messrs., W. L. Ammon, York; Harvey Gross, York; H. W. Ramsay, Delta; John Robinson, Bel Air; Thomas Seitz, Stewartstown; S. J. Barnett, Delta.

THE ADDRESSES

The exercises began with prayer by Rev. Dr. S. H. Treadway, of Fawn Grove, who was followed by Mr. Milton E. Smith, of Norrisville, Md., who delivered the address of welcome. John B. Gemmill, of York responded. He said:

"We are here to celebrate the completion, and to formerly open the New Park and Fawn Grove railroad from Stewartstown to Fawn Grove, which a few years ago was a quiet little quaker village with a meeting house, store, a doctor, blacksmith shop, wheelwright, saddler, an undertaker and a hotel. Today it is a thriving borough, with new industries springing up on every side. It is the terminal of a standard gauge railroad with its burnished bands of steel sending out and away into busy marts of commercial and manufacturing centres, bringing you into closer touch and business relations with the outside world.

"Some twelve years ago a railroad meeting was held at New Park on the very ground where this road now passes. The very efficient general manager of the Stewartstown railroad and now operating manager of your road, Mr. M. W. Bahn was chairman of that meeting. Some of the speakers failed to be present and I was drafted into service. Among other things which I said on that occasion I made a prediction, and it has come to pass, it has been verified this day. I said that in 1885 I had helped build a railroad into Stewartstown and run the first train over it, carrying 2500 persons on opening day, and I expected to live to see the day when there would be a railroad at New Park, and there would be carried on the opening day 5000 passengers. You have done even better than I predicted, you have built it into Fawn Grove, three miles further and you have bidden us come and see what great things you have wrought. We are here 5000 people strong to congratulate you, and to share with you the pleasures of your great achievement."

A letter of regret was read from Rev. R. L. Clark, Lancaster, who was to have been one of the speakers.

Hon. John W. Bittenger, president judge of the courts of York county, was the next speaker. He said that a railroad was a blessing to any community, if it was conducted in the interest of the people. He complimented the people of the lower end on their enterprise in building the new road. Judge Bittenger, during the course of his remarks, referred to the abuses of the laws by railroads and other corporations, and said that the time was near at hand when the people would not submit to corporate domination and also predicted that during the session of the next state legislature a law would be enacted fixing the maximum railroad rate at two cents a mile.

Thomas Mackenzie, Esq., of Baltimore, was the first speaker in the afternoon. He said the road was not built by dreams or idle wishes, but by the active energy of the progressive farmers and others who set to work to help themselves. He believed the road would prove the best instrumentality for advancing the interests of the section which it reached, and hoped it would always be operated for their good. He broadened the view - county, state and national reforms for the benefit of the whole people.

Rev. Robert Reed Gailey, a former resident of the community, but for several years a missionary at Tientsin, China, brought the congratulations of 400,000,000 Chinese. He made a forcible address, on a high plane. He emphasized the importance of the individual man, in his private capacity, in developing and uplifting the community in which he resides. He entered a strong plea for better public roads, better schools and other public improvements.

All of the addresses on the occasion were unique and interesting and we regret our inability to present them in full to our readers.

ADDRESS BY J. H. ANDERSON, PRESIDENT OF THE COMPANY

This is an occasion of great personal satisfaction to me as it marks the realization of one of my fondest hopes.

I am not here to make a speech; my early education consisted largely in driving a big team to Baltimore and Shrewsbury and Peach Bottom which you will all admit is poor training for a public speaker.

To you who are stockholders of the road I want to say that we have collected your money and used it, and have succeeded in building over nine miles of railroad and have it in operation; in the prosecution of this work we met with many things which were very encouraging and pleasant, and of course, other things which were quite the reverse.

W began operating regular trains on the 5th day of July, in the midst of harvest when very little freight or passenger travel could be expected; but, not withstanding these conditions we have done a very encouraging business up to date.

We have built the road both better and longer than was at first intended and our expenses have naturally been greater than the original estimate. There is an indebtedness of about $35,000 on the property; this debt must be raised by a small issue of bonds, or carried in the local banks unless sufficient stock is raised to meet it.

I would recommend an issue of bonds and advise the stock holders to take them; there is $400,000 in the banks of Stewartstown and Delta at 3 per cent. interest, enough of which could be safely and profitable invested in, our bonds at 4 ½ per cent, to buy the entire issue.

Since we began running regular trains two unexpected sources of freight have developed; the Standard Oil company has 25 or 30 cars of building material on the road and will necessarily use a great deal of coal in the future, and 2,000 telephone poles are being hauled from a single tract of woodland in Harford County, Md.

Let me advise you to be careful what you do with your stock, don't sacrifice it.

Your board of directors are unanimous in the opinion that we have a valuable

it cost and bound to be a money maker as well as a great convenience.

ADDRESS OF CHARLES A. HAWKINS, ESQ., OF YORK

"We celebrate today because at last we have a railroad, and we take special pride in the fact that we built it ourselves. That is true, we did build it. But are we the only ones that are responsible for its existence? Not by any means. Our fathers and grandfathers labored before us. They contributed their part in procuring the conditions which have made this road possible. Every stroke of the axe of the pioneer in clearing off his little patch of forest in which to sow his bit of wheat or rye, was a stroke which aided in making this country what it is today. We enjoy the benefit of their labor, as well as our own, and therefore we are richer than they. It is said that gratitude is the rarest virtue. Our chief duty, it is true, is to remember the debt of gratitude we owe our predecessors.

"And what was this country like a century and a half ago? Can we imagine it? Hardly, I think. Until 1815 Peach Bottom township was included as a part of Fawn, and the whole of it in 1783 had but 783 inhabitants, and it will be of special interest to note that 39 of these were slaves. Probably not more than 200 to 250 persons lived within the present limits of Fawn. Only 18,100 acres out of 50,000 or more had been taken up. There were still Indians living in the neighborhood. It is, indeed, said that there was at one time an Indian village on the place now owned by L. E. Allen.

"Mr. Allen's property is a part of the land which has so long been in the Webb family. It was bought by James Webb on the 18th day of the sixth month, 1774, from William Matthews, of York. Both were subjects of George III, then, and the reference to the "sixth month" in the deed indicates that one or both of these men were members of the Society of Friends. The tract pruchased contained 133 acres and allowance. James Webb was the grandfather of the Richard Webb, whom some of us knew when small boys. James in 1784, conveyed this property to Richard Webb, father of the Richard Webb just mentioned, and in the deed the property is called "Small Gain," a name which does not well comport with the size of the crops that are grown or it today, or with the contented smile worn by our worthy contemporary, the Webbs who now owns the greater portion of it. The property is described as adjoining lands late of Josiah Hitchcock, the province line, the barrens, Benjamin Johnson's heirs, Isaac Jones and other land of James Webb.

"When James Webb was a young man, transportation was conducted chiefly by pack horses. Indeed few, if any, roads suitable for wagoning had been established in the neighborhood and in this connection I propose to tell you a story, and if it isn't true it might as well have been. James sometimes made journeys to Baltimore, and less frequently to Philadelphia, for the purpose of trade. On this particular occasion referred he had gone to Philadelphia in charge of a pack train of ten or twelve horses in company with another man, one of them leading and the other bringing up the rear. Their route was by way of McCall's Ferry, crossing on an old Indian trail, and was an important artery of travel at the time I refer to. Indeed, the portion of the road from Philadelphia to the ferry, and for a part of the distance from there to the locality of Fawn Grove, was open for wagon travel, a fact which the pack horsemen deplored, for already these wagons were interfering with their business. Its the old story, you know, there are always some pulling ahead in the line of progress and others pulling back, according as their interests dictate. Well, after a long day's travel through mud and rain on a summer evening, James and his party of horses reached the river and put up for the night. He and his companions relieved the horses of the loaded sacks and wallets and panniers or baskets which had been placed across their backs, fitted up to carry anything from a live calf to a barrel of molasses or even iron bars crooked around the body of the beast. They fed their horses and stabled them, went into the tavern; had a bite to eat, and laid down on the hotel floor in their wet clothes, as they could do no better, for a night's rest. Under such conditions sleep could scarcely be otherwise than fitful and disturbed. As he sought the comforts of slumber, his mind recurred to his home and his young wife and little children who were expecting even at that moment. The next thing he seemed to realize was that he was passing up the hill just by, in eager anticipation of his homecoming, for a trip in those days to Philadelphia was a journey. But the scenes had strangely altered since he had left some eight or ten days before. Instead of forest to the right of him and forest to the left of him, as he climbed the hill, he saw beautifully cultivated land. A crop of wheat, such as he had never seen or heard of had been evidently taken from one of the fields adjoining, for there were the heavy thick stubbles, the best possible evidence. A field of corn was growing and shooting forth into ear with evident promise of 75 to 90 bushels to the acre. Was anything so astounding? Comfortable, attractive dwellings and well-filled barns appeared before his eyes that he had never seen before. When about half up the hill he heard a strange sound; off to the West arose a loud, unexpected and unheard-of shriek, or he thought possible it might be better described as a whistle. He stood still; following this, was a rumbling, clanging sound which approached nearer and became louder and louder, and of a sudden, without warning, 200 feet before him from out of a cut at the roadside rushed across his pathway a monster piece of mechanism, a puffing, snorting iron horse, with wheels turning, smoke lifting and more powerful and more terrible in aspect than any of the monsters he had read about in mythology. James Webb and his retinue were stricken with fear. Unable to go either forward or backward, he stood as if turned to a pillar of salt. He was a man of ordinary courage, but this was too much for him, he called out in terror and immediately he realized he was back in McCall's Ferry tavern in his wet clothes and that it was all a dream. As you think you have a railroad but wouldn't you better get your next neighbor to pinch you hard? Perhaps you, too, are dreaming.

NEW PARK & FAWN GROVE RAIL ROAD
AUGUST 9, 1906 THRU OCTOBER 1, 1934

Appendix No.6

Stewartstown Railroad Company.

ACCOUNTING DEPARTMENT.

C. W. Shaw, Auditor, Gen'l Freight and Pass. Agt.

OFFICE OF THE AUDITOR OF PASSENGER AND FREIGHT.

Stewartstown, Pa., Nov 13. 1906 190

PROPOSITION

1st That we sell the N.P.&.F.G.RCo, Engine No 3 at the purchase price plus rhe interest on the investment from the date of purchase to the time when full settlement has been made,

2nd That we sell the N.P.&.F.G.R.Co. 9/16 of coach no,3 for $1125.00

that all future repairs and renewals, on coach or coaches used on joint traffic shall be divided on same basis or. as 9is to 7,

Settlement for past serviceof pperation shall be charged at the rate of $2.50 per day this charge to cover the charge for use of coaches cost of management, less charge of auditor whose cost of service shall be based on percentage of business done, The above to cover cost of agencies,

4th
That the charge for the agent at NEw Freedom shall be divided 1/3 to the N.P.&.F.G.R. and 2/3 to the S.R.R.

N P F G RR shall keep ... ...
one leg of the y viz the one leading from
Ey House to ... ...

Charge for use of ... ...
40c per ... ...

Appendix NO.7

NEW PARK & FAWN GROVE RAILROAD
LIST OF CHECKS ISSUED
1906

CHECK NO.	DATE	NAME	AMOUNT
515	Aug.10,1906	H. S. Merryman	$23.20
517	Aug.15,1906	H. T. McCallister	$6.00
518	Aug.15,1906	H. N. Dirk	$28.25
519	Aug.15,1906	C.M. Almoney	$24.80
520	Aug.15,1906	W.A. Scott	$12.30
521	Aug.15,1906	L. Harman	$13.95
523	Aug.15,1906	J.H. Allen	$14.10
524	Aug.15,1906	C. Channell	$10.05
526	Aug.15,1906	L.M. Lane	$12.00
527	Aug.15,1906	H.S. Merryman	$5.85
529	Aug.15,1906	W.M. McCallister	$7.65
530	Aug.15,1906	H.B. Hopkins	$4.20
531	Aug.15,1906	G. Channell	$8.90
533	Ayg.15,1906	C. Channell	$9.75
534	Aug.16,1906	Adams&Mettake Co.	$6.70
536	Aug.29,1906	R.G. McDonald	$40.60
537	Aug.29,1906	C.C. Jones	$10.65
538	Aug.29,1906	W.M. McCallister	$8.40
514	Aug.07,1906	Ella R. Edie	$11.16
50	Julu18,1906	E.A. Mayne	$5.46
57	July26,1906	Wm. M. Baton	$16.59
181	June21,1906	J.S. Jones	$18.00
170	Junr06,1906	C.E. Strawbridge	$7.50
315	Mar.06,1906	Jacob Lanins	$28.00
557	Oct.-01,1906	Augustus Neller	$4.82
558	Oct.12,1906	W.A. Scott	$36.15
176	Jume20,1906	Dispatch Publ. Co.	$15.00
566	Oct.12,1906	W.W. Wilkerson	$7.80
15	July04,1906	H.N. Dirk	$27.75
52	July18,1906	H.R. Brooks	$3.00
39	July18,1906	J.M. Fletcher	$5.25
512	Aug.02,1906	J.H. Allen	$4.50
513	Aug.13,1906	James Agens	$5.00
572	Oct.18,1906	Dr. Vallie Hawkins	$54.00
549	Sept.17,1906	John H. Anderson	$13.00
506	Aug.01,1906	Lewis Harman	$13.95
507	Aug.01,1906	W.R. Almoney	$12.00
508	Aug.01,1906	J.H. Allen	$11.40
509	Aug.01,1906	C. Channell	$7.05
510	Aug.02,1906	A.H. Morris	$3.70
504	Aug.01,1906	W.A. Scott	$14.70

NEW PARK & FAWN GROVE RAILROAD
LIST OF CHECKS ISSUED
1906

CHECK NO.	DATE	NAME	AMOUNT
505	Aug.01,1906	A.L. Thompson	$7.20
501	July30,1906	American Iron &Steel	$259.00
597	Dec.01,1906	Lewis Harman	$$14.12
598	Dec.01,1906	Frank Trout	$16.50
646	Dec.19,1906	George Channell	$34.60
573	Oct.13,1906	J. I. McDermott	$22.00
574	Oct.13,1906	William Libney	$6.00
575	Dec.14,1906	Ellan N. Edie	$6.85
576	Oct.29,1906	S.M. Manifold	$205.09
577	Oct.29,1906	William M. Barton	$21.16
578	Oct.30,1906	Grafton Devoe	$26.18
579	Oct.30,1906	Verona Tool Works	$32.57
580	Oct.09,1906	John E. Myers	$6.15
581	Nov.09,1906	A. Neal	$14.70
582	Nov.09,1906	W.E. Almoney	$12.20
583	Nov.09,1906	W.C. Channell	$14.10
584	Nov.09,1906	W.J. Wise	$15.45
585	Nov.09,1906	Frank Trout	$11.85
587	Nov.09,1906	W.A. Scott	$21.90
589	Nov.09,1906	L.L. Kinard	$40.50
590	Nov.090,1906	H.N. Dirk	$21.52
591	Nov.09,1906	B.F. Morris	$10.75
592	Nov.09,1906	B.F. Morris	$35.00
593	Nov.09,1906	B.F. Morris	$10.12
594	Nov.10,1906	F.P. Strawbridge	$13.00
595	Nov.10,1906	J.C. Wiley	$12.00
596	Nov.17,1906	J.T. Hoster	$14.00
600	Dec.13,1906	L.P. Day	$8.70
602	Dec.13,1906	E.H. Jones	$15.75
603	Dec.13,1906	J.W. Tomkins	$11.85
604	Dec.13,1906	E.A. Waine	$15.60
605	Dec.13,1906	C.W. Alloway	$21.80
606	Dec.13,1906	G.F. Mathews	$20.10
608	Dec.13,1906	Robert Myers	$35.40
611	Dec.13,1906	R.B. Mattews	$37.20
616	Dec.14,1906	Fred Repo	$61.00
617	Dec.14,1906	N.A. Manifold	$121.16
618	Dec.14,1906	H.T. McCalister	$15.90
619	Dec.18,1906	George Giley	$25.65
620	Dec.18,1906	W.B. Hawkins	$11.25
622	Dec.21,1906	Ross Grove	$5.50

Appendix NO.8

NEW PARK & FAWN GROVE RAILROAD

TIME TABLE IN EFFECT MAY 25, 1907.   DAILY EXCEPT SUNDAY.

No. 7 P.M.	No. 5 A.M.	No. 3 A.M.		No. 4 A.M.	No. 6 P.M.	No. 8 P.M.
3.35	11.20	7.00	Leave FAWN GROVE Arr.	10.32	3.10	7.15
			KISNER			
3.50	11.35	7.15	NEW PARK	10.17	2.54	7.00
4.00	11.45	7.25	STRAWBRIDGE	10.07	2.44	6.50
			WILEY			
			GEMMILL			
			ANDERSON			
4.20	12.05	7.45	STEWARTSTOWN	9.47	2.24	6.30
			S. R. R.			
4.30	12.20	8.00	STEWARTSTOWN	9.37	2.14	6.25
4.57	12.47	8.25	NEW FREEDOM	9.10	1.47	5.58
			N. C. R.			
5.50	1.44	9.54	YORK	7.50	12.52	4.55
7.15	3.15	9.30	Arr. BALTIMORE Lve	7.30	11.44	4.55
P. M.	P. M.	A. M.		A. M.	A. M.	P. M.

Trains No. 5 and 6 run Wednesday and Saturday. Freight and Express agencies at Fawn Grove, New Park, Wiley, and Stewartstown. Trains stop at Way Stations only when signaled, or on notice to conductor.

J. C. WILEY, General Manager.

B. F. MORRIS, Supt.

Appendix NO.9

NOTICE.

MARKING

Less than Carload Shipments.

Attention is directed to the following rules, which will take effect on July 1, 1908:

Each package, bundle or piece of less than carload freight must be plainly marked by brush, stencil, pasted label or securely fastened tag, showing the name of consignee and the name of the Station, Town or City, and the State to which destined. (See Note.)

The marks on packages, bundles or pieces must be compared he shipping order and bill of lading, and corrections, if ary, made by the consignor or his representative before ipt is signed. Old marks must be removed or effaced before kages, bundles or pieces will be accepted for transportation.

Freight consigned to a place of which there are two or more he same name in the same State, must have the name of the nty marked on each package, bundle or piece, and also shown he shipping receipt.

When freight is consigned to a place not located on the line of a Railroad, each package, bundle or piece must be marked with the name of the station at which the consignee will accept delivery, or if routed in connection with a water line with which there are no joint rates in effect, the name of the place at which delivery is to be made to such water line must be marked on each package, bundle or piece.

Freight not marked in accordance with the foregoing rules will not be accepted for transportation.

NOTE : Pasted labels or securely fastened tags should be used only when the character of the freight prevents marking by brush or stencil.

Appendix NO.10

New Park & Fawn Grove R. R.

Conductor's Train Report

Train No.	DISPATCH	ARRIVAL
CAR OWNER	CAR NUMBER	RECEIVED	DELIVERED
Trips of RR coach #4			
Dec 22 – 1 round Trip			
" 26 – 1	"	"	
" 27 – 1	"	"	
" 28 – 1	"	"	
" 29 1	"	"	

Remarks:

Date 12/31/1940   R H Morris
Conductor

Appendix NO.11

153

Appendix NO.12

Stewartstown Railroad Company,

Office of the General Manager.

C. W. SHAW, General Manager.

Stewartstown, Pa., Sep 17/10

The Executive committee of the Stewartstown Railroad Co met for purpose of considering the station question and the application of the Norrisville people for help toward the building of a piece of STATE road from the foot of Hughs hill to Wileys station.

1st   In looking over the ground at Penna Ave we find that we do not have a a proper location on wich to build a suitable building that would meet present and future requirements that would be accessible

that the only available ground we have at all is on the lot bounded by the N P & F G Track , the street and the property of Lawrence Shaw and this is undesirable for the following reasons.

2nd   It is on the wrong side of the track for the majority of our patrons.

3rd   In coming to and from the station passengers would have to go around the and cross over the tracks.

4th   It would necessitate the necessity of cutting the train every time we come up to the station to avoid blocking the crossing.

5th   If excavated to bring the station down to the track level it would come below the grade of the street and make it inconvenient to get to and from the station.

OUR RECOMMENDATIONS THEREFORE IS AS FOLLOWS

If the New Park & F G R R Co will give us the assurance that they will not seek a physical connection with another line for the purpse of diverting at least part of the traffic unless it was mutually agreeable to both lines.

That we change the location of the station to meet the views of the N P & F G people to the most available site possoble at or near Penna. Ave.

be involved in making the change as other questions of eual importance are confronting us some of wich are relaying of our line with heavier steel to accomodate heavier equipment.

Better passenger service to accomodate the traveling public.

We recommend in the request of the Norrisville people that the S R R Co & N P & F G Co should take an active interest in the building of the state road from Hughes hill to Wileys station and if necessary make a contribution,

Appendix N0.13

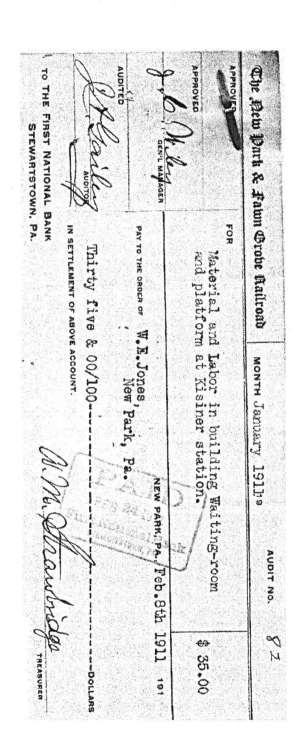

Appendix NO.14

Stewartstown Railroad Company,

Office of the General Manager.

C. W. SHAW, General Manager.

Stewartstown, Pa., June 2nd 1911

EXECUTIVE COMMITTEE REPORT AND RECOMMEND THE FOLLOWING.

That we pay our trainmen for all extra trips made before and after regular trains one third (1/3) of a days wages for each round trip.

That we pay our engineer and fireman $1.00 each per month for a washout of the Locomotive Boiler, to be done between the 1st and 15th of each month (If not done no pay) That the engine must be kept more cleanly.

That we demand the total abstinance from strong drink whether on or off duty by the trainmen, a violation of this rule means discharge.

Approved by the board
June 10th 1911

C.W.Shaw
T B Fulton
J W Anderson
W J P Gemmill

Exec. Committe.

156

Appendix NO.15

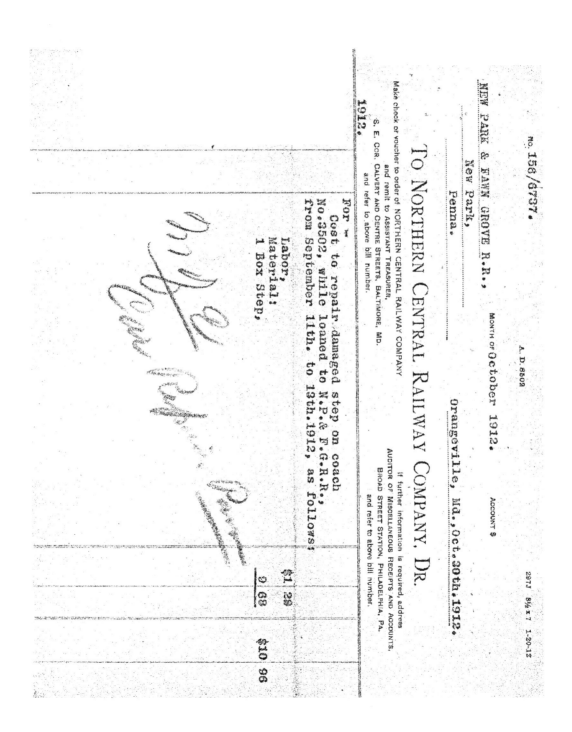

Appendix NO.16

Fawn Grove, Pa. Mar. 3 1913

M N. P & F. G. R.R.

— IN ACCOUNT WITH —

C. E. Orr,

General Blacksmith

Sept.	3	Rep to engine rake	.20
Sept.	12	rep to pump irons	.35
Sept.	20	dressing 6 big ends for pick	.60
Sept	20	dressing 5 small " pick	.30
Sept	21	steeling small end pick	.25
Sept	27	steeling big & little " pick	.75
Sept	27	dressing 3 cutting hammer	.30
Oct.	23	dressing 2 big 2 little pick	.30
Oct.	24	dressing 2 big 2 little bits	.30
Oct.	24	4 ends on picks	1.50
Oct.	25	dressing 2 big 2 little P.	.30
Nov.	1	rep to engine poker	.10
Nov.	14	dressing 2 big 2 little Pick	.30
Nov.	19	dressing 3 big 3 little pick	.45
Nov.	19	rivets	.05
Nov.	20	dressing 3 big 3 little bits	.45
Nov.	28	dressing 4 big 4 " bits	.60
Nov.	28	plating pick eye	.15

Bill now due . . Please remit at once

Appendix NO.17

Your account stated to date. If error is found, return at once.
W. E. WILEY,
GENERAL MERCHANDISE,
HAY, FLOUR, FEED & FERTILIZER.
Specialty: Potatoes in Car Load Lots.

Stewartstown, Pa. _____ 191_

M _____

McCASKEY, ALLIANCE, O.

Reg. No. _____ Clerk _____

ACCOUNT FORWARDED	3	76

5 gal gas _____ 75

4 51

NO 26

Appendix NO.18

No. M1sc.118/404

A. D. 3500

MONTH OF September 1914   ACCOUNT $

New Park & Fawn Grove Railroad,

J. C. Wiley, General Manager,

New Park, Pa.

Make check or voucher to order of THE PENNSYLVANIA RAILROAD COMPANY
refer to above bill number and remit to Treasurer,
BROAD STREET STATION, PHILADELPHIA, PA.

To THE PENNSYLVANIA RAILROAD COMPANY, DR.

Philadelphia, September 23rd, 1914

If further information is required, address
Auditor of Miscellaneous Accounts,
BROAD STREET STATION, PHILADELPHIA, PA.
and refer to above bill number and month.

For rental of P.R.Co's passenger coach 3353,
in use by the New Park & Fawn Grove Railroad, account
Stewartstown Fair, from 9.00 a.m. September 10th to
5.00 p.m. September 11th, 1914;
    2 days at $5.00 per day, $10.00

For empty mileage made necessary for the delivery
of this car to the New Park & Fawn Grove Railroad, and
the return to service on P.R.R.   One car Baltimore to
New Freedom and return, total 74 miles:
    74 miles at 10¢ per mile,   7.40
                                                               _____
                                                               $17.40

160

Appendix N0.19

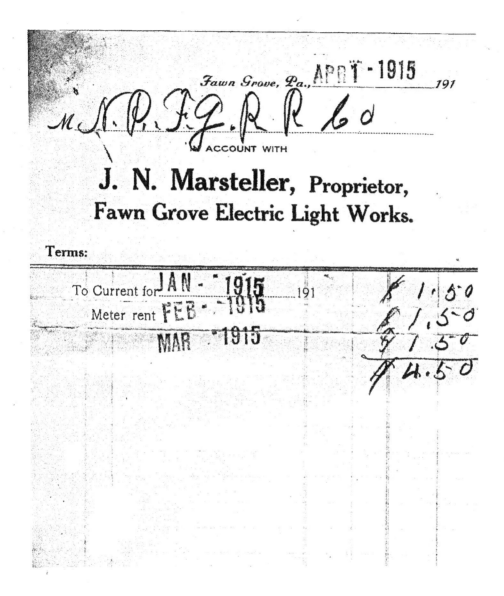

Fawn Grove, Pa., APR 1 - 1915 _____ 191

M N. P. F. G. R R Co

ACCOUNT WITH

J. N. Marsteller, Proprietor,
Fawn Grove Electric Light Works.

Terms:

To Current for JAN - 1915 _____ 191	$	1.50
Meter rent FEB - 1915	$	1.50
MAR - 1915	$	1.50
	$	4.50

Appendix NO.20

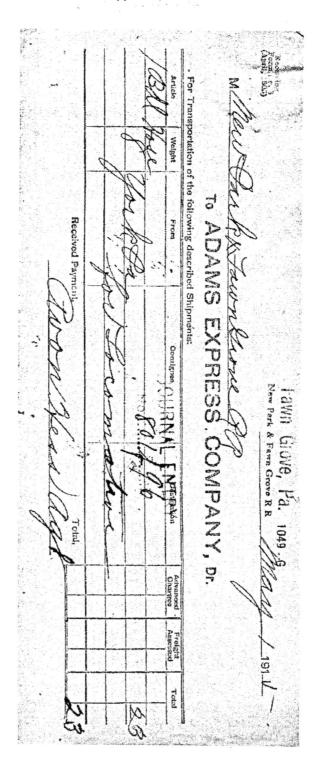

Appendix NO.21

TERMS 30 DAYS.

Best Goods.   Lowest Prices.

New Park, Pa., June 30, 190_

Mr. _J. A. Gailey_

To J. A. GAILEY,

Dealer in

Dry Goods, Notions, Groceries, Hardware, Boots, Shoes, Hats, Clothing,
Agricultural Implements, Fertilizers and Feed.

1 Years Rent, Heat and Light for General Office, Year ending June 30 1915		$60.00

Doz. Eggs
Lbs. Butter
Lbs. Chicken

№ 1

Highest Market Price Paid for Produce.
Ask for anything you want, we have it, or we will get it quick.

New Park, Pa., July 1 1915

At New Park & Fawn Grove R.R.Co

— IN ACCOUNT WITH —

ANDERSON BROS. CO.,

Grain, Hay, Feed, Fertilizers, Wagons, Farm Implements, Etc.

1915		To Bill Rendered			
Feb 6	To	2 ft Hose ¾" @15		30	
" 6	"	2 " 1" Pipe	8	16	
" 26	"	5 Gal Gaso	15	75	
		Amt due	-	$1 21	

Appendix NO.23

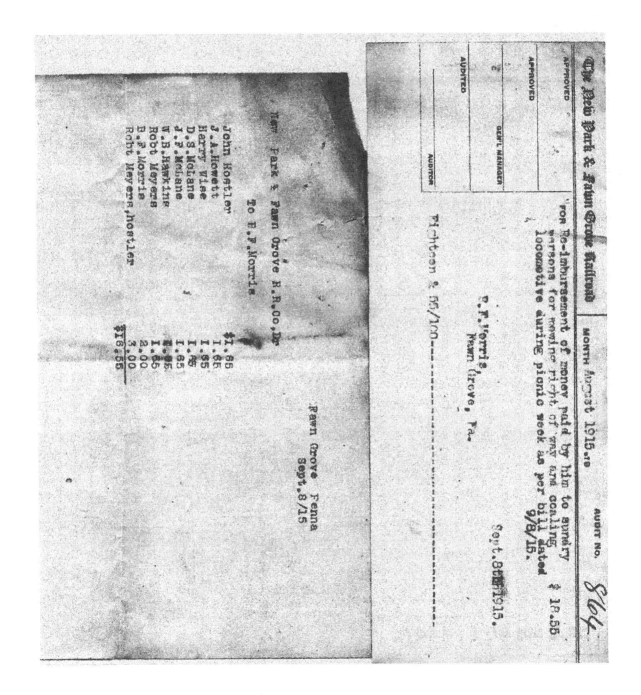

Not responsible for loss or damage to goods after obtaining Shipping Receipt or Bill of Lading in good order.   Report all errors promptly on receipt of goods.

Philadelphia, Pa., ___Aug. 11th, 1915.___ 191___

New Park & Fawn Grove Railroad .

New Park, Penna.

Bought of **KEYSTONE LANTERN COMPANY**

Manufacturer of

"Casey" Lanterns, Tin Boxes; Screw-Caps and Specialties in Light Metal Stamping

TACONY AND COTTMAN STREETS, TACONY

Our Order No. __14250__

Your Order No. _____   Req. No. __8/9/15.__

TERMS:—30 days net, or _____ per cent. discount for cash in _____ days from date of this invoice.

½ Doz. — Standard #39 "CASEY" R.R.Hand Lanterns, @ 7.50 per dozen, f. o. b. Philadelphia,	1.88	
½ " " Extra burners for same, @ 60¢ per doz.f.o.b.Phila.	.15	2.03

"Order completed-
Shipped via Adams Express.

Appendix NO.25

New Park & Fawn Grove R. R.
TRACK FOREMAN'S REPORT

Fawn Grove	*Sept* Left *1915*	A. M.
(Place of Work)	Arrived	A. M.
Time Allowed at Noon	*Tie Inspection and*	Hr. Min.
Stopped Work	*taken up at* Left	P. M.
Fawn Grove	*Davis siding* Arrived	P. M.
Number of Men Working		
Time Made	*Jacob Grove*	Hrs.

Place and kind of work done

Sept 8th

78 – 1st class chestnut ties
12 – 2nd " " "
90   3 ties con'd

REMARKS (Plans for next day's work, discoveries as to roadway conditions, materials needed, etc.)

Date *Sept 8* 1915

E. Grove, Foreman.

Appendix NO. 26

NEW PARK AND FAWN GROVE RAILROAD

—o—

Time Table in Effect Dec. 27, 1915.   Daily Except Sunday.

Westward—Read down			Eastward—Read up	
No. 7.	No. 3.		No. 4.	No. 8.
P. M.	A. M.		A. M.	P. M.
3.20	6.45	Leave FAWN GROVE Arr.	10.30	7.00
		KISINER		
3.30	6.55	NEW PARK	10.15	6.45
		STRAWBRIDGE		
3.36	7.01	WILEY	10.10	6.40
		GEMMILL		
		ANDERSON		
4.15	7.25	STEWARTSTOWN	9.55	6.25
		S. R. R.		
4.20	7.40	STEWARTSTOWN	9.55	6.25
4.50	8.07	NEW FREEDOM	9.30	6.00
		N. C. R. R.		
5.55	9.45	YORK	8.35	5.08
6.05	9.15	Arr BALTIMORE Lve	7.25	4.20
P. M.	A. M.	(Union Station)	A. M.	P. M.

Freight and Express agencies at Fawn Grove, New Park, Wiley, and Stewartstown. Trains stop at Way Stations only when signaled, or on notice to conductor.

J. C. WILEY, General Manager.   B. F. MORRIS, Supt.

Appendix N0.27

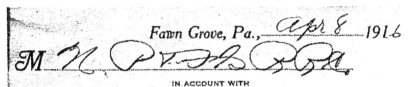

Fawn Grove, Pa., *Apr 8* 1916

M

IN ACCOUNT WITH

𝔚. 𝔈. 𝔐𝔞𝔫𝔦𝔣𝔬𝔩𝔡 & ℭ𝔬.,

DEALERS IN

Grain, Hay, Feed, Produce, Fertilizers, Coal, Farm Machinery, Etc., Etc.

Terms Cash: Interest on all over-due accounts
Discounts not allowed after 3d day from date due

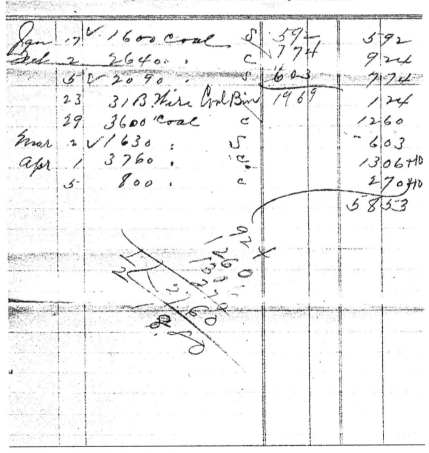

Appendix NO. 28

FAIRBANKS, MORSE & CO.
(INCORPORATED)

TERMS

S.D. B/L

SOLD TO

NEW YORK May 18, 19 15

The New Park and Fawn Grove RR,
New Park, Pennsylvania.

Order Fairbanks, Morse & Co.,

PURCHASER'S ORDER NO.
5/8/15.

IN REFERRING TO THIS INVOICE PLEASE MENTION OUR REGISTER

SHIPPED TO
Notify The New Park and Fawn Grove RR,
New Park, Pennsylvania.

OUR ORDER NO.

NO.

VIA

MC & P R % NC- Stewartstown   Sheffield Jones 5/10/15.

RUSH ALL POSSIBLE

QUANTITY ORDERED	QUANTITY SHIPPED	IN NO CASE ALLOWED TO COLLECT OR MAKE DRAFTS WITHOUT OUR WRITTEN AUTHORITY	PRICE	DISCT	PAYABLE IN NEW YORK EXCHANGE		
	1	#1 standard section hand car. #94396			27	00	
		fob THREE RIVERS, MICH.					

INVOICE

Appendix NO.29

Stewartstown, Pa., *Dec 10* 1914

Mess N. P v J G R R

IN ACCOUNT WITH

James Fulton & Sons' Co.,

DEALERS IN

General Merchandise, Grain, Feed, Produce,

Coal, Fertilizers, Farm Implements and Wagons.

1912

Oct 17 20 1 Ell		05
Sep 5 " 1 Bush 1 Sleeve		.10
Oct 3 " 1 " 1 Nip		.10
295 Coal		.98
3' 3/v Hose 16	48	
1 /v Nip	10	60
1 Bush	4	62
		1,85
1913 July 28 To Cover Injector Screw	25	
1914 July 13 2 Scythes 75	1 50	
" " 1 Snath	85	
Aug 26 1 File	20	
Dec 11 1 Stove Grate	25	3.05
		4.90

Appendix NO.30

Mogul Type Locomotive for the New Park & Fawn Grove Railroad

THE BALDWIN LOCOMOTIVE WORKS

Baldwin Class 8-26-D, 196

Code Word, REDIMESSI

GENERAL DIMENSIONS

GAUGE	4' 8½"
CYLINDERS	16" x 24"
Valves	Balanced slide
BOILER—Type	Wagon top
Diameter	54"
Working pressure	180 lbs.
Fuel	Soft coal
FIREBOX—Length	70⅞"
Width	33⅜"
Depth, front	61"
back	60"
TUBES—Diameter	2"
Number	211
Length	9' 0"
HEATING SURFACE—Firebox	102 sq. ft.
Tubes	985 sq. ft.
Total	1087 sq. ft.
Grate area	16.3 sq. ft.
DRIVING WHEELS—Diameter	48"
Journals	7" x 8"
TRUCK WHEELS—Diameter	28"
WHEEL BASE—Driving	11' 0"
Total engine	18' 0"
Total engine and tender	42' 10½"
WEIGHT—On driving wheels	77,500 lbs.
Total engine	93,000 lbs.
Total engine and tender	162,000 lbs.
TENDER—Water capacity	3,000 gals.
Coal capacity	6 tons
TRACTIVE FORCE	19,580 lbs.
SERVICE	Passenger and Freight
	Rails, 65 pounds per yard; sharpest curves, 19 degrees; grades, 2 per cent.

732 5C-2-15

THE BALDWIN LOCOMOTIVE WORKS

Know all Men by these Presents, That THE BALDWIN LOCOMOTIVE

WORKS, Philadelphia, a company incoroporated under an Act of the General Assembly of the Common-

wealth of Pennsylvania, for and in consideration of the sum of One Dollar to it in hand paid by

- - - - - - - - - - The New Park and Fawn Grove R. R. - - - - - - - -

the receipt whereof is hereby acknowledged, has granted, bargained, sold, assigned, transferred, and

set over, and by these presents does grant, bargain, sell, assign, transfer and set over, unto the said

- - - - - - - - - - The New Park and Fawn Grove R. R. - - - - - - - -

in fee simple, the following described locomotive

Builder's Class 8-26 D 196   Construction No. 41462

Road No. 2

In Witness Whereof, THE BALDWIN LOCOMOTIVE WORKS has caused its

corporate seal to be hereto affixed, duly attested by the signatures of its President and its Secretary

this   Fifth   day of   January   191 7

THE BALDWIN LOCOMOTIVE WORKS

_____
President

_____
Secretary

J.A.Gailey,Auditor.   New Park, Pa.

THE NEW PARK AND FAWN GROVE RAILROAD.

New Park, Pa. February 8th 1917.

The Baldwin Locomotive Works,
        Philadelphia, Pa.

                Gentlemen:-

                        We are in receipt of your Bill of
Sale,dated ~~JANUARY~~ January 5th 1917,for our Road Locomotive No.2,
Builder's Class 8-26 D 196, Construction No.41462, for which we are
thankful.

                Yours Respectfully,

                                Auditor.

Appendix N0.32

Whereas the Board of Directors of the New Park and Fawn Grove Railroad have called a SPECIAL MEETING of the Stockholders of the New Park and Fawn Grove Railroad at New Park, Pa. on the 6th day of August 1919,for the purpose of authorizing the execution and delivery of a contract or contracts between this company and the United States or its representatives and all questions and matters pertaining thereto;

Resolved, " That the Board of Directors of the company is hereby authorized to enter into a contract with the Director General of Railroads, respecting the possession,use and control of the company's railroad and its appurtenances,respecting the operation of such properties,and respecting any other matter connected with or growing out of the relationship between the company and the Director General of Railroads,or arising out of the Federal Control Act,upon such terms,conditions and stipulations as the said Board may approve.

"The Board of Directors is hereby furthur empowered to authorize at any time and from time to time alterations,amendments,or additions to the terms and provisions of the said agreement in any manner that may be therein provided; and to take all such other and further action as the said Board shall deem necessary in the premises; and generally to consider and act upon any and all questions and matters incidental to the purposes aforesaid or growing out of the Federal control of the properties of this company.

"Any such agreement,when approved by the Board of Directors of the Company,may be executed by such officer of the Company as the Board may designate for the purpose.

175

Appendix NO.33

New Park and Fawn Grove Railroad

Time Table in Effect June 13, 1921. Daily Except Sunday.

Westward—Read down			Eastward—Read up	
No. 7.	No. 3.		No. 4.	No. 8.
P. M.	A. M.		A. M.	P. M.
2.55	6.45	Leave FAWN GROVE Arr.	10.50	7.00
3.05	6.55	KISNER / NEW PARK	10.35	6.45
3.11	7.01	STRAWBRIDGE / WILEY	10.25	6.40
3.50	7.35	GEMMILL / ANDERSON / STEWARTSTOWN	10.10 *	6.25
		S. R. R.		
4.00	7.40	STEWARTSTOWN	10.10	6.25
4.27	8.07	NEW FREEDOM	9.40	6.00
		N. C. R.		
5.22	9.50	YORK	8.48	5.13
6.10	9.15	BALTIMORE (Union Station) Lve	7.20	4.20
P. M.	A. M.		A. M.	P. M.

Freight and Express agencies at Fawn Grove, New Park, Wiley, and Stewartstown. Trains stop at Way Stations only when signaled, or on notice to conductor.

B. F. MORRIS,
Supt. and Gen. Manger.

J. A. GAILY,
Gen. Pass. Agent.

Appendix NO.34

INTERSTATE COMMERCE COMMISSION.

Washington, D. C.

Valuation Docket No. 255.

RECEIVED

JUN 24 1922

BUREAU OF VALUATION

June 21, 1922.

The Honorable,
    The Attorney General of the United States.

The Honorable,
    The Governor of Pennsylvania,
        Harrisburg, Pa.

Public Service Commission,
    Harrisburg, Pa.

The New Park and Fawn Grove Railroad,
    New Park, Pa.,
        Care J. A. Gailey, Auditor.

    You are hereby notified that the Interstate Commerce Commission
has completed the tentative valuation of the property of The New
Park and Fawn Grove Railroad, as of June 30, 1916, and that said
valuation is set forth in the tentative valuation report which is included in the order adopting the same, a copy of which is attached
to this notice and made a part hereof.

    You are required to file with the Commission at its office in
Washington on or before thirty (30) days from the 1st day of July,
1922, any protest which you may desire to make to such valuation or
to any part of such valuation.

    You will file in connection with such protest specification
setting forth in detail each particular thing against which the protest is directed.

    You are further required to transmit a copy of such protest
to each of the other parties to whom this notice is addressed and
to file with the Commission for its official use twenty-five (25)
additional copies of the same.

    By the Commission, Division 1.

                                    George B. McGinty
                                    Secretary.

O R D E R.

At a Session of the Interstate Commerce Commission, Division 1, held at its office in Washington, D. C., on the 21st day of June, A. D. 1922.

Valuation Docket No. 255.

THE NEW PARK AND FAWN GROVE RAILROAD.

It is ordered, That the following be, and it is hereby declared to be, the tentative valuation of the property of The New Park and Fawn Grove Railroad, as of June 30, 1916:

Location and general description of property.- The railroad of The New Park and Fawn Grove Railroad, hereinafter called the carrier, is a single track, standard gauge, steam railroad, located in the southern part of Pennsylvania. The owned mileage extends in an easterly direction from Stewartstown to Fawn Grove, Pa., a distance of 9.234 miles. The carrier also owns yard and side tracks totaling 1.141 miles. Its road thus embraces 10.375 miles of all tracks owned. In Appendix 1 will be found a general description of the property of the carrier.

Jointly used property.- The carrier has no jointly owned and used property except minor facilities, the carrier's portion of the reproduction costs being included with property classified as wholly owned and used. In Appendix 2, under the caption Leased Railway Property, will be found a statement showing the property used jointly with others and the terms of the use.

Traffic connections.- The railroad of the carrier connects at Stewartstown with the line of The Stewartstown Railroad Company.

Physical conditions affecting construction.- The country traversed is rolling farm land. The soil is of clay and the rock is mainly a mica schist with infrequent outcrops of quartz.

Economic conditions relating to traffic.- The principal products of the region are those of the farm.

Corporate history.- The carrier was incorporated on May 11, 1905, under the laws of Pennsylvania. The principal office is at New Park, Pa..

The detailed facts as to the development of fixed physical property are given in Appendix 2.

History of corporate financing, capital stock, and long-term debt.- The carrier has issued a total of $89,050 par value of stocks and bonds, of which amount $86,450 was actually outstanding on date of valuation. Of the securities actually outstanding $49,050 represents capital stock and $37,400 first mortgage bonds.

In addition to the above outstanding capital obligations, there is held by or for the carrier $2,600 par value of first mortgage bonds.

The carrier issued a total of $52,602.20 par value of short-term notes, of which amount $9,622.18 was outstanding on date of valuation.

Appendix NO.35

Upon motion of T B Fulton Seconded by S H Smith the following
was accepted.
STOCKHOLDERS MEETING.

Office of the Stewartstown Railroad Company, January 8,
1923, upon motion duly made and seconded, and by the
affirmative vote of all present, they bring a majority in interest,
the following preamble and resolutions were adopted.

Whereas the New Park and Fawn Grove Railroad Company has
offered to sell, transfer, and convey to the Stewartstown Railroad Company, its successors and assigns, all of its coporate
property, real, personal and mixed, rights and credits, owned,
possessed, hold, used, belonging to, and all debts due of what-
ever kind, choses in action, as well as other things in action,
belonging to the New Park and Fawn Grove Railroad Company, and
all real estate, buildings, machinery, piping, boilers, engines,
passenger and freight cars, poles, wire, tools, rails, ties,
switches and tracks, implements, motors, leases, lease-hold
interest, right of ways, contracts, claims, demands, money and
property of every kind, description, name and nature, belonging to
said New Park and Fawn Grove Railroad Company, for and in
consideration of the Stewartstown Railroad Company, assuming and
paying the first mortgage outstanding bonded indebtedness of the
said New Park and Fawn Grove Railroad Company amounting to
$34,300.00 and the bills and amounts payable of the said New Park
and Fawn Grove Railroad Company, amounting to approximately
$12,000.00 and the sum of One Dollar in cash.

Resolved that the Board of Directors of this Company
be and they are hereby authorized and directed to purchase the
said property mentioned, for the price, and upon the terms and
conditions stated, and to pay out of the funds of this Company
the said first mortgage outstanding bonded indebtedness and the
said bills and accounts, due and payable.

In motion of T B Fulton Seconded by S H Smith it was decided to accept
offer stated below .

MINUTES OF DIRECTORS MEETING.

Upon motion duly made and seconded, it was
Resolved, That this Company, accept the offer of the New Park
and Fawn Grove Railroad Company to sell and convey to this
Company, the property described in the resolution of the
stockholders passed January 8, 1923 authorizing the purchase,
and the Board of Directors do hereby adjudge and declare that
the consideration mentioned is a fair value of the same.

Further resolved, That the proposed agreement for the sale
of said property presented at this meeting be and the same is
hereby approved as to form, and the President and Secretary of
the Company are hereby authorized and directed to execute said
agreement in the name and on the behalf of this Company, and to
affix the corporate seal thereto.

Appendix NO.36

We the undersigned agree to pay the amount set opposite our names for the purpose of helping grade the piece of road between Manifold's bridge and Anderson's siding.

The sum of $5,000 must be raised immediately in order to have this piece of road built this summer, and if not built this summer the amounts subscribed will be returned to the subscribers.

NAME	ADDRESS		AMOUNT
Harry Fulton	M.F.	Paid	10.00 X
Melvin Fulton	M.F.	Paid	10.00 X
Ernest L. Brenneman	Mar.		2.00
W.S. Fulton		Paid	5.00 X
Richard Waltimyer		Paid	5.00 X
John Sipe			10.00
H. Robert M. Mull	M.F. 7/6/23	Paid	5.00
Jno. Streett	M.F. 7/6/23	Paid	1.00 X
Kreamer Bros	M.F.	Paid	24.00 X
Roy Norris		Paid	5.00 X
Guy Brown		Paid	5.50 X
H.L. Trout	Cross Roads	Paid	5.00 X
	Red Lion	Paid	5.00 X
Waltimyer	M.F. 7/6/23	Paid	2.00 X
J.H. Brennaan			2.00
Kenneth J. Orr			1.00
Roland Waltimyer		Paid	10.00 X
Robt. Hamilton		Paid	10.00 X
Fulton	M.F.	Paid	5.00 X
Ray. Bartenslager	M.F.	Paid	10.00 X
People Baking Co.		Paid	5.00 X
Atlantic Refining Co		Paid	25.00 X

180

Appendix N0.37

APPLES
Yellow Transparent
Wealthy
Mackintosh
Jonathan
Grimes
Stayman
York Imperial

PEACHES
Carman
Belle of Ga.
Elberta
Salway
White Heath

H. W. Anderson
GROWER OF
FANCY APPLES AND PEACHES
IN CAR LOTS
STEWARTSTOWN, PENNA.

July, 9, 1923.

Mr. Thos. J. Simons,
York,
Pa.

Dear Sir:-

The work of grading and moving the Rail Road, so as to be able to lay the State Road is nearing completion. This work must be paid for in next few days. Without your help this work would not have been completed.

The amount of your subscription is $10.00 A prompt remittance will be greatly appreciated. Thanking you for your part and trusting to be of service to you in the near future, I am,

Yours very truly,

H. W. Anderson

Paid Thank you
H. W. Anderson

Appendix NO.38

Stewartstown Railroad Company

Freight and Passenger Office

Stewartstown, Pa., Sep 25,1923 *192*

To the board of directors6

        Gentlemen your General manager wishes to make the
following report_ since our last meeting we have had three
very expensive wrecks: more damage being done than in all our
38 years of railroading , On SepII ththe new bus operated by
John Barton ran into an open switch at New Park Pa and struck
a box car on the siding damaging theEngine and pilot to the
extent probably of $ 700. dollars the repairs are being made
as rapidly as possible and we hope to have thh car in service
this P M while this was an accident had the operator been
watching his business more carefully the damage would have not
been so great, on the same day we ahd a derailment at Keeney
that tore up about 300 feet and held up traffic for 2 days
  the cost of track , machinery and stone car will probably
reach $400 dollars of which must be credited a car of 55 tOns
stoneth t we ahd to unload .
    Sep the 19th the worst disaster occured in our 38 years of
Our existence when the freight train struck the passenger
train rounding the curve at Zeiglers telescoping and practically
destroying the body of coach and at the same time injuring
Mrs Reeling Mrs Anderson, Mrs Diehl and Miss Rose Rigdon,
The injuries consist of Bruises burns and shock no bones broken
The engine pilot Smoke box door and front bumper were broken
also the cab practically ###### wrecked, the cab was in pretty bad
shape so am having an entire new one put on . The loss can only be estimatd
Coach cost$2300 , 7 years ago damage to engine will probably reach $800
From my investigation of the cause I have arrived at the following
conclusion That conductor Mc Elwain did not take the proper precaution
to safe guard his train . That Engineer Roseberry and fireman Few were

---

running reckless and were not on the lookout as they should hsve been
when following a passenger train ?.   My recommendation is that the
chair appoint a commitee to look after the injured and to make the
best adjustment possible , my further recommendation is that we make
Stewartstown the stabting point for the freight train as we will have
better control and get better service than under the present plan.

                    C F Shaw

Appendix 38b

N O T I C E

STEWARTSTOWN RAILROAD COMPANY hereby gives notice that on the 8th day of April, 1924, it filed with the Interstate Commerce Commission at Washington, D. C., its application for authority to acquire control of the New Park and Fawn Grove Railroad Company, by purchase of capital stock, and for a certificate that the present and future public convenience and necessity require the acquisition by the applicant, by purchase, of the railroad of the New Park and Fawn Grove Railroad Company, which extends from Stewartstown to Fawn Grove, a distance of approximately nine (9) miles, all in York County, Pennsylvania.

W. B. Gemmill,
    Attorney.

STEWARTSTOWN RAILROAD COMPANY.

By Thomas B. Fulton,
        President.

Courtesy PENNSYLVANIA STATE ARCHIVES (PHMC)

Agreement for the merger and consolidation of The Stewartstown Railroad Company into and with The New Park and Fawn Grove Railroad, forming one corporation to be known as The Stewartstown Railroad Company.

THIS AGREEMENT, made this 14th day of March,
1922, between The Stewartstown Railroad Company, party of the first
part, and The New Park and Fawn Grove Railroad, party of the second
part.

WHEREAS, The Stewartstown Railroad Company, party of the
first part, is a corporation in the State of Pennsylvania, chartered
and organised under an Act of Assembly entitled, "An Act to organise
and authorise the formation and regulation of Railroad Corporations,
approved April 4, A. D. 1868, and the several supplements thereto."
and was duly organised for the purpose of constructing and operating
a railroad. That the said Stewartstown Railroad Company was incorporated on September 22, 1884 and that said Company has since accepted
the provisions of the Act of April 29, 1874 and is now engaged in the
business authorized by its charter; and

WHEREAS, The New Park and Fawn Grove Railroad is a corporation of the State of Pennsylvania, chartered under an Act of General
Assembly of the Commonwealth of Pennsylvania, entitled "An Act to
authorise the formation and regulation of Railroad Corporations, approved April 4th, A. D. 1868, and the Acts supplementary thereto." for the
purpose of building and operating a railroad. That said Company was
duly incorporated May 11, 1905. Amended and supplemental Articles of
Association of the said New Park and Fawn Grove Railroad were approved
and Letters Patent issued thereon by Edward C. Stewart, Governor of
Pennsylvania, on August 11, 1930. That the said Company has accepted
the provisions of the Act of April 29, 1874 and is now engaged in the
business authorized by its charter; and

This is the first page of the sale agreement of the NP&FG RR to the Stewartstown RR circa 1922.

Courtesy PENNSYLVANIA STATE ARCHIVES (PHMC)

BUREAU OF
PUBLIC CONVENIENCE

of the

Commonwealth of Pennsylvania

E. M. VALE
CHIEF OF BUREAU

Harrisburg, Penn'a., **May 7, 1924.**
File A.10759, 10760-1924.

In re: Stewartstown Railroad Company for approval of the acquisition of the control of the New Park and Fawn Grove Railroad Company, by purchase of its capital stock. A.10759-1924.

In re: Stewartstown Railroad Company for approval of the purchase and acquisition of the New Park and Fawn Grove Railroad Company. A.10760-1924.

W. B. Gemmill, Esq.,
Security Building,
York, Pa.

Dear Sir:

I acknowledge receipt of original and **three copies** of the petitions in the above cases (docketed to the above numbers); also filing fees, receipted bill for which is enclosed herewith.

The Commission has fixed as the time and place of hearing on said applications: **Thursday, May 29th, at 9:30 A. M. Standard Time, in the Commission Building, 112 Market Street, Harrisburg.**

You are directed to publish notice of the time and place of hearing in form enclosed herewith, marked "Notice to be Published". in a newspaper of general circulation printed in **York** in the issues of said paper on **May 15th and 22d.**

Proof of publication of notice of hearing in form enclosed, marked "Proof of Publication of Notice of Hearing" must be filed with the Commission on or before **May 26th.**

Kindly acknowledge receipt of this communication.

Very truly yours,

E. M. Vale

Chief.

JSH: C
Encls.

P. S. The notices of these applications and hearings may be combined in one notice covering both cases, to be published as above directed.

Stewartstown Railroad Company
Office of the General Manager
Stewartstown, Pa.

C. W. SHAW, Gen. Manager

12/6 1924

W B Gemmill Esq
Dear sir

Original Bond issue dated Oct 1 1908   40,000 00

Redeemed by N P & F G R R   5200 00
      "   & S R R   31,200 00   36400

            Balance outstanding.   3600 00

Items of interest is shown on the
memorandum I gave you
Bonds are due & payable Oct 1, 1933   31,700
                                        3600
                                       34810

            yours C W Shaw

Appendix N0.39

NOTICE

No Trespassing or Stealing Allowed

THIS IS PRIVATE PROPERTY. All Persons are hereby notified and warned neither to trespass on these premises under a penalty of a fine not exceeding $10.00, as provided by the Act of April 14, 1905, P. L. 169; nor to take, steal or carry away any property whatsoever under a penalty of a fine not exceeding $500.00 and imprisonment not exceeding 3 years, as provided by the Act of May 1, 1925, P. L. 440.

Appendix NO.40

Pennsylvania Railroad System

General Office, Broad Street Station,

A. J. County,
    Vice President in charge of Accounting.

Philadelphia, June 16th, 1925.

Geo. J. Adams,
    Asst to Vice President in charge of Accounting.

Mr. H. E. Anstine,
    Secretary, Stewartstown R.R.Co.,
        Stewartstown, Pa.

Dear Sir:

I have your letter of the 15th instant requesting the Pennsylvania R.R.Co. to forward its proxy for use at the special meeting of the stockholders of the Stewartstown R.R.Co. to be held on Tuesday next, the 23rd instant, in favor of proposed leasing of the New Park and Fawn Grove Railroad.

Will you kindly advise me the terms of the proposed lease and such other facts as may be pertinent to the matter? My recollection is that in 1922 this Company furnished its proxy in favor of the purchase by the Stewartstown R.R.Co. of the New Park and Fawn Grove Railroad, and, I assume that said purchase was never consummated and that the lease will be resorted to in lieu thereof. Kindly advise why the purchase has not been carried out.

Yours truly,

Vice President - Accounting and
Corporate Work.

Appendix NO.41

The Public Service Commission

of the

Commonwealth of Pennsylvania

BUREAU OF
ACCIDENTS

JOHN P. DOHONE
CHIEF OF BUR

Harrisburg,   March 30th, 1928.

C. W. Shaw, Gen. Mgr.,
          Stewartstown Railroad Company,
          Stewartstown, Pa.

Dear Sir:

          This Bureau is in receipt of your report on
State Highway grade crossings on your lines, and they are
being returned herewith for the reason that the crossing
numbers as listed with the Commission are not correctly
notated thereon.

          We are also sending you a copy of the lists
as filed with the Commission during 1922, of the above named
company as well as The New Park & Fawn Grove railroad company
with the request that you carefully examine same and note ther
any changes that may have occurred in the intervening period,
and return to this Bureau.

          You will notice that State Highways are marked
in red "S.H.X.", and the State Aid Roads (S.A.X.) if these
markings are not correct, kindly advise.

          An early compliance with the above request wil
be much appreciated.

                              Very truly yours,

                              John P. Dohoney

                                        Chief.

JPD/c

Appendix NO.42

STEWARTSTOWN RAILROAD
TIME TABLE

Connecting with the Pennsylvania Railroad at New Freedom, Pa.

Daily, except Sunday—In Effect April 29, 1928

	Going West--Read down			STATIONS	Going East--Read up			
Motor Bus No. 7	Freight No. 5	Motor Bus No. 3	Freight No. 1		Freight No. 2	Motor Bus No. 4	Freight No. 6	Motor Bus No. 8
P. M.	A. M.	A. M.	A. M.		A. M.	A. M.	P. M.	P. M.
3 25	10 00	6 45		Lve FAWN GROVE Arr	9 40	10 47		7 12
3 28		6 49		KISINER		10 44		7 06
3 30	10 15	6 57		NEW PARK	9 25	10 36		7 03
3 40		7 02		STRAWBRIDGE		10 32		7 00
3 45	10 30	7 05		WILEY	9 10	10 28		6 55
3 49		7 09		GEMMILL		10 24		6 53
3 51		7 11		MAPLE HILL		10 21		6 50
3 53		7 14		ANDERSON		10 18		6 48
3 57		7 17		MANIFOLD		10 16		6 45
4 00	12 20 P.M.	7 22	6 45	STEWARTSTOWN	8 35	10 12		6 40
4 03	12 22	7 24		ZEIGLER		10 09	2 17	6 37
4 07	12 24	7 27		REIMOLD		10 06	2 14	6 34
4 09	12 27	7 30		ORWIG		10 03	2 11	6 31
4 12	12 30	7 33		ANSTINE		10 01	2 08	6 29
4 16	12 34	7 37	7 05	SHEFFER	8 15	9 56	2 06	6 24
4 19	12 37	7 40		KEENEY		9 52	2 01	6 20
4 23	12 42	7 45	7 20	TURNPIKE	8 05	9 49	1 57	6 17
4 28	12 47	7 52	7 30	NEW FREEDOM	7 55	9 42	1 54	6 10
				———— P. R. R. ————			1 47	
5 22	1 30	9 50		YORK		8 56	1 02	5 11
6 13	3 20	9 00		BALTIMORE		7 20	12 00 P.M.	4 27
P. M.	P. M.	A. M.		Arrive Leave		A. M.	A. M.	UNION P. M.

Trains stop at way stations only when signaled or on notice to conductor. Tickets sold and Baggage checked to all points on P. R. R. between Baltimore and Harrisburg. All trains carry Mail, Express and Baggage.

Passengers wishing to leave Fawn Grove and intermediate points between morning and evening passenger trains can do so by using the freight train leaving Fawn Grove 10:00, New Park 10:15, Wiley 10:30.

C. W. SHAW,

    General Manager

THOS. B. FULTON,

    Supt.

Appendix NO.43

FREIGHT BILL

To The New Park & Fawn Grove Railroad, Dr. For charges Advanced, Receiving, Weighing,
Storage, Transportation, Delivery, Etc. on the Articles named below:

Shipped by _____ Original Point of Shipment _____ Original Car No. _____

Waybill No. _951_ Date _____ From _____ Car No. _____

Bill No. _____

MARKS	ARTICLES	WEIGHT	RATE	FREIGHT CHARGES	ADVANCES	TOTAL
				15 —	1.11	1.51

Received the above named goods in good order and condition by _____ 19___

All Claims for Overcharge on this Shipment must be Presented to the Agent, Accompanied by Bill of Lading and this Freight Bill, within Forty-eight Hours after Delivery of Property.

MAKE CHECKS PAYABLE TO THE NEW PARK & FAWN GROVE RAILROAD

Appendix NO.44

ENCLOSE THIS TO AUDITOR

Station Agent's Report

TO THE AUDITOR OF THE

Stewartstown Railroad Company

From _New Park Pa_ Station

Made _Feb 20th_ 19_33_

For Month of _January_ 19_33_

REMITTED ON ACCOUNT OF

	Dollars	Cents
Passenger		50
Freight _Reed levl f_	218	22
Freight PP ford, omitted from December 1932		69
Express Commission	3	97
Total	223	38

DUPLICATE OF LAST PREVIOUS REPORT

Remitted Treasurer 19____

Passenger _2/20/33, 1st Nat Bk Stewartstown_ 223.38

Freight _in full for January_

_1933_

Total _____ $ 223.38

J. H. Bailey Agent

This must agree with the report sent to the Treasurer and be forwarded at the same time.

Agents will enter the MONTH in which they will claim the remit-
tance on their Monthly Reports to the Auditor.

Appendix NO.45

STEWARTSTOWN, PENNA.

~~MAY 29~~ 1935.
June 3

-------LEASE AGREEMENT.-------

This agreement made by and between C.W.Shaw for account of The Stewartstown Railroad Company, to be hereafter known as the party of the first part: and Kenneth Manifold for account of Full Moon Club, to be hereafter known as party of the second part.

The Party of the second part being desirous of leasing part of building known as old station for use as a club room from the party of the first part, the party of the #### second part hereby agrees and covenants, to wit:-

The Party of the second part agrees to vacate the above described premises on sixty (60) days notice from party of first part or on ten (10) days notice from party of first part if the party of first part is able to rent or lease the entire building for industrial use or for any use that will employ labor.

The Party of the second part agree to furnish their own heat, light and water and if the present installed facilities of same are use the party of the second part agrees to keep same in repair at no cost to party of first part and further that party of second part shall be responsible for any and all costs created by the use of said faciliti

The Party of first part agrees to permit the party of second part to remove on vacating the premises any and all improvements installed by party of second part during the period of occupancy of said building and party of second part agrees to have building in as good or better condition on vacating same as found when occupied as of June 1st 1935.

The Party of second part agrees to pay($4.00) Four Dollars per month, payable quarterly in advance, for use of first floor of building west of that portion of building used by Boy Scout Troop as of June 1st 1935.

And so we mutually agree and covenant.

C. W. Shaw.
Per Fay Shaw
_____
Party of first part

& Ken. S. Manifold
Party of Second Part

John Amherman
Witness

STEWARTSTOWN

RAILROAD

THE STEWARTSTOWN RAILROAD

-*-

CHRONOLOGICAL HISTORY
1883 TO 1940

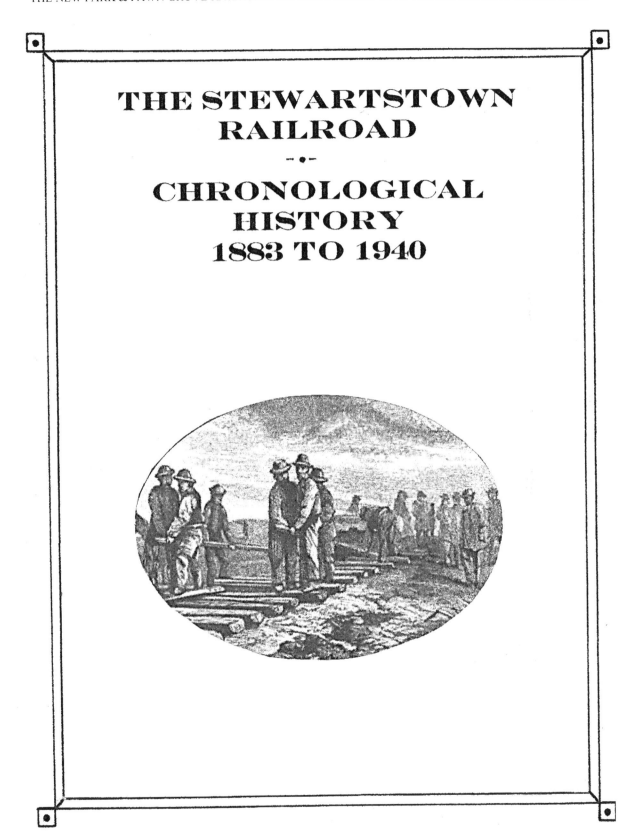

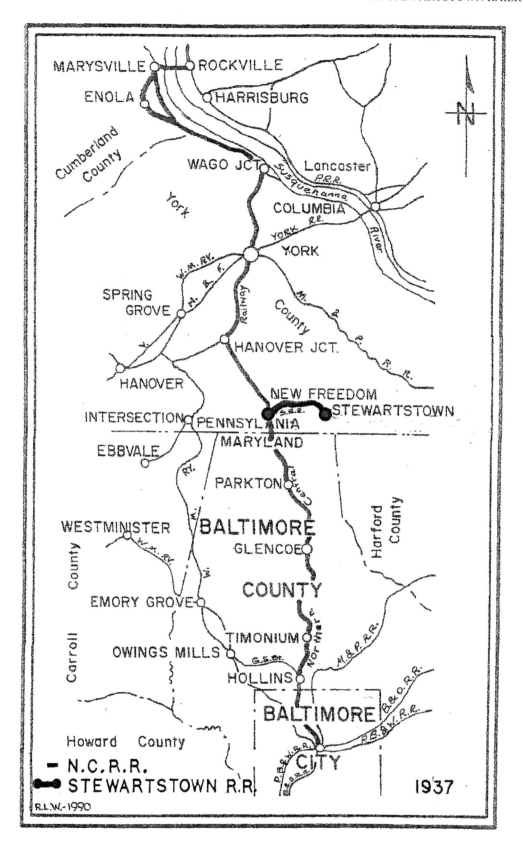

JAMES FULTON
The first elected president of the Stewartstown Railroad
1884–1894

STEWARTSTOWN RAILROAD
Chronological History
1883 to 1940

Apr. 21, 1883	New Freedom, Pa. Items.
	It would be interesting to the readers of the Advocate, perhaps, to read a brief account of our village. We have present two blacksmith shops, two wheelwright shops, three dry goods stores, one ice cream saloon, two saddler shops, one cigar factory, one cabinet shop, five churches —Lutheran, Evangelical, Methodist, Baptist and Catholic; one school house, two doctors and one huckster. The Northern Central Railroad passes through the heart of the village, making everything convenient and pleasant. It is about 1,300 feet above the level of the sea, and it also divides the waters which flow north and south. A new railroad is expected from Stewartstown, to connect with the Northern Central Railroad, which will still add to the improvement of our village. (DA)
May 26, 1883	Stewartstown RR Meeting Minute Notes convey that each share of stock will cost $50 per share. (see Appendix No. 1)
Aug. 4, 1883	M. W. Bahn writes a letter addressed to the president of the Stewartstown Railroad, James Fulton, informing Mr. Fulton that he was not able to make the meeting. (See Appendix No. 2)
Jun. 9, 1883	There was a meeting held at Stewartstown recently on behalf of the new railroad from Stewartstown to New Freedom. According to the report of the engineers, the route surveyed is an excellent one and can be graded, bridged and the iron put down for about $63,000. The people of Stewartstown are determined to have a railroad either to New Freedom or to the narrow-gauge. (DA)
1884	A list of individuals that subscribed and became stockholders in the Stewartstown Railroad. (See Appendix No. 3)
	A list of individuals who contributed land to establish the right-of-way for Stewartstown Railroad. (See Appendix No. 4)
Mar. 22, 1884	A Projected Railroad – The Bel Air *Democrat* of 14th inst., says: "Another move is being made in the direction of furnishing the good people of Stewartstown, York County, with railroad facilities — this time, however, not in the direction of the Northern Central, but the Maryland Central Railroad. Messrs. Rufus Lowe and John McElvain, near Fawn Grove, and James Fulton, of Stewartstown, and other wealthy and enterprising citizens will start this week a preliminary survey from Stewartstown to a point on the Maryland Central near Pylesville. This proposed road will probably run near St. Mary's Church and Five Forks, Fawn Grove, crossing the Maryland line near John L. Glenn's; thence about a mile north of Norrisville, near New Park, and thence to Stewartstown.

The road will be about 15 miles long. The country traversed is a fertile agricultural section, without railroad facilities, and it is believed the fertilizers used and grain produced will furnish a large amount of freight, which, together with the passenger travel, will pay a good interest on the outlay necessary to build the road. The route selected, it is believed, will not be an expensive one. With terminal facilities already secured, there is a fair prospect for the success of the enterprise." (U)

May 3, 1884	The project of building a narrow-gauge railroad from Stewartstown to Pylesville or the Rocks of Deer Creek, to connect with the Maryland Central Railroad, is being pressed vigorously. The people of Stewartstown and the neighborhood have subscribed liberally. The road will be 15 miles in length and will pass near Norrisville. (U)
July 6, 1884	Meeting was held at the Fulton Hotel whereby the stockholders elected a provisional Board of Directors and Company Officers. John B. Gemmill was elected president. (EB)
Aug. 14, 1884	The stockholders met again and elected James Fulton as the permanent president of the Stewartstown Railroad. (EB)
Aug. 16, 1884	Stewartstown Railroad — The Glen Rock *Item,* referring to this enterprise, says: "There is now being made a last effort to secure the balance of the necessary funds to build the Stewartstown and New Freedom Railroad. There are but a few thousand dollars remaining to be subscribed, and this the people in that section should subscribe, without delay. If the present effort should fail, the chances for a road will be delayed a long while. The friends of the enterprise have worked faithfully, and the people of that section will all be benefitted; they of the new railroad should therefore contribute all they possibly can spare. Let this last effort be made a success." (U)
Aug. 30, 1884	Stewartstown Railroad — The contemplated railroad from Stewartstown to the Northern Central Railroad, which has been hanging fire for some time, has now taken shape, and we are told that it is to be built. The capital stock of $57,000 has all been subscribed but about $3,000, and the right-of-way is nearly all secured. James Fulton is the president; A. S. Bowman, secretary, and Andrew Anderson, treasurer. It will intersect the Northern Central near Shrewsbury. (U)
Sept. 1, 1884	The survey for the location of the Stewartstown RR is nearly compete, and it is hoped that the new railroad will pass through Shrewsbury to get the trade of that place. (Letter from Shrewsbury) (YD)
Sept. 3, 1884	The vice president of the Northern Central Railway Company acknowledged Mr. James Fulton (president of the Stewartstown Railroad) [in a] letter pertaining to proposed railroad. (See Appendix No. 5)
Sept. 9, 1884	The 3rd vice president of the Pennsylvania Railroad Company acknowledged Mr. James Fulton (President of the Stewartstown Railroad) [in a] letter pertaining to proposed railroad. (See Appendix No. 6)

Sept. 10, 1884	Gitt, Stewart, & Wood are the [civil] engineers locating the Stewartstown Railroad. (YG)
Sept. 15, 1884	The Stewartstown Railroad has been located and it will cross the turnpike ¾ miles south of the center square of Shrewsbury giving no help to the people of that community. This will be the funeral for Shrewsbury as commerce will by-pass the town. Time will tell. (YG)
Sept. 20, 1884	The New Freedom and Stewartstown railroad being considered again. There was a meeting in M. W. Bahn's Hall on Tuesday evening for the purpose of ascertaining what could be done financially. It requires money to build the railroad and not talk. The people of New Freedom have a railroad and if the Stewartstown folks want one let them build it. (DA)
Sept. 22, 1884	The Stewartstown Railroad was granted a charter from the Commonwealth of Pennsylvania. (EB)
Oct. 1, 1884	A notice was issued to all prospective bidders when the bids are due for the construction of the Stewartstown Railroad by James Fulton, President. (See Appendix No.7)
Oct. 9, 1884	L. L. Bush Co. submit a bid of $62,000 to construct the Stewartstown Railroad. (See Appendix No. 7)
Oct. 15, 1884	A quote was submitted by the Pennsylvania Steel Company for 56-pound steel rail at $28.50 per ton. (See Appendix No. 8)
Oct. 31, 1884	Work on the Stewartstown and New Freedom Railroad was begun on Monday, Oct. 20, by E. Y. Diller, contractor for the grading and masonry. The work is progressing rapidly and will probably be completed by March or April. (AI)
Nov. 15, 1884	Proposal submitted to Stewartstown Railroad from the Billmeyer & Small Company to provide a combine passenger and baggage car. (See Appendix No. 9)
1885	List of property owners that provided the land for the construction of the Stewartstown Railroad. (See Appendix No. 4)
	Stewartstown Railroad check issued to Mrs. R. S. Strong for purchases [for the] railroad for the amount of $51.25. (See Appendix No. 8)
Jan. 19, 1885	Baldwin Locomotive Works submits a proposal to the Stewartstown Railroad for one locomotive as per Specification No.2092 – Class 8/24¼ C for a price of $5,400. (See Appendix No. 10)
Feb. 21, 1885	The Northern Central Railroad Company will build a railroad depot at New Freedom for the benefit of the Northern Central Railroad and the Stewartstown and New Freedom railroad. It is to be completed by July. By that time the new railroad will be in operation. The grading is rapidly approaching completion. (DA)
Feb. 24, 1885	Grading on the Stewartstown RR has been impeded by bad weather of late. (YG)

May 16, 1885	The grading of the Stewartstown Railroad is approaching completion. A month or six weeks will complete that part of the work. It is supposed the connection with the Northern Central Railroad at New Freedom will be affected about July 1. (DA)
May 23, 1885	Jacob Rider submitted a Letter of Application for the position of engineer on the Stewartstown Railroad. The company soon hired him. (See Appendix No. 11)
May 30, 1885	The Stewartstown RR is securing the intersection with the Northern Central RR and track laying will commence soon. Sam Keeney complained over squealing wheels and railroad officials promised to grease them. (YG)
June 8, 1885	Empire Car Works submits a proposal for two gondola cars at $350.00 each to the Stewartstown Railroad. (See Appendix No. 12)
June 9, 1885	Baldwin Locomotive Works General Specification for No. 2092 – Class 8:24¼ C Locomotive as submitted by a proposal submitted on Jan. 19, 1885. (See Appendix No. 13)
June 12, 1885	The Stewartstown Railroad — Track-laying on the new railroad from New Freedom to Stewartstown began on the 21st instant and is progressing at the rate of half a mile a day. The road is seven miles in length, but will not be completed until about July 1, owing to some grading to be done near Stewartstown and some trestle work yet to be finished. (AI)
June 22, 1885	The first engine has arrived and the track is laid to Keeney's east of the turnpike. We suspect that the station on the turnpike will be called Shrewsbury and we suggest that a switch be located there. (YG)
June 27, 1885	The Stewartstown Railroad is on a rapid approach to completion. The company has a new engine running on the road as far as it is built. Its completion extends about miles or more. It is expected to be finished by July. (DA)
June 29, 1885	The Stewartstown RR is spiked down for three miles from the junction with the Northern Central RR at New Freedom. The engine "Hopewell" is the charge of Jacob Rider, engineer, and Mr. Griffith, fireman. A large force is at work laying track. Mr. Diller, the contractor for grading and masonry, is keeping ahead of the track layers. Some have predicted that the road would not be built — foolish expression. (YG)
July 18, 1885	The Stewartstown Railroad is pushing the work of track laying along as rapidly as possible. By the first of September, the road will be finished and in working order. Freight is carried to points along the road in car loads to places where switches are put down. The road will do a good freight business when finished. The outgoing freight will not be so heavy until a full crop comes around. The crop this year will be short, hence the surplus for sale will also be short of former years.

The borough of Stewartstown is improving very rapidly in view of the advantages of the railroad in erecting new buildings and repairing others when finished. (U) |

July 27, 1885	A letter from the Northern Central Railway informing President Fulton of the Stewartstown Railroad that Capt. Frank Gisse will be arriving in New Freedom at 8:30 a.m. to make a connection with the SRR train to Stewartstown. (See Appendix No.14)
Aug. 31, 1885	William Harman requested 12 complimentary tickets from the committee that is handling the opening of the Stewartstown Railroad. (See Appendix No. 15)

Sept. 4, 1885   OPENING OF THE STEWARTSTOWN RAILROAD

The Stewartstown Railroad will be formally opened on Thursday, the 10th of September, and a grand time is expected. A great many invitations have been extended to prominent people. The exercise will be held in a grove at Stewartstown, where addresses will be delivered and a collation served. The ladies of Stewartstown and vicinity are exerting themselves in getting up a handsome banquet for all those who attend the opening. (DA)

Sept. 5, 1885   The Stewartstown Branch Railroad — The Shrewsbury correspondent of the York *Gazette* says: "The Stewartstown Railroad is nearing completion. Mr. Diller, the contractor, has finished his work. The grading having been finished; the track will soon be laid to its terminus." (U)

Sept. 7, 1885   Author of "Letter from Shrewsbury" predicted the "funeral" of that town when it was by-passed by the Stewartstown RR. Ha had received many complaints but little proof is possible. Only time can tell. (A)

Sept. 11, 1885   In all probability the little burg of Stewartstown never witnessed such an invasion as took place Thursday, September 10th with the opening of the Stewartstown RR. At York, the southbound Northern Central train to New Freedom was delayed 15 minutes as people waited in long lines to purchase tickets for New Freedom. There was standing room only in the cars due to the large and unexpected crowd. At New Freedom, the Stewartstown RR was also caught by surprise not expecting such a large crowd. They had only three cars which were not enough to carry everyone so many had to wait for the train to go to Stewartstown and then return. At Stewartstown, the train was met by the Stewartstown Band which escorted the passengers to a beautiful grove at the edge of town. President Col. Fulton was introduced followed by Strawbridge, the railroad attorney, who gave a brief speech dealing with the history of the project. The dinner bell than rang and everyone thronged to tables which groaned under the weight of the food — meat, chicken, ham, rolls, cakes, etc. 3,000 were fed. At 2 P.M. H.C. Wiles gave an address followed by Judge [Adam] Ebaugh. (A)

Sept. 14, 1885   The opening of the Stewartstown RR which occurred on Thursday last was the absorbing topic for the pass week all over the lower end of the county. The occasion was a grand success in every particular. The people of Stewartstown have reason to rejoice and be glad. It was the largest body of men ever assembled in the vicinity with people coming from Baltimore, York, and Hanover. The train was run by engineer Jacob Rider and conductor John B.

Gemmill. It was taxed to its utmost capacity by the crowds but handled well. The Shrewsbury Cornet band provided music. Judge Ebaugh is reported to have made remarks disparaging of Shrewsbury. (A) (See Appendix No. 16)

Nov. 11, 1885 — A new station was opened at New Freedom on the Northern Central RR to handle the increased traffic occasioned by the opening of the Stewartstown RR. Little traffic for Shrewsbury is moving over the SRR as the NC is just about as close to the village. Consideration should be given to opening a railroad from the NCR to Shrewsbury! (A)

Nov. 24, 1885 — LETTER FROM SHREWSBURY – The Northern Central Railway Company has completed the new station house at New Freedom and all trains will stop at this station from and after today. The building is a substantial one and has sufficient dimensions for the freight and passenger traffic contemplated at that station, which connects with the Stewartstown railroad at this point. The building has a neatly finished office, on each side of which is a waiting room, and a large and commodious freight room at the north end of the building. A platform extends around the entire structure, the whole being covered with slate and handsomely painted inside and outside.

The tracks of the Stewartstown Railroad extend to the east side of the main tracks of the N.C.R.R. opposite the new station house. Mr. M. W. Bahn, the agent at New Freedom, will move the office from its present location in his business place to the new station building today. He will no doubt feel very proud of his new quarters. The business of the company will be materially advanced at New Freedom under superior management. Col. John Wesley Koller, his popular and efficient clerk, will go with him into the new station, where he will always be ready with a broad smile and a stern business look to wait on and attend to the wants of the patrons of the railroad company. Mr. H. W. Kapp, superintendent of the N.C.R.R., has given this improvement special attention with a view to securing first-class accommodations at this point. I do not think there is a station along the line of the road that will be looked upon in the future with greater pride by him than New Freedom. I am pleased to congratulate our worthy superintendent on the completion of this much-desired improvement, and Mr. Bahn on his advancement. (YG)

Nov. 24, 1885 — The extension of the Stewartstown Railroad to New Park and Fawn Grove, as per survey now being made, and the building thereof contemplated, has tickled the mules heal with a straw, and the way he kicks is a sin. The good people of Stewartstown have shown their neighbors further what's nice thing it is to be let out by rail, and now they want to let out too. We say to those people penned up down to Fawn, push the road through; you have rights too that other people are bound to respect. The extensionist must be careful not to cross any farms where kickers own or their damages demanded will be more than the cost of constructing the road. The extension to New Park will no doubt pay handsomely; it would give an outlet to all that vast region of the country surrounding it, which is the richest portion of the county along the line.

As the road does not benefit us any and as many of those people south of Stewartstown put their money into the new road, we would like to see them benefit, which could be done by its extension to New Park and Fawn Grove.

Since the completion of the Stewartstown Railroad, the tracks around Shrewsbury Station have been materially relieved of the burthen of too many cars, as has been the complaint very often — the business at our depot can be conducted now with ease. This subject I apprehend will strike the pockets of our good people at no distant day, but just how it will strike them I am unable to state. K (YG)

Dec. 4, 1885	It is stated that a survey is being made for the extension of the Stewartstown Railroad, which runs from Stewartstown, York County, to New Freedom, N.C.R.R., to New Park and Fawn Grove. (AI)
Dec. 12, 1885	LETTER FROM SHREWSBURY PA. – Shrewsbury, Pa., December 8th 1885. Editors *Union*: The trial of the case of Jacob Lanius vs. the Stewartstown Railroad Company, for damages done to his farm by locating their road diagonally through the heart of it, and which excited so much interest, was disposed of in our court last week, the jury giving Mr. Lanius $1,643 damages. The former viewer gave him $2,125. The verdict costs and attorney's fees in the last trial will amount to the same or more, as there were over forty witnesses summoned in the case. The company has now no ground to put up a station on his property at the pike, and they must secure it in some way before any business can be done there. There is considerable opposition to the road, developing itself recently, which, if the extension to Fawn is opposed, may embarrass the new enterprise to a damaging extent. In the matter of coal, for instance, they have caught on to discrimination already and boast that they can sell coal cheaper at Stewartstown than along the main stem of the N.C.R.R., where they connect, or farther north. (U)
April 1, 1886	Stewartstown Railroad, Stewartstown to New Freedom, 7.3 miles. Rail is 50# steel. Equipment: 1 Steam Locomotive, one passenger car/baggage combination car, one stone car. Operation for 6 ½ months ended April 1.1886: Passengers carried 9,586, Tons of freight moved, 6,974. Earnings: Passenger $1,526.04, Freight, $3,454.37, Other, $1,094.05, total $6,074.46. Operating expenses $3,680.56 leaving net earnings of $2,393.90. The cost of road and equipment is $71,620.93 (Poor's)
April 3, 1886	Since the completion of the New Freedom and Stewartstown railroad, the latter place is getting to be an important tobacco market. One day last week 105 wagon loads of tobacco changed hands there and 118,000 lbs. were shipped by the railroad the same day. (U)
Apr. 17, 1886	The Stewartstown Railroad continues to do good business. The spring trade is unusually heavy. By harvest, the country around the ancient town of Stewartstown will be stripped of the surplus produce. The building seems to be going wild in and around the town. Every foot of ground for building purposes is

eagerly bought up at fabulous prices. (U)

July 20, 1886	The Stewartstown Railroad Company adorned their office at this place with a large and commodious safe bought from York Safe and Lock Company.
	There has been a petition gotten up by the stockholders of the S.R.R. to the directors and general manager to run a train on Sunday during camp at Summit Grove, but we hope they will consider the evil of desecrating the Sabbath to railroading. (YG)
July 24, 1886	The Shrewsbury folks made another attempt on Tuesday to survey a route Shrewsbury for the Stewartstown Railroad run to that place. (DA)
Nov. 6, 1886	Pike Station, on the Stewartstown Railroad, south of Shrewsbury, will be ready for business by the 15th of this month. Mr. James H. Hendrix will have charge of the station. He is a thorough business man, has many friends, and will give the people entire satisfaction. (BCU)
Nov. 23, 1886	Pike Station on the Stewartstown Railroad, is about ready for business. Though a good deal of shipping has been done from that point within the last week. The station presents a very desirable appearance to transact business, and it is fair to suppose that a good deal of business will be done at this point if the necessary facilities are furnished by the company. It seems to me the first point to be made is, to secure as much travel as possible from the station, otherwise the old route will be maintained profitably. We shall wait and see what inducements will be offered by the railroad or made known to the public. (YG)
Mar. 5, 1887	The report of the Stewartstown Railroad Company for nine months ended Dec. 31, 1886, shows gross earnings of $8,669.34; operating expenses, $3,826.43; net earnings, $4,842.82. The road is seven miles long and extends from New Freedom, N.C.R.R., to Stewartstown, York County. The original cost of the road was about $74,000, and a debt of about $21,000 remains. (U)
1888	Stewartstown Railroad Rail Pass issued to G. H. Moorehouse, Asst. Superintendent of Adams Express. (See Appendix No. 17)
	REPORT ON THE STEWARTSTOWN RAILROAD, 1888 (Poor's)
	Line of Road: New Freedom, Pa. to Stewartstown, Pa. 7.2 miles, Sidings –1.05 miles, Gauge – 4 ft, 8½ in., Rail Steel – 50 lbs.
	Rolling Stock: December 31, 1887: Locomotive engine – 1, Cars: Passenger – 1, Platform – 1.
	Operations for the year ending December 31, 1887: Passengers carried was 14,977, tons of freight moved was 12,587. Earnings – passenger was $2,476.48, freight was $6,428.59, and mail was $327.04.
	President and General Manager: James Fulton Vice President: Joseph W. Anderson
	From January to December 1888, the Stewartstown Railroad carried 15,535

passengers. (SRRRB)

Jan. 28, 1888	The Stewartstown Railroad paid a dividend of 3 percent on the capital stock of the company. (Poor's)
Feb. 4, 1888	The Stewartstown Railroad Company has escaped bonding its road for the balance of indebtedness due on account of its construction, by selling stock sufficient to pay the debt. They also on a stock debt declared a 3 percent dividend. This is a remarkably good showing for the new road. (DA)
Mar. 2, 1888	STEWARTSTOWN, March 1, 1888 Mr. Davis Edie, of Hopewell, has in the course of construction, an extensive warehouse for storage of canned fruit and cans of milk, near the Station of the Stewartstown Railroad. Mr. Edie deals very extensively in this line, and this building will enable him to keep his stock secure preparatory to shipment to city markets. Mr. Robert M. Richey is the contractor and builder of the structure, which will be completed at an early day. (G)
March 1889	Stewartstown Railroad purchased a velocipede rail car from the Sheffield Velocipede Car Company for $110. (A.R. of S.R.R.)
Mar. 16, 1889	Notice — To all interested in the extension of the Stewartstown Railroad. There will be a meeting at New Park, Pa., on Saturday, March 16, 1889, at 11 p.m., to discuss the proposed extension of the Stewartstown Railroad to New Park. Col. W.W. Stewart is expected to be present and exhibit the profile and give an estimate. (YG)
Mar. 22, 1889	RAILROAD MEETING AT NEW PARK, PA. — Pursuant to a call quite a large number of farmers met at New Park on Saturday last to discuss the proposed extension of the Stewartstown Railroad to New Park and ultimately to Fawn Grove and Delta. John B. Gemmill called the meeting to order and stated the object for which it was called. Reed W. Anderson was chosen president and John M. McElwain secretary. A profile of the proposed route was exhibited showing cuts and hills. A very good route can be obtained at a cost of about $7,000 per mile: distance to New Park, 5½ miles. Speeches were made favoring the project by Hon. L. Allen Leib, John A. Anderson, Thos. Sykes, John S. McElwain and others. Messrs., John Wiley, Jas. C. Jordan, A.W. Strawbridge, John S. McElwain, and John B. Gemmill were appointed to a committee to secure the right of way from Fawn Grove to Stewartstown, Pa. John Marsteller and John S. McElwain were appointed to wait on the Stewartstown Company and see if they would extend their charter and what terms could be affected with them in reference to the extension. Adjourned to meet on April 20, at 8 p.m. (GRI)
May 15, 1889	Stewartstown Railroad Timetable. (See Appendix No. 17)
June 5, 1890	Stewartstown Railroad Timetable. (See Appendix No. 18)
1891	For the year of 1891, the Stewartstown Railroad carried 15,384 passengers (SRRRB)

Nov. 13, 1891	PROPOSED RAILROAD EXTENSION — The *Delta Herald* of the 6th instant says: "For some time there has been talk of a railroad to run westerly from Delta, through Fawn Grove, New Park, and Stewartstown and connecting with the N.C.R.R. The question has lately been revived, and some of the public-spirited men of Delta and others along the route are manifesting an interest. The proposed road would join the Stewartstown Railroad and would make a valuable outlet for our famous Peach Bottom roofing slate, and the people all along the route would appreciate their increased railroad facilities. Should the Susquehanna be bridged at Peach Bottom, all lower York County and upper Harford would have ready access to Philadelphia." (AI)
1892	From February to October of 1892, the Stewartstown Railroad carried 13,892 passengers. (SRRRB)
Jan. 8, 1892	The Trestle Bridges on the Stewartstown R.R. — In view of a possible increase in the weight of locomotives that may be put on the road in the near future, a few weeks ago the directors secured the services of J. Minsker, Esq., an expert on wooden superstructures in employ of the Pennsylvania Co., to inspect the trestles and bridges of the Stewartstown Road and suggest such repairs for the improvement and strengthening of the structures as in his mature judgment and experience might be considered necessary. Mr. Minsker after making a very careful and thorough examination of all the trestles and bridges on the road specifically pointed out such additions and improvements as he deemed necessary for giving the required additional strength and security to the long span over the road crossing, with suggestions in detail, for making other less important repairs for maintaining the good condition of the structures. In his general report, Mr. Minsker describes the timbers in the trestles as being in good condition, and pronounces "the trestles to be strong enough to carry safely a Pennsylvania railroad engine, class E, ten-wheel freight." This class of engine weighs some fifty or sixty percent more than the locomotive now used on the road.
	The Company is now arranging to make the improvements suggested without delay, which when made will give the management of the road full assurance of the capacity of the trestles to carry safely any increased weight in the equipment that the traffic of the road may require, and doubtless will give renewed assurance of safety to timid passengers when traveling on the road. (SN)
Mar. 4, 1892	After the first of February the post office department will establish a mail route from New Freedom to Stewartstown, by the way of the Stewartstown Railroad. (AI)
Jan. 25, 1897	A List of Individuals (Stockholders) Receiving Dividend Checks from the Stewartstown Railroad Company (See Appendix No.19)
Feb. 13, 1897	Jacob Rider, Engineer, receives a wage pay voucher from the Stewartstown Railroad for the amount of $56.34. (SHS)

Sept. 25, 1897	The Stewartstown Railroad Company has built a new fence around their cattle yard and a new gangway for loading and unloading cattle. (SN)
Nov. 18, 1897	Jacob Rodgers is the conductor on the Stewartstown Railroad during the absence of Jesse Kennedy. (SN)
Feb. 21, 1898	A Ticket Sales Report was issued by the station master at New Freedom. (See Appendix No.20)
June 25, 1898	Stewartstown Railroad purchased a new hand car from the Robert Thorp Company for the sum of $39. (SHS)
Apr. 14, 1899	The early train is soon to be resumed on the Stewartstown Railroad, much to the satisfaction of the "upper-end citizens." (AI)
June 23, 1899	The Stewartstown Railroad Company proposes to erect a new and modern station house in that enterprising town during the summer. The news will be hailed with joy by the patrons of the road. (AI)
July 28, 1899	A NEEDED IMPROVEMENT — The Stewartstown Railroad Company is about to build the greatly needed new station house at Stewartstown. It will be located where the present freight warehouse stands and will be 24 feet wide by 60 feet in depth, and will contain a waiting room, ticket office, freight warehouse, and directors' room. A projecting roof will cover the track, ensuring the passengers' protection from the weather in boarding and alighting from all trains. (AI)
1900	Statement of Record that the postal service was carried out by the Stewartstown Railroad Company as per the standards of the United States Postal Office Department. (See Appendix No. 21)
Apr. 7, 1900	The Stewartstown Railroad Company has under consideration a change from steam to electric motive power. (U)
Mar. 31, 1901	Stewartstown Railroad Articles of Incorporation filed under the laws of Pennsylvania. (ICC)
Aug. 20, 1901	Information was also received at Union Station (Baltimore) that the Stewartstown Railroad, which runs from New Freedom to Stewartstown, a distance of about 12 miles, had been badly washed, and that freight and passengers could not be received until further noticed. (BS)
Aug. 21, 1901	YORK — The loss in the vicinity of Stewartstown from the recent flood is estimated at $250,000. On Deer Creek nine wooden county bridges and all the dams were washed away. The Stewartstown Railroad is damaged to an extent of $6,000 or more. The non-passenger train at a thirty-foot trestle at Zeigler's has passed over it barely two minutes before it tottered and fell into the torrent. (YD)
Aug. 22, 1901	THE FLOOD AT STEWARTSTOWN — Loss to Stewartstown Railway Not as Great as First Reported. Editor Evening Dispatch

Noting the erroneous statement in your paper last evening relative to the extent |

of damage and consequent loss to the Stewartstown Railroad by the recent flood it is due the public and the company, that a more accurate statement of the damage and loss should be made. The washout at the Zeigler embankment is about sixty feet at the top and thirty feet at the bottom, and to repair will entail a cost of probably one thousand dollars. The low bridge at Keeney's which was carried away will cost probably two hundred and fifty dollars to replace. To repair damage to the track at various other places will conservatively estimate the cost of two hundred and fifty dollars. This will aggregate a total loss of fifteen hundred dollars and not six thousand dollars, nor four hundred feet of embankment washed away as your inst. informant makes. We of course regret that the loss is as heavy as I have already stated, but the fact that there was no loss of life or train equipment may well be considered as very fortunate.

Should the company decide to place an iron span at the first mentioned place which matters are now under consideration, the above estimate cost may be slightly exceeded, but not materially changed in the aggregate at least. The temporary suspension of its train service is a matter of much regret to both the company and its patrons, but this of course is unavoidable and it is expected will be resumed in the course of a week.

M. W. Bahn, General Manager

Nov. 16, 1901	Stewartstown Railroad freight bill for one case of cigars. (See Appendix No. 22)
Dec. 30, 1901	Stewartstown Railroad: Notice was sent out to all stockholders that dividends will be paid annually on July 1st instead of semi-annually. (See Appendix No. 23)
1903	REPORT ON THE STEWARTSTOWN RAILROAD, 1903 (Poor's)

1903 — Line of Road – New Freedom Pa. to Stewartstown, Pa. 7.2 miles, Sidings –1.25 miles, Gauge – 4ft. 8½ in., Rail Steel – 56 lbs.

Rolling Stock, December 31, 1902 – Locomotive engine – 1, Cars- Passenger – 2, Platform – 1.

Operations – for the year ending June 30, 1902 – Passengers carried was 16,930; tons of freight moved was 17,265. Earnings – Passenger was $2,694; Freight was $9,336; and Mail was $1,055

President: J. W. Anderson
Vice President and General Manager: M. W. Bahn

Feb. 11, 1905	Old engine to be sold for $1,100. (MMN)
June 17, 1905	A furniture factory is about to be erected at Turnpike Station, on the Stewartstown Railroad. It will be necessary to raise $15,000 to get the enterprise underway, and it is said that most of this sum has already been subscribed. (U)
Dec. 19, 1905	TIED TO WRECK TRAIN ON STEWARTSTOWN ROAD.

Stewartstown, Dec. 18 — The detectives employed by the directors of the

Stewartstown Railroad to run down the person or persons who attempted to wreck the Stewartstown Railroad train last Wednesday evening, think they have a clue, and arrests are looked for any day.

The attempt to wreck the passenger train which reaches this place at 6 o'clock was a most bold one, and was attempted at a place where the loss of life would have been great had the attempt been successful.

Near Reimold Station a heavy, green oak tie was placed across the tracks and apparently fastened. The engineer saw the obstruction and reversed his throttle, but as he was on the road's heaviest grade, he could not stop his engine and crashed into the obstruction. Luck seemed to be with the crew, as the cowcatcher raised the big tie and carried it along the tracks for one hundred and fifty feet before the engine could be stopped.

Just where the tie was placed on the track, there is the highest embankment on the entire railroad and the train, had it been thrown from the track, would have turned a somersault. Both the directors of the road and the train crew which makes the daily run are much worked up over the occurrence, as it was feared that some fiend has an imaginary grievance and thinks by wrecking the train he can "get square". (G)

Jan. 5, 1906	The Stewartstown RR gave a banquet for the New Park and Fawn Grove RR and SRR employees at the Leader House Monday afternoon. It was a turkey dinner followed by a ride over the 3-mile portion of the NP&FGRR which has been completed. Grading has nearly been completed to New Park. (SN)
Apr. 13, 1906	It is said that a movement is on foot to purchase the Stewartstown Railroad and that the purpose of the prospective buyers is to extend the line by way of the New Park and Fawn Grove Road, across the Susquehanna River to Oxford. (AI)
May 1906	The Stewartstown Railroad purchased another locomotive from the Northern Central RR in anticipation of additional traffic from the New Park and Fawn Grove RR line. (SN)
May 12, 1906	Used engine to be purchased from the Northern Central RR for $1,450. (MMN)
July 5, 1906	Regular service between Fawn Grove and Stewartstown was inaugurated Thursday. The line is being operated by the Stewartstown Railroad. The crew includes A. T. Cox, engineer, Smith Jones, fireman, Ollie Morris, conductor, and George W. Channell, brakeman. (SN)
Aug. 11, 1906	SRR Board authorized the purchase of its first gas power section car. (MMN
Aug. 18, 1906	Dr. A. C. McCurdy, [chairing] a special committee appointed for the purpose, has arranged with the Maryland & Pennsylvania Railroad for reduced rates for the Timonium Fair. The rate from Delta to Baltimore and by the Northern Central to Timonium, including admission to the fairgrounds, will be $1.83, with corresponding rates from all stations along the road. Dr. McCurdy expects to make a similar arrangement with the Stewartstown Railroad. (U)

Nov. 10, 1906	Authorized the sale of Engine No.3 to the New Park and Fawn Grove RR. (MMN)
Nov. 13, 1906	SRR proposition for selling to the New Park and Fawn Grove Railroad the following: 1.) sell Engine No. 3, 2.) sell 9/16 of coach No.3, 3.) business transaction between both railroads and 4.) shared cost of agent at New Freedom. (See Appendix No. 24)
Mar. 15, 1907	Stewartstown: Last Tuesday was a busy day for the farmers and tobacco buyers. Quite a number of loads were delivered at the railroad station here. (SN)
Aug. 2, 1907	Special Trains — On account of the Summit Grove Camp, the Stewartstown Railroad will run special trains on Thursday and Saturday evenings, Aug.1st and 3rd, leaving Stewartstown at 7:00 p.m., returning leave New Freedom at 10:15 p.m. W.H. Fulton, Supt. (SN)
Dec. 14, 1907	Purchased used Pennsylvania RR engine for $1,300. (2nd No. 3) (MMN)
Jan. 11, 1908	New engine house reported complete and in use. (MMN)
Feb. 8, 1908	Purchased a new combine car (No.4) from Wilmington, DE, for $4,200. (MMN)
Mar. 8, 1908	Petition received to move the Stewartstown depot to Pennsylvania Ave. This is a result of the New Park and Fawn Grove RR coming into town. Conflicts over the cost of the move and who will pay the bills. No action was taken. (MMN)
Mar. 29, 1908	LEAP FROM RUNAWAY CAB. — Passengers Hurt in Their Wholly Unnecessary Panic — York, Pa. March 28 — Several Yorkers who were passengers on a runaway coach on the Stewartstown Railroad, near New Freedom, had an exciting experience and received slight injuries in jumping to escape. While the engine was engaged in shifting, the car was left standing on a steep grade and started off. The passengers jumped, and one of them, Charles Sayres, badly sprained his right leg. An upgrade stopped the runaway about a mile away. (T)
Mar. 4, 1909	20" of snow closed the Stewartstown RR all day; however, several gangs of snow shovelers were able to open the line the next day. (SN)
June 30, 1909	During the year-end, the Stewartstown Railroad hauled over 33,000 tons of freight and carried over 39,000 passengers. (G)
July 7, 1909	Milton Witman Bahn, Manager of the Stewartstown Railroad, passed away last evening at the age 70 years. 1864 – Mr. Bahn moved to New Freedom, this county, where he engaged in mercantile business and became an agent of the Northern Central Railway. 1886 – Mr. Bahn was a big promoter of the construction of the Stewartstown Railroad so after the completion of the road, Mr. Bahn was given the position of General Manager and served in that capacity until his passing. 1896 – Relinquished his mercantile interest to his son, Walter D. Bahn, but continued his service with the Northern Central until he removed to [York].

Mr. Bahn was also one of the directors for the Stewartstown Railroad and also for the New Park and Fawn Grove Railroad which he held until his passing. (YD)

Oct. 1, 1909	A special train to the New Freedom Fair leaves Stewartstown at 7:00 P.M. and returns from New Freedom (where the fairgrounds will be well-lighted) at 9:45 P.M. Suggest Stewartstown hold a fair. (SN)
Nov. 27, 1909	BECAME SICK AT FUNERAL AND DIED — Baltimorean Receives Attack of Heart Disease at Anstine Station.

Shrewsbury, Nov. 26 — Coming to Anstine Station on the Stewartstown Railroad to attend a funeral, Michael Gill, of Baltimore, was himself taken suddenly sick and died from heart disease. Undertaker [W.I] Mumma, of Stewartstown, took charge of the body and shipped it to Baltimore. Mr. Gill was a relative of the White family. He was about 50 years old. (YD)

Dec. 31, 1909	A special train from Fawn Grove to Stewartstown. Fare is 25 cents and is for reserved seats only to see a juggler and magician. Other special trains were run for [the] Summit Grove Camp, baseball games, fairs, and other community activities. (SN)
Feb. 12, 1910	Construction of the passenger train shed located in New Freedom, Pa., is progressing. (MMN)
June 11, 1910	First offer was made to buy out the New Park and Fawn Grove RR. Offer is $12.50 a share for NP&FGRR stock or exchange 4 shares for 1 Stewartstown RR share. (MMN)
Aug. 13, 1910	New Park & Fawn Grove RR declines to sell out — will pay $10 per month towards joint agency at Stewartstown. (MMN)
Aug. 15, 1910	Trains started to run on a regular schedule on the Stewartstown Railroad from New Freedom to Zeigler's Station. (YD)
Aug. 30, 1910	RAILROAD WITHOUT DEBT WILL CELEBRATE — The Twenty-fifth Anniversary of the Stewartstown Railroad will be combined with the town's first fair.

The first annual fair and twenty-fifth anniversary of the Stewartstown Railroad will be held by the Stewartstown and Farmers' Improvement Association at Glenwood Park, Stewartstown, on September 8, 9, and 10. On Saturday afternoon the 10th, the silver anniversary of the Stewartstown RR will be observed. Joseph W. Anderson will deliver a speech on the history of the railroad, followed by John B. Gemmill who will speak about the railroad and other roads. State Highway Commissioner Joseph W. Hunter will speak on the roads of Pennsylvania and improvements. Miss Mildred and Muriel Kurtz will sing a duet and Miss Emma Fulton will give a recitation. (G)

Sept. 19, 1910	SRR Executive Committee suggests that a new depot be built on Penn. Ave. if the New Park & Fawn Grove RR does not extend its line to connect with another railroad. (MMN)
Dec. 10, 1910	STEWARTSTOWN RAILROAD WINS — Lower York County Railroads Hear

Commission's Verdict. — York, Pa., Dec. 7

The State Railroad Commission has handed down a report to the effect that it has no jurisdiction in the matter of the differences between the Stewartstown and the New Park and Fawn Grove railroad companies.

This is regarded as a victory for the Stewartstown company since the commission found no evidence of discrimination by this company against the New Park and Fawn Grove Railroad in the handling of its passengers or freight. Both railroads are located in the lower end of York County. (YD)

Jan. 25, 1911,	Anstine's Station will be discontinued as a passenger station by the Stewartstown Railroad after April 30, 1911. (YD)
Mar. 1, 1911	Anstine's Station was abandoned as a passenger stop. As a result of complaints, it was quickly decided to stop train No.8, the westbound evening train, at that station. (MMN)
Dec. 9, 1911	It is agreed to run one train on Sundays in order to handle the growing milk business if necessary. Consideration is being given to the purchase of a gas motor passenger car jointly with the NP&FGRR. (MMN)
Jan. 25, 1912	American Telephone and Telegraph Company addressed a letter to Thomas Fulton, treasurer of the SRR, pertaining to pole yard rental fees. (See Appendix No. 25)
Feb. 10, 1912	Unable to reach an agreement with the NP&FG RR so the motor car will not be purchased. A shed for passengers at Anstine is reported to have been built. (MMN)
Nov. 8, 1912	Management ordered to sell Engine No.3 (later reported that SRR sold Engine No.3 for $2,000, Apr. 13, 1913). Consideration was given to purchase a passenger car jointly with the NP&FG RR. (MMN)
Apr. 12, 1913	SRR Board authorized to completely relay the line from New Freedom to Stewartstown with 70# rail. (MMN)
May 10, 1913	Purchased a new 54-ton engine from Baldwin for $9,350. (Engine No.4) (MMN)
June 14, 1913	Equipment Report: Coach No.3 (jointly owned) is out of service until May 1914. Coach No. 5 is to be sold. 60' coach with 6 wheels trucks purchased secondhand for $2,350. Locomotive No.2 is to be rented to the NP&FG RR for $12.50 per day and engine No.4 for $18 per day. (MMN)
1914	SRR Board decided to build a new depot on Pennsylvania Ave. in Stewartstown. (MMN)
Jan. 17, 1914	Spikes were placed on the track at Orwig Station derailing the locomotive on train No.7. The Incident is being investigated. (MMN)

Jan. 19, 1914 — The New Park & Fawn Grove Railroad proposed to run their train and crew over the Stewartstown RR to New Freedom for $10 per day. The offer was declined by the SRR board members. (MMN)

Mar. 14, 1914 — Stewartstown, March 14 — This borough is to have a new railroad station, built on modern lines, which will be used by both the Stewartstown and the New Park and Fawn Grove railroads. Work will begin on the station as soon as the plans can be completed. The new station will be located on Pennsylvania Avenue, where the NP&FG RR crosses that thoroughfare. Pennsylvania Avenue runs west from Center Square.

A new traffic arrangement has been entered between these roads. The new station is one of the first results of this agreement. It will be built by the Stewartstown Railroad. As a result of the new traffic agreement, the train service over both roads will be greatly improved. Negotiations for the sale of the NP&FG RR to the Stewartstown Railroad have been abandoned. (YD)

Aug. 25, 1914 — GLEN ROCK — Aug. 25 — The singing class organized and conducted by Prof. J.R. Eaton, of Tolna, is planning to hold a picnic on Saturday, Aug. 29, in Waltermeyer's Grove, near Orwig's Station, on the Stewartstown Railroad. A special train will carry the picnickers to that place. The Shrewsbury Band will furnish the music. Rehearsals have been held at Shrewsbury, Waltermeyer's, and King's. (YD)

Nov. 2, 1914 — Shrewsbury, Nov. 1 — H. W. Rehmeyer, merchant at Turnpike, near here, has shipped 15 carloads of potatoes to the city markets since last Monday. The cars contained 8,000 bushels. Fourteen cars were consigned to Baltimore, and one car to Marysville. The potatoes were all shipped over the Stewartstown Railroad to New Freedom. (YDLY)

Dec. 29, 1914 — Moved into the new station located at Pennsylvania Ave. located in Stewartstown. (MMN)

Dec. 31, 1914 — NEW STATION FINISHED — Serves Two Railroads at Stewartstown, Has Many Modern Improvements

Stewartstown, Dec. 31 — The new station of the Stewartstown Railroad Company is completed and the office was moved from the old building to the new one on Tuesday. The new building is located on Pennsylvania Avenue. Trains now pull into the station from both the Stewartstown and New Park and Fawn Grove railroads and take on or let off passengers. Passengers may alight on either side of the track, as suits their convenience. Concrete walks are on each side of the track.

The building is of good size, made of brick with a slate roof. There is also a second story over the middle part of the building for the directors' room and the auditors' office. The first floor is all concrete and there is a concrete porch around the whole building, the roof extending out over the porch. The interior of the office is finished in yellow pine and is lighted with electricity. The equipment is modern. The freight warehouse is roomy and sufficient to take care of all local traffic. The location has advantages over the old one as the walks up town from that place are much better. (YD)

Jan. 2, 1915	NEW FREEDOM — Jan. 2 — An engine off the track at Tolna Thursday morning tied up traffic on the Stewartstown Railroad for more than six hours. A broken flange on the engine of the train leaving here at 9:32 a.m., on the return trip to Stewartstown, caused it to jump the track. The engine of the New Park and Fawn Grove Railroad was brought into service and made the trip to this place last evening, arriving here at 4:55 p.m. (YD)
Feb. 13, 1915	SRR authorized the construction of a small passenger shed at Keeney. (MMN)
June 18, 1915	SRR Directors inspect the railroad. (MMN)
Dec. 15, 1915	S. F. Sheffer resigned as agent at Sheffer's — Chas. Diehl appointed agent. (MMN)
Aug. 12, 1916	Secondhand coach purchased for $2,300. (MMN)
July 11, 1918	20-year-old Raymond Almoney, a youthful conductor on the NP&FG RR, died at his mother's house in Fawn Grove from pneumonia stemming from a fall from a box car that caused a brain hemorrhage. (SN)
July 8, 1919	Stockholders, at a special meeting, voted 891 to 0 to go under Federal control. (MMN)
1919	Stewartstown Railroad reports the following to the Interstate Commerce Commission:

> 2 Locomotives
> 3 Coaches
> 2 Freight Train Cars
> 2 Gondolas – work equipment
> 1 Motor Car – No.14 Fairbanks Motor Car purchased in 1910
> 2 Push Cars – 6'x7' and 6'x8' purchased in 1910

Oct. 30, 1919	C. W. Shaw, General Manager of the SRR, issues a Notice of Storage Charges. (See Appendix No.26)
Mar. 21, 1921	PASSENGERS FINISH RIDE ON ENGINE AS TRAIN STALLS — York, March 12 — Many stories have been told about the Stewartstown Railroad, and of how the trainmen sometimes stop the trains to shoot rabbits in Winter and fish in Summer, but Walter A. Saylor, an automobile dealer of this city, gives an experience which befell him this week and which puts most of the other stories into the shade. Saylor says he had occasion to go to Stewartstown to bring an automobile back to York, and he made the forward trip over the Stewartstown Railroad.

From the moment the train left New Freedom, there was trouble with the steam, and after the train had stopped several times to "get steam up," and after the train had been cut once or twice to enable the engine to pull it a car or two at a time to get over the hill near Turnpike Station, matters became bad that the passengers were advised that if they wanted to finish their trip to Stewartstown they should pile on the engine, and this they did — men and women to the number of more than a dozen. The remainder of the trip was completed amid a shower of coal dust, black water, and general discomfort and since they were all riding on the engine or in the tender, among the coal, every one of them needed a bath when they reached Stewartstown. (EN)

July 8, 1921

Several fires have sprung up along the Stewartstown Railroad near Turnpike and Sheffer stations in hay fields that are close to the tracks. Several acres of land were burned over on the farm of Elmer Rehmeyer near Turnpike. It is supposed that the dry grass caught fire from hot cinders that escaped from the railroad engine as it passed by. (YD)

July 25, 1921

WRECK AT NEW FREEDOM — 200 feet of track torn up on the Stewartstown Railroad

Railroad, July 25 — Practically the worst wreck in the history of the Stewartstown Railroad Company occurred Saturday afternoon at about 2 o'clock while the train was rounding a sharp curve between Keeney's and Sheffer's stations about two miles from New Freedom. The train was making its regular noon run from New Freedom having left New Freedom at 1:45 with one passenger coach, three empty, and one loaded box car, which was loaded with empty tin cans for James T. Smith, canner at Fawn Grove. As the train rounded the curve making fairly good time, something went wrong with box cars and all four of them jumped the track, tearing up the track as they passed along. Before the engineer could stop the train, about two hundred feet of track was torn up, and about a hundred or more ties were rendered useless. The engine and passenger coach stayed on the rails. No occupants of the coach were injured except when experiencing shock.

Word was immediately dispatched to the General Manager C. W. Shaw at Stewartstown who immediately secured workmen and hastened to the accident, and work was begun on reconstructing the road and placing the cars back on the rails. Fortunately, none of the cars turned over which was a great benefactor to the company as they do not have a derrick to lift cars but have to do all their lifting with jacks worked by hand, thus it was a difficult task to replace the road and place the cars back on the rails, and much time was consumed. The workforce was compelled to work all Saturday night up until Sunday noon until the road was ready for service again.

Immediately after the accident, notice was sent to the agent at New Freedom to notify the ticket agents at Baltimore, York, Harrisburg, and other local points that there would be no train service in the evening over the road and that passengers desiring should be notified accordingly.

The mail was transported by automobile from Stewartstown and Turnpike to New Freedom for the Pennsylvania Railroad connections. Passengers who already were on their journey when the accident occurred and also the express goods were hauled in an auto truck from New Freedom to Stewartstown.

Several carloads of freight could not be moved Saturday night on account of the accident. The cars delivered to the company at Stewartstown from the New Park & Fawn Grove Railroad were left in Stewartstown until Monday morning. The company resumed business this morning filling all regular runs. (YD)

1922	2 flat cars were purchased for $225 each. Track scales purchased for $1,100. (MMN)

Jan. 6, 1922 — The Stewartstown train, running thrice daily over the Stewartstown Railroad, from Stewartstown to New Freedom, Sundays excepted, may be up-to-date in some particulars, but the coach which was on the train on Friday has a unique lighting system. Where the baggage is supposed to be kept, along the coach and above the seats, there was a presto tank and this is what is used for lighting the coach, providing the train runs when it is dark. There was a strip of wood placed from one side of the coach to hold up the presto tank. George Hale, the conductor on the train, says the system is not modern, but up-to-date. (YDR)

Jan. 18, 1922 — TURNPIKE — George Hale, the conductor on the Stewartstown Railroad, resumed his duties yesterday after being off several days on account of sickness. During his absence, Lawrence Shaw acted as conductor.

Frank Mantz, route agent of the American Railway Express Company, located in York, visited several of the stations on the Stewartstown Railroad and the New Park and Fawn Grove Railroad yesterday in the interest of the company. (YD)

Jan. 25, 1922 — The Stewartstown Railroad is carrying heavy passenger traffic at present, owing to the many persons en route to the Summit Grove camp meeting, near New Freedom. (YDR)

Jan. 25, 1922 — ONCE UPON A TIME — Reimold Station on Stewartstown Railroad, Was Named After A Man Who Committed Suicide, Sunday

Tolna, Jan. 24 – Reimold Station on the Stewartstown Railroad, near this place, derived its name from Julius Reimold, the 79-year-old man who committed suicide by cutting his throat with a razor Sunday night at the home of his son-in-law and daughter, Mr. and Mrs. Lewis Thoman, near Glen Rock, with whom he made his home. This fact was recalled by some of the older residents of this locality. Mr. and Mrs. Reimold came from Germany when quite young and settled near this place before the Stewartstown Railroad was built. He was a shoemaker and built up quite a business of repairing shoes at his home. He built a home on the property and became quite progressive. (YDR)

Jan. 26, 1922 — TURNPIKE — Jan. 23 — A proposal to consolidate the Stewartstown and New Park and Fawn Grove railroad companies was discussed at a joint meeting of the directors of both companies held yesterday afternoon. If an agreement can be made with the New Park and Fawn Grove Railroad, by the Stewartstown Railroad, the consolidation will take place in the near future. There will be better services on the road with both passenger and freight trains. (YDR)

Feb. 11, 1922

Harry Anstine, agent of the Stewartstown Railroad at Stewartstown, and William Duncan, conductor on the New Park and Fawn Grove Railroad, were visitors at the Pennsylvania Railroad station at New Freedom yesterday.

The canners located at various places along the Stewartstown Railroad and the New Park and Fawn Grove Railroad are slowly getting their supplies for the canning season. (YD)

April 13, 1922

It was reported that a special meeting was held on Tuesday, April 11. Stockholders of the NP&FG RR met at New Park at 1 P.M. with President J. W. Anderson presiding at the meeting. Stockholders of the SRR met at Stewartstown at 9 A.M. with Anderson chairing the meeting. The vote at both meetings was unanimous to merge the two railroads. Officials from the PRR attended the meeting at Stewartstown arriving at New Freedom on a special train in order to catch the morning Stewartstown train. Following the meeting, they were returned to New Freedom via a special SRR train. The PRR owns a considerable amount of stock in the SRR. It is expected that the railroad will be able to provide better service with one crew doing all the freight work. (SN)

June 25, 1922

Box Car purchased for use as a caboose to carry LCL for $290.00 (MMN)

June 27, 1922

A COMMUNICATION — C. W. Shaw answers criticism against himself and the Stewartstown RR on the "Good Road Movement."

Editor, The Gazette and Daily:

There seems to be some criticism of the writer and the Stewartstown Railroad Co., in connection with the Good Road movement and the program of the committee of the Good Roads association, of which the writer is a member. First, the committee labored hard and long on a comprehensive building program that would cover the most used roads, and give each section of the county a fair share. The available funds were limited, only a small percentage of the total mileage can be improved, and no member of the committee got all he wanted for his section, but the members of the committee are all broad-gauge businessmen and as such were considerate of each other's interests, and substituted a program that had the unanimous approval of the committee and was ordered by the county commissioners. Owing to the extremely high pieces of labor, freight rates, materials, and high interest charges, the carrying out of the program has been delayed, and earnings now be done at once. Route 333 Road, Red Lion to Rinely, a part of which was on the first-year building program, is still on. The county commissioners have been criticized for not going ahead and spending the two and half million dollars at once. The committee felt this would have been a business mistake and commended the commissioners for their good business judgment, in not paying $50,000 per mile for roads, or our money would have been spent only on a few miles, or not completed. With declining prices of materials, labor, and freight rates, we all will be able to build a greater mileage and accommodate a greater number of people. The writer as general manager of the Stewartstown Railroad has been vitally interested and the end was one of the pioneers in the good roads movement, and I want to assure the public that with good roads we may lose a few tons of freight and a few passengers. But the management of the Stewartstown Railroad Co. is too broad-minded to stand in the way of progress, but at all times stand ready and willing to cooperate in any way that will advance or benefit our county. As proof of this, the Stewartstown Railroad has run special trains to the good road's meetings carrying everyone interested free. C. W. Shaw. (YDR)

Jun. 29, 1922	During this past week, many improvements to properties have been made. Cement walks were laid in front of the property of H. W. Rehmeyer. The local crossing of the Stewartstown Railroad has also been improved. (YDR)
Dec. 30, 1922	We don't know how often George B. Hale, conductor on the Stewartstown Railroad, between New Freedom and Stewartstown chases chickens off the track, but a reporter for The Gazette and Daily caught him in the act this week. Some shifting was done and after that the train pulled, out for New Freedom, but six chickens were on the track and Hale was on top of a box car. He waved his hand and silently murmured "shoo" with wonderful success. So great a success, we will say, that the left front wheel of the freight car missed one of the chickens by about three inches. Of course, this is no worse than shooting rabbits from the cab of an engine which was done two years ago on the New Park & Fawn Grove Railroad, now consolidated with the Stewartstown. (Great Eastern) (YDR)
1923	Stewartstown Railroad recommended wage rates for the year 1923. (See Appendix No. 27)
Jan. 9, 1923	TURNPIKE — Jan. 7 — Much progress is being made by the Superior Wire Cloth Company for the erection of their $100,000 plant at this place. It was reported Friday that the switch from the Stewartstown Railroad has been laid out and also the building. As soon as the elevation is secured, the foundation for the building will be dug. (YDR)
Jan. 9, 1923	TURNPIKE — Jan. 7 — Owing to the melting of the snow, the roads in this section are in bad condition. For instance, during the past week, salesmen take the train on the Stewartstown Railroad from here to New Freedom, leaving their machines at this place, to avoid the bad road. (YDR)
Feb. 12, 1923	SRR Board of Directors authorized the purchase of a rail motor bus. (MMN)
Feb. 14, 1923	RAILROAD BRIEFS — A broken rail was reported as the cause of the wreck on the Stewartstown Railroad, near York, yesterday morning. Conductor W. L. Duncan was injured and a score of passengers were shaken up and cut by flying glass when a coach of the train was derailed and turned over on its side. Duncan was not injured seriously. (EN)
Mar. 13, 1923	SRR purchased a White Motor Bus out of Philadelphia, Pa. for $12,690. (MMN) (See Appendix No. 22)

Mar. 15, 1923	C. W. Shaw announced that the Stewartstown Railroad 2 has purchased a gasoline motor bus. The rail bus will be used to provide the people served by the railroad with better and more frequent passenger service which will now be divorced from the mixed passenger and freight trains. It is experimental and it is hoped that traffic will increase to cover the extra costs. It will now be possible to make a round trip to York or Baltimore in half a day instead of a whole day as presently required.

Two new stops have been added — Jordan Crossing and Jos. Manifold's. If the service is not patronized, it will be withdrawn. (SN) |
| Mar. 22, 1923 | The first combined line schedule appears in the newspaper. (SN) |
| Apr. 5, 1923 | (Thursday) Our two local railroads are united in one line. After long negotiations and lots of red tape, the merger is finally complete. A new schedule of trains went into effect last Monday. The new motor bus was delayed in arriving at Stewartstown but arrived on Tuesday, and will be put into operation as soon as the instructor arrives. Three round trips will be operated each weekday from New Park (make that Fawn Grove) to New Freedom with George B. Hale as a motorman and Charles McElwain as conductor. The freight schedule now calls for two round trips each weekday and at present the train is being operated by the Fawn Grove crew since it must start at that point. Most of the Stewartstown men took other employment: brakeman Lawrence Shaw is working at the lumber company and engineer George Gibbs is working for carpenter Ben Busler. (SN)

The Motor Bus is painted maroon, is 35 feet long, will carry 42 people, will run 35 m.p.h., weighs 2,000#, and costs $14,000. The gas tank holds enough gas to run 180 miles. The bus has an electric starting and lighting system and is a handsome piece of railroad "furniture". (SN) |
| Apr. 6, 1923 | J. G. Brill Company sends a letter along with a diagram showing the dimensions of the motor car, and photographs of the interior of the Motor Car. (See Appendix No. 28) |
| Apr. 6, 1923 | STEWARTSTOWN R.R. INAUGURATES MOTOR SERVICE

The Motor Car passenger service was inaugurated on the Stewartstown Railroad between Fawn Grove and New Freedom, yesterday, with two round trips being made, the test proving satisfactory, and the runs being made on schedule. On the last trip, the car carried thirty-five passengers between Stewartstown and New Freedom. The car left Fawn Grove at 11:50 a.m. and 3:00 p.m. There is no change in schedule from Stewartstown, but from Fawn Grove hereafter there will be three trains daily, the additional one leaving at 11:50 a.m. The car which was bought by the Stewartstown Railroad from the White Company, of Cleveland, Ohio, through the Penn Motor-Craft Company, local distributors for the White Company, is a handsome piece of equipment, as much interest was manifested along the line on the first run. It is the first car of its kind operated in this county. The motor is of the standard four-cylinder type. The same as used |

on the five-ton truck. The car is operated the same as a motor truck and contains a hot water heating system. It was delivered on Tuesday of this week and has been accepted by the company. Standing on the rear platform of the car is the general manager of the company, C. W. Shaw, George B. Hale the motorman, and Charles McElwain, conductor. The freight train will make two round trips per day and will be in charge of the crew that operated the New Park and Fawn Grove Railroad now consolidated with the Stewartstown Railroad. Mr. Hall has been a conductor on the Stewartstown Railroad for several years. The run from New Freedom to Stewartstown in the evening was made in 24 minutes. (G&D)

Apr. 12, 1923   (Thursday) The motor bus was put right into service and is working very satisfactorily. Last Friday evening it carried 60 passengers plus 3,000# of express and stopped at every station. It was only 3 minutes late arriving here.

The schedule:
7:00 am 11:50am 3:25pm Fawn Grove 10:47am 2:52pm 7:15pm

7:37 12:25pm 4:00 Stewartstown 10:12 2:17 6:30

8:07 12:52pm 4:28 New Freedom 9:42 1:47 6:00

C. W. Shaw, General Manager; Thos. B. Fulton, Superintendent

Stops are made at Fawn Grove, Kisiner, New Park, Strawbridge, Wiley, Gemmill, Maple Hill, Anderson, Manifold, Stewartstown, Zeigler, Reimold, Orwig, Anstine, Sheffer, Kenney, Turnpike, and New Freedom. (SN)

Apr. 14, 1923   Stewartstown Railroad purchased $2,000 worth of common stock from the Hopewell Furniture Company. (MMN)

June 26, 1923   Special meeting was held by the Board of Directors of the Stewartstown Railroad to hear the committee report on relocating the right-of-way between the highway bridge at Manifold to the H. W. Anderson grade crossing. After a lengthy discussion, the board of directors agreed to the change and will lay the ties and tracks along, as the right-of-way has been secured and the roadbed has been prepared. (MMN)

Sept. 19, 1923   The worst accident in the 38-year history of Stewartstown Railroad. (See Appendix No. 29)

Sep. 21, 1923   Mrs. Charles M. Kidd, a trained nurse of New Freedom, is staying at the home of Mr. and Mrs. Allen G. Trout caring for Mrs. Trout's mother, Mrs. Jemima Reeling, who was injured in the wreck on the Stewartstown Railroad. (YD)

Sept. 25, 1923   Mr. C. W. Shaw, General Manager, reported 3 very expensive wrecks during September — the worst experience in 38 years of operation.

On September 11 the new bus operated by John Barton ran through an open switch at New Park striking a box car. Barton was reported as "not paying attention". His accident caused $700 in damage to the engine and pilot and put the bus out of service until September 25.

On September 11 a derailment at Keeney tore up 300 feet of track and forced a suspension of service for two days until $400 worth of repairs could be made.

On September 19, the worst accident occurred. The freight train stuck a passenger coach which had accidentally disconnected from the passenger train near Zeigler, telescoping and practically destroying the coach. The injured included — Mrs. Reeling, Mrs. Anderson, Mrs. Diehl, and Rose Rigdon — all suffering from bruises and shock, but no broken bones. Damage to the engine cab, pilot, smoke box, etc. was $800, and to the coach $2,300. Passenger conductor McElwain did not protect his train, and freight engineer Rosenberry and fireman Few were not on the lookout.

General Manager Shaw suggested that Stewartstown be the starting point for all freight trains to maintain better control. That change was authorized on September 25. (MMN)

| Dec. 6, 1923 | TURNPIKE — Dec. 5 — The coach on the Stewartstown Railroad is draped in mourning, on account of the death of Joseph W. Anderson, president of the Stewartstown Railroad Company, which occurred yesterday. (YDR) |

| Dec. 13, 1923 | Resolutions of respect and sympathy on behalf of Jos. W. Anderson our President who died December 3, 1923. |

Whereas — It has pleased Almighty God to remove from our midst the last one of the original members of the Board of the Stewartstown Railroad Company, who first served as a director, then Treasurer and has been our faithful President for nearly twenty-nine years, elected President Jan. 14th 1895, and wishing to pay tribute to the memory of the deceased do earnestly resolve that in the death of our associate member and President we feel and mourn his loss very keenly as he was always deeply interested in the welfare of the Stewartstown Railroad Company. (SN)

1924 — Stewartstown Railroad reported the following to the Interstate Commerce Commission:

TRACK

7.343 miles of Main Track
1.602 miles of Yard and Side tracks
Total of 8.945 miles of track owned
Bessemer Rail – 70 lbs. per liner foot

EQUIPMENT

Steam Locomotives – 2
Freight Train Cars – 2
Passenger Train Cars – 4
Work Equipment – 3

One of the passenger cars is owned jointly with the New Park and Fawn Grove

	Railroad. (ICC)
June 9, 1925	"BUS" trains 5 and 6 were discontinued. Passengers to be carried on freight trains 3 and 4. (MMN)
June 16, 1925	Pennsylvania Railroad System responded to a letter sent by H. E. Anstine, secretary of the SRR, requesting a proxy for an upcoming meeting about the New Park and Fawn Grove Railroad. (See Appendix No. 30)
June 23, 1925	The Board of Directors of the Stewartstown Railroad ratified the lease agreement drawn up by the New Park and Fawn Grove Railroad to be leased by the Stewartstown Railroad for 99 years for one dollar. (MMN)
July 1925	During the month, the railroad quit advertising its passenger schedule as it had done almost every week since it opened. (SN)
July 2, 1925	A new schedule has been announced. The noon rail bus trip has been discontinued. Passengers may ride from Fawn Grove to Stewartstown on the regular freight train leaving Fawn Grove at 10:55 A.M. or on the mixed train leaving Stewartstown at 12:25 P.M. The noon bus had carried few passengers on the lower end. (SN)
Sept. 1, 1925	New station at Turnpike completed. (MMN)
Sept. 19, 1925	NEW TURNPIKE STATION IN USE — Stewartstown Railroad's $6,000 Depot Opened to Public Yesterday
	Turnpike, Sept. 18 — The new station house, built here by the Stewartstown Railroad Company, is finished and today was occupied. The old station house was located in a building owned by H. W. Rehmeyer, a local produce dealer. The new station house is a modern one, being built of brick and one story high. The cost of construction was $6,000. On one end is the freight warehouse and on the other end is the waiting room. (YDR)
Sept. 24, 1925	(Thursday) The new station at Turnpike opened last Friday. (SN)
Oct. 23, 1925	M. W. Bahn, general agent for the Northern Central and Stewartstown railroads at New Freedom, moved to Linden Avenue, this city [York]. (YDR)
Dec. 9, 1925	TURNPIKE — R. E. Bollinger, a contractor of New Freedom, is doing the interior finishing at the newly erected station of the Stewartstown Railroad Company at this place. (YDR)
Dec. 14, 1925	Stewartstown RR Motor Car hits the automobile of Dr. Free – No one hurt.
	Railroad, Dec. 14. The gasoline motor car in the Stewartstown Railroad operated by Charles Heaton, motorman, and Millard Almoney, conductor, struck the automobile owned and driven by Dr. [John L.] Free, of Stewartstown, near the crossing at Zeigler's station on Saturday evening as the car was making its evening run from Fawn Grove to New Freedom. The car did not move more than about the length of itself after it struck the automobile, but the contact was so great that the motor car was derailed and stopped with the front trucks

about four feet from the rails. The automobile landed against a telephone pole of the railroad company's line, breaking it off. No injuries were sustained by any. The traffic was at a standstill on the line as the steam train could not be operated to New Freedom because of it being only a single track. It was several hours before the car was again placed back on the rails and service resumed. (YD) *Editor's note*: Conductor Millard R. Almoney, a WWI naval veteran, died in November 1939 from serious injuries after being struck by a car in Baltimore.

Dec. 17, 1925	Dr. Free and the Stewartstown RR rail bus collided at a crossing just beyond Zeigler's Station. The bus was on the evening run to New Freedom. There is poor visibility at the crossing and neither vehicle was able to stop in time. The bus was derailed and the pilot broken. The doctor's car was also seriously damaged but fortunately, no one was hurt. (SN)
Jan. 11, 1926	The siding at Reimold is to be discontinued. Action was reconsidered in June and July and it was decided to leave the siding in. (MMN)
Apr. 26, 1926	Stewartstown Railroad Timetable issued by C. W. Shaw, General Manager (See Appendix No. 31)
Dec. 11, 1926	Lawrence Shaw, conductor on the freight train on the Stewartstown Railroad, between Fawn Grove and this place, is off duty, suffering from an injury to a leg, which was bruised and became sore. George Schminkey, a brakeman, is substituting as conductor. (YDR)
Jan. 20, 1927	NOTICE is hereby given that the stock certificate issued by the Stewartstown Railroad Co., for two shares of capital stock of the said Stewartstown Railroad Co., has been lost, destroyed, or stolen, and the undersigned administratrix of the estate of J. V. Winemiller, deceased, has made application for a new certificate. Sophia Ann Winemiller, Administratrix. (SN)
Apr. 12, 1927	General Manager Shaw is directly to notify the track foreman that the next time they get drunk they shall be considered for dismissal from service. (MMN)
May 10, 1927	Declining traffic on the New Park and Fawn Grove RR noted. A certificate issued to the residents are to be notified by a circular. A meeting will also be held to drum up business. (MMN)
Nov. 22, 1927	Lawrence B. Shaw, of town, a brakeman on the Stewartstown Railroad between New Freedom and Fawn Grove, has served 31 years as an employee of the company. (YD)
Nov. 22, 1927	Pennsylvania Railroad sent a letter along with the corrected plans for the construction of the overhead bridge at Zeigler, Pa. (See Appendix No. 32)
Dec. 22, 1927	The SRR board issued a series of resolutions memorializing Harry E. Anstine, a long-time employee who recently passed away. He began his decades-long career as an assistant agent and then served variously as an agent, secretary of the board, director, and freight claims agent. Railroad officials characterized Anstine as "active, interested, and on the alert." (SN)

Jan. 28, 1928	Bridge and fill completed at Zeigler at a cost of $6,000. (MMN) (See Appendix No. 24)
1929	It was reported that a truck line, Southern Freight Company, was preparing to haul milk and general freight between York and Fawn Grove. (MMN)
Apr. 8, 1929	Trackman Arthur Barnett was killed near Turnpike when a telephone pole fell on him (3,250 feet west of Turnpike). He died at the hospital and was the first fatality ever on the railroad. (MMN)
1930	There were two minor collisions between the motor bus and an automobile. (MMN)
Sept. 11, 1930	Jacob Orwig gave written permission to the Stewartstown Railroad to enter his property to clean up all the weeds and debris on his property and the SRR right-of-way to reduce fire spreading. (See Appendix No.33)
Feb. 10, 1931	The SRR account declined in traffic. There was a 5% reduction in wages. (MMN)
Jan. 9, 1932	Railroad account shows further decline in traffic. Wages were reduced by 10% while the section forces were reduced to 2 men on the NP&FG RR and 4 men on the Stewartstown section. (MMN)
Feb. 1932	Train crew reduced to 3 men. (MMN)
Apr. 14, 1934	Reported I.C.C. authority to abandoned NP&FG RR received. (MMN)
Oct. 1, 1934	NP&FG RR operations to cease. (MMN)
Nov. 20, 1934	Engine No. 5 to be offered for sale. (MMN)
May 14, 1935	NP&FG RR property to be liquidated by the Stewartstown RR. (MMN)
June 3, 1935	Stewartstown Railroad and Kenneth Manifold entered into a lease agreement pertaining to the old New Park and Fawn Grove Railroad station located into Fawn Grove, Pa. for the sum of $4 per month, payable quarterly. (SHS)
June 5, 1935	DAILY MEMORANDUM – Fifty Years Ago: The laying of the track of the Stewartstown Railroad to New Freedom has started. The line will be about seven miles in length. (YDR)
1938	Stewartstown RR purchasing PRR common stock as an investment. (MMN)
Mar. 18, 1939	NEWS OF THE PAST – Fifty Years Ago – Citizens of New Park and Stewartstown vicinity met at the latter place and launched a movement for the extension of the Stewartstown Railroad to New Park, and possibly to Fawn Grove and Delta. The road to Fawn Grove became a reality, but that to Delta did not materialize. (YDR)
Mar. 28, 1939	SRR Directors undertake a study of changing from steam power to gasoline power. (MMN)
Apr. 17, 1939	President H. W. Anderson calls a special meeting. The East Berlin Railway is reported to be folding up and they have a small gas engine for sale. No action is

	taken. (MMN)
Nov. 27, 1939	Engine No.5 is reported to have a defective fire box sheet. It is out of service and the Maryland & Pennsylvania RR is being contacted to make the repairs. Ma. & Pa. RR loans a steam engine to the Stewartstown RR. Pressure is on to purchase a new engine. (MMN)
Nov. 29, 1939	Representatives of Plymouth Locomotive Company come to Stewartstown to meet with the SRR directors. The representative advised that Plymouth has a suitable engine that can be made ready for shipment in 10 days for a price of $11,385 f.o.b. Stewartstown. It will pull 190 tons up the Stewartstown 1.8% grade and around 16-degree curves. Plymouth will help unload and set up engine. The deal was made. (MMN)
Dec. 19, 1939	The Fate-Root-Heath Company sends the Stewartstown Railroad dimensions and photograph of Plymouth Gasoline Engine. (See Appendix No. 34)
1940	The Stewartstown Railroad creates a shipping order for the Stewartstown Furniture Company. (See Appendix No. 35)
Jan. 8, 1940	Plymouth No.6 hauled 188 tons to Stewartstown meeting the performance guarantee. The SRR directors moved to junk Engine No.4. Engine No.5 will still be on hand. (MMN)

The Stewartstown Railroad Company continued to operate well after 1940. One of its major purchases was No.9 "Mighty Mo," a vintage-1943 Plymouth gasoline-fueled switcher engine purchased in 1960 from the South Carolina Port Authority. In the two decades after World War II, the SRR saw a steady decline in its freight business as trucking became the norm. A loyal cadre of companies and individuals (some of them stockholders) kept the ailing railroad alive. When Hurricane Agnes wrecked the Northern Central Railway in 1972, the destruction severed the Stewartstown Railroad's connections to outside markets in Baltimore, York, Harrisburg, Philadelphia, and elsewhere. The SRR, instead of folding, stayed active by maintaining its right-of-way and keeping its engine and rolling stock.

Once the NCR reopened, the SRR again ran trains regularly from 1985 until 1992. The railroad found a new market as a passenger excursion line until 2004 when that enterprise halted. The Stewartstown Railroad resumed partial operations as an excursion line a few years later and continues to expand that effort today. For more information, please visit the company's website at www.stewartstownrailroadco.com or its Facebook page at www.facebook.com/StewartstownRailroadCompany/.

Founded in 1884

STEWARTSTOWN RAILROAD

21 WEST PENNSYLVANIA AVE. * STEWARTSTOWN, PA * (717) 746-8123

Sources:

(YD) *York Dispatch*, York, PA.

(SN) *Stewartstown News*, Stewartstown, Pa.

(Poor's) *Poor's Manual of the Railroads of the United States*, New York, N.Y.

(YG) *York Gazette*, York, Pa.

(A) *The Age*, York, Pa.

(MMN) Stewartstown RR Directors Meeting Minute Notes

(A.R. of S.R.R.) Auditor Records of the Stewartstown Railroad

(G) *The Gazette*, York, Pa.

(YDR) *York Daily Record*, York, Pa.

(G&D) *Gazette and Daily*, York, Pa.

(YDLY) *York Daily*, York, Pa.

(T) *Tribune-Sun*

(GRI) *Glen Rock Item*, Glen Rock, Pa.

(EN) *Evening News*, Harrisburg, Pa.

(BS) *Baltimore Sun*, Baltimore, Md.

(BCU) *Baltimore County Union*, Towson, Md.

(U) *The Union*, Towson, Md.

(AI) *Aegis & Intelligencer*, Bel Air, Md.

(DA) *Democratic Advocate*, Westminster, Md.

(EB) *The Story of the Stewartstown Railroad* by Eric J. Bickleman

(SHS) Stewartstown Area Historical Society

(ICC) Interstate Commerce Commission

(SRRRB) Stewartstown Railroad Receipt Book 1888 to 1892

(AR-SRR) Auditor Report for the Stewartstown Railroad

Note: All appendices are from the collection of the Stewartstown Area Historical Society except where noted.

THE STEWARTSTOWN RAILROAD

~ o ~

PHOTOGRAPHS

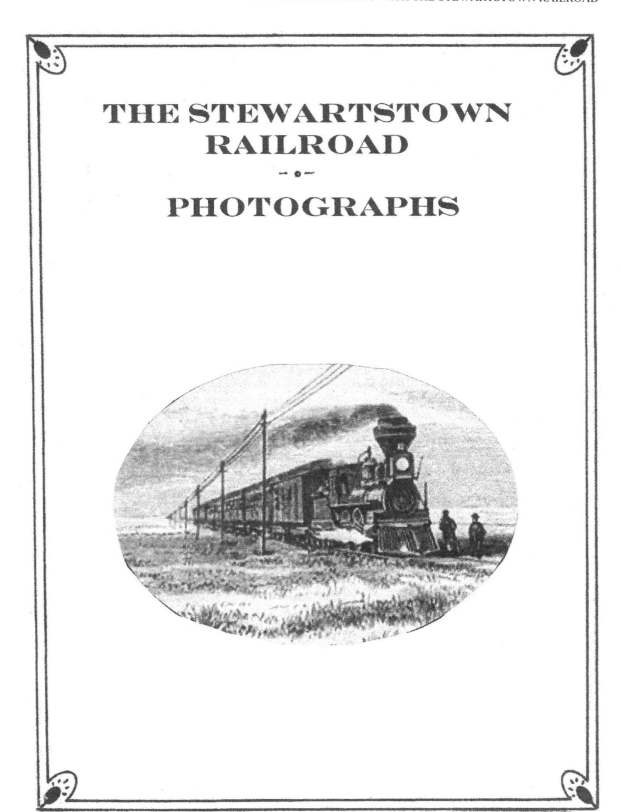

ROUTE MAP OF STATIONS, SHELTERS, AND FLAG STOPS
ON THE STEWARTSTOWN RAILROAD

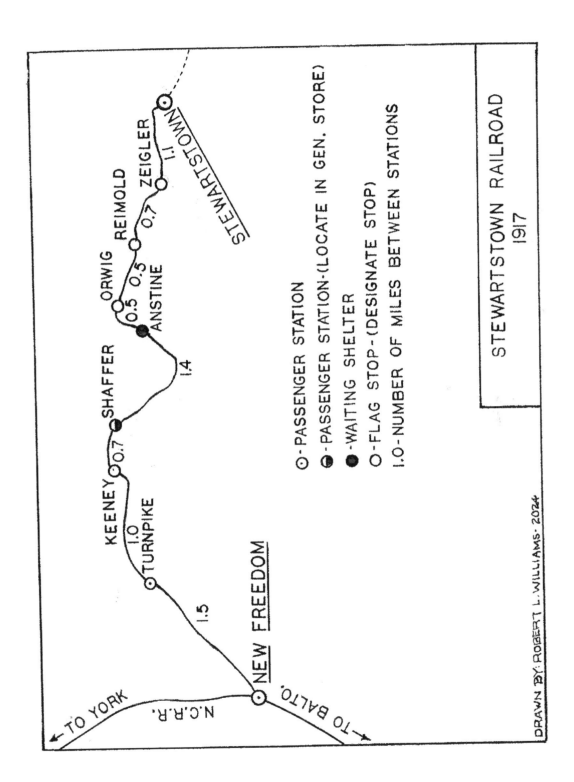

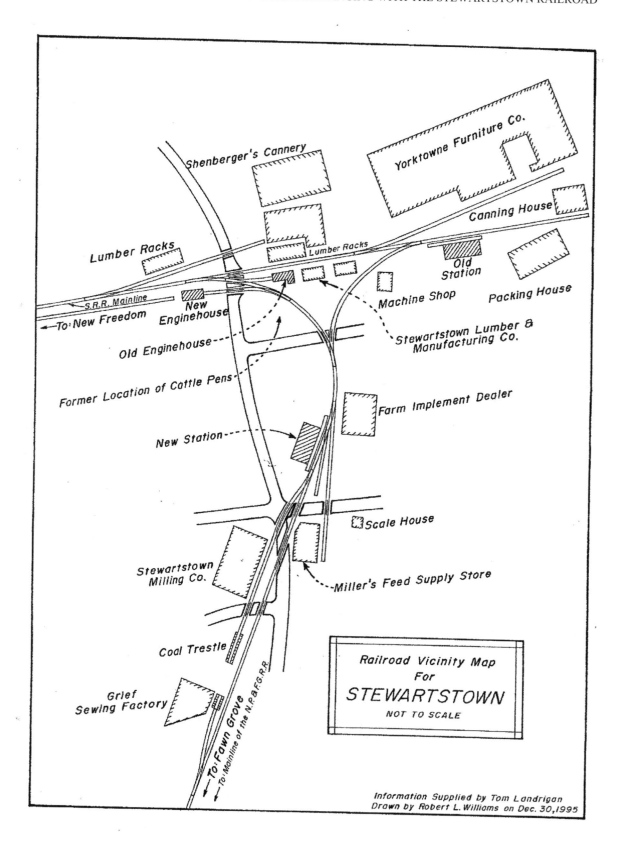

Shenberger's Cannery

Yorktowne Furniture Co.

Canning House

Lumber Racks

Lumber Racks

Old Station

S.R.R. Mainline

To New Freedom

New Enginehouse

Machine Shop

Packing House

Old Enginehouse

Stewartstown Lumber & Manufacturing Co.

Former Location of Cattle Pens

Farm Implement Dealer

New Station

Scale House

Stewartstown Milling Co.

Miller's Feed Supply Store

Coal Trestle

Grief Sewing Factory

To Fawn Grove

To Mainline of the N.P.&F.G.R.R.

Railroad Vicinity Map
For
STEWARTSTOWN
NOT TO SCALE

Information Supplied by Tom Landrigan
Drawn by Robert L. Williams on Dec. 30, 1995

STEWARTSTOWN

Grand opening of the Stewartstown Railroad's new station in Stewartstown in July 1899.

From the collection of the Stewartstown Area Historical Society

Postcard view of the Stewartstown Railroad Passenger Station – ca.1910.

From the collection of the Stewartstown Area Historical Society

Postcard view of the Stewartstown Railroad Passenger Station – ca.1915.

From the collection of the Stewartstown Area Historical Society

Round trip ticket from Stewartstown to New Freedom – ca.1920. Calvin Webster Shaw (1866–1944) was the company's general passenger agent. He and his wife were quite active in local affairs.

From the collection of the Stewartstown Area Historical Society

Stewartstown Railroad station stamp dated January 30, 1915. C. W. Shaw and other passenger ticket agents used these stamps for official company business.

From the collection of the Stewartstown Area Historical Society

The Stewartstown Railroad's first engine house was put into use on January 11, 1908. The extension to the wooden frame structure was added in 1916.

From the collection of the Stewartstown Area Historical Society

The Stewartstown Railroad opened its second passenger station on December 29, 1914.

From the collection of the Stewartstown Area Historical Society

Interior view of the Stewartstown passenger station that was completed on December 29, 1914.

From the collection of Robert L. Williams

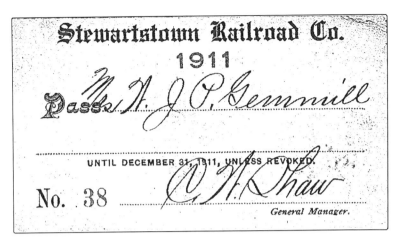

General Manager C. W. Shaw issued this Stewartstown Railroad Company yearly pass for 1911.

From the collection of the Stewartstown Area Historical Society

Unloading a freight car in Stewartstown – ca.1910.

From the collection of the Stewartstown Area Historical Society

General view of the Stewartstown Planing Mill: After the new train station was completed in 1914, the old station seen in the photograph (left-center) was rented out to various businesses.

From the collection of the Stewartstown Area Historical Society

Postcard view of Mill Street looking east at the general railroad business district of Stewartstown.

From the collection of the Stewartstown Area Historical Society

Bird's-eye view of the railroad business district in Stewartstown – ca.1930.

From the collection of the Stewartstown Area Historical Society

Vintage early 20th-century postcard showing the Stewartstown Planing Mill, which was one of many local businesses serviced by the Stewartstown Railroad.

From the collection of the Stewartstown Area Historical Society

J. C. Leib & Co. constructed this feed mill in 1887 at the corner of West Pennsylvania Avenue and Hill Street in Stewartstown. Owner J. Calder Leib often partnered with Anderson Bros. in New Park to promote new products of interest to the farmers in the region, including the newly introduced "Gold Medal Flour." In 1906 the land behind this business would become the tie-in point between the New Park & Fawn Grove Railroad and the Stewartstown Railroad.

From the collection of the Stewartstown Area Historical Society

This poster advertised the Stewartstown Fair held from September 13–15, 1915. This popular event helped boost revenues significantly for the Stewartstown Railroad and New Park & Fawn Grove Railroad. Both companies rented additional equipment from the Northern Central Railway and Pennsylvania Railroad to handle the increased passenger traffic during the fair.

From the collection of the Stewartstown Area Historical Society

Left: Stewartstown R.R. Baggage Tag.   Right: Report of Lock Pouches carried between station, 1948.

From the collection of the Stewartstown Area Historical Society

Stewartstown R.R. clerical pass.

From the collection of the Stewartstown Area Historical Society

Officials and workers pose at the groundbreaking ceremony in 1903 for the new Hopewell Furniture Factory on Hill Street in Stewartstown. The company frequently shipped its products on the S.R.R.

From the collection of the Stewartstown Area Historical Society

A view of the Hopewell Furniture Factory after its completion in 1904.

From the collection of the Stewartstown Area Historical Society

Two unidentified dapper passengers strike a pose on the platform of an S.R.R. passenger car.

From the collection of Kurt Bell

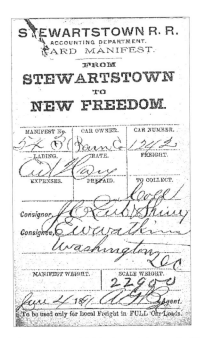

Card Manifest for a shipment on freight car no. 1242 dated June 4, 1891.

From the collection of the Stewartstown Area Historical Society

Tool House for storage of the railroad's tools and equipment – ca. 1920.

From the collection of the Stewartstown Area Historical Society

Track crew from left to right – George Schminkey, John Shaw, and Thomas Heaton.

From the collection of the Stewartstown Area Historical Society

Drawing of an oak-and-iron, human-powered velocipede purchased by the Stewartstown Railroad from the Sheffield Velocipede Company in 1889. The velocipede was stored in a barn in Gatchellville for 48 years before being on display at the Stewartstown Railroad Museum in 2021. It was capable of speeds up to 10 mph but had no brakes.

From an advertisement for the Sheffield Velocipede Car Company (collection of Robert L. Williams)

Time Account for the Stewartstown R.R.'s trackmen, including George B. Schminkey (pictured on the previous page), from June 16–30, 1919.

From the collection of the Stewartstown Area Historical Society

A view looking east toward the first engine house (left-center) and the steam engine (left) proceeding west on the main track of the Stewartstown Railroad.

From the collection of the Stewartstown Area Historical Society

Engine No.2 on the "wye" track passing the first engine house built by the Stewartstown Railroad. Notice the passenger coach in the background sitting on the main track waiting for pick up.

From the collection of Benjamin F.G. Kline/Stewartstown Area Historical Society

One of two passenger coach cars that ran on the Stewartstown Railroad in the early 20th Century.

From the collection of the Stewartstown Area Historical Society

The new engine house was built in 1915. It is presently in service housing the equipment of the modern Stewartstown Railroad.

From the collection of the Stewartstown Area Historical Society – ca.1960

Passenger train Engine No.2. Crew from left to right: Jacob Rider – engineer, Lawrence Beldon Shaw – fireman, Clarence E. Yost – conductor, and Peck Hartman – brakeman. Rider, an engineer on the Northern Central Railway, moved to Stewartstown in 1885 and then was an engineer for the SRR for the next 36 years. Shaw ran as a Republican for a judgeship in 1923 but remained with the railroad. He and his father also raised prize-winning hogs. Yost served from 1904 until resigning in February 1918 to take a position with a manufacturing firm in Waynesboro, Pa. George B. Hale of New Freedom replaced him.

From the collection of the Stewartstown Area Historical Society – ca.1913

Charles W. "Charlie" Heaton stands at the controls of the gasoline combination passenger and baggage car. The native of Harford County, Md., began his long career on July 3, 1915, with the N.P.&F.G. R.R. He worked for the railroad until 1932 when he resigned to take a construction job in Maryland. He returned to engineering for the S.R.R. in 1936 and served until his retirement in January 1962. He and his family lived in Norrisville, Md.

From the collection of the Stewartstown Area Historical Society

Engineer George Edwin Gibbs (1886–1962) is shown in this image taken about 1938. After retiring from the railroad, he worked for the Stewartstown Furniture Company. He also was part of the Eureka Volunteer Fire Company for several years.

From the collection of the Stewartstown Area Historical Society

Bank voucher addressed to Jacob Rider, an S.R.R. engineer, dated February 13, 1897.

From the collection of the Stewartstown Area Historical Society

A locomotive, possibly S.R.R. Engine No.4, pushing snow drifts away from the tracks – ca.1915.

From the collection of Eric Bickleman

Possibly Engine No.4 sitting in New Freedom after pushing snow drifts away from the track.

From the collection of Eric Bickleman

Engine No.1 (*Hopewell*) is at the coal station just west of Zeiglers. The SRR purchased this American-style 4-4-0 from the Baldwin Locomotive Works for $5,300 in 1885.

From the collection of the Stewartstown Area Historical Society

Engine No.2, a Baldwin 4-4-0 purchased in December 1904 for $7,675, sits in Stewartstown. It was scrapped during the Great Depression.

From the collection of the Stewartstown Area Historical Society

Engine No.3, a Renovo 4-4-0 built in 1888, sits in Fawn Grove.

From the collection of the Stewartstown Area Historical Society

Engine No.4, a Baldwin 2-6-0 constructed in June 1913, is shown with the combination freight and caboose car (Market Car) in front of Stewartstown's passenger station.

From the collection of the Stewartstown Area Historical Society

Engine No.5, a Baldwin 2-6-0 constructed in June 1914, sits with the Market Car in Stewartstown.

From the collection of the Stewartstown Area Historical Society

Second Engine No.3, a Renovo 4-4-0 constructed in 1888. The man standing on the locomotive is believed to be W. Earl Fulton, the son of William Fulton and the grandson of the company's first president, James Fulton.

From the collection of Eric Bickleman

Railbus Car No.7, constructed by the J. G. Brill Company of Philadelphia, sits in front of the Stewartstown passenger station in March 1923. The company was founded in 1868 to make horsecars.

From the collection of the Stewartstown Area Historical Society

Engine No. 6, a gasoline engine constructed by Plymouth in December 1939, is at the engine house.

From the collection of the Stewartstown Area Historical Society

ZEIGLERS

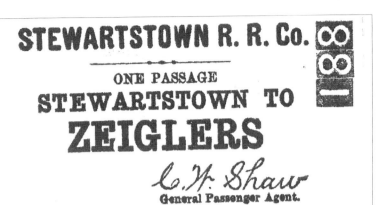

A one-way passenger ticket from Stewartstown to Zeiglers – ca.1920.

From the collection of the Stewartstown Area Historical Society

Passenger train sitting across from the coaling station just east of Zeiglers Station.

From the Schminkey collection/Stewartstown Area Historical Society – ca.1920

A Sunday outing for this couple near the coaling station just east of Zeiglers.

From the Schminkey collection/Stewartstown Area Historical Society – ca.1920

This stone foundation once supported a 7,500-gallon water tank just east of Zeiglers.

From the collection of Robert L. Williams

A view looking east at the switch leading to a siding at Zeiglers Station.

From the Schminkey collection/Stewartstown Area Historical Society – ca.1920

A young couple stands on the Pratt wrought iron truss railroad bridge over Valley Road near Zeiglers. The Keystone Bridge Company originally constructed the span in 1870 for the NCR. After a devastating flood in August 1901 destroyed the previous wooden trestle bridge at this location, the SRR bought this iron bridge from the NCR and installed it at Valley Road.

From the Schminkey collection/Stewartstown Area Historical Society – ca.1920

The bridge over Valley Road is one of the oldest remaining entirely wrought iron bridges in the country. Photo is from a federal government study in 1968. (Library of Congress Photographs Division)

In this view also from the 1968 series, the photographer is standing on the eastern side of the bridge as the line runs toward New Freedom. (Library of Congress Photographs Division)

This sturdy stone-arch culvert crossed over Ebaugh's Creek in rural Hopewell Township.

From the collection of the Stewartstown Area Historical Society

This deck plate girder bridge was rebuilt in 1895. It crossed over Ridge Road near Stewartstown.

From the collection of the Stewartstown Area Historical Society

REIMOLD

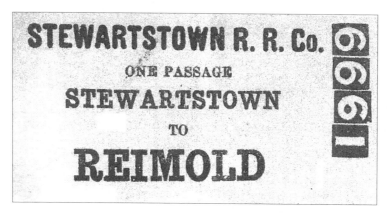

One-way passenger ticket from Stewartstown to Reimold.

From the collection of the Stewartstown Area Historical Society

Bill of Sale from W.E. Manifold addressed to the Stewartstown Railroad on December 20, 1940.

From the collection of the Stewartstown Area Historical Society

ORWIG

One-way passenger ticket from Stewartstown to Orwig.

From the collection of the Stewartstown Area Historical Society

This privately-owned general store doubled as the S.R.R.'s train station in Orwig.

From the collection of Eric Bickleman

ANSTINE

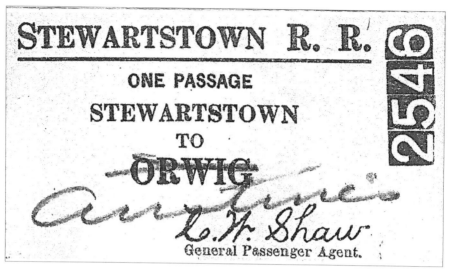

One-way passenger ticket from Stewartstown to Anstine.

From the collection of the Stewartstown Area Historical Society

John Y. Keeney operated a shingle mill that appears in the left of the photo. His farm is to the right.

From the collection of Robert H. Shaub/Stewartstown Area Historical Society

Engine No.5 proceeds westward from Anstine Station.

From the collection of Eric Bickleman

The Stewartstown Railroad erected this high wooden trestle bridge in 1885. The increased weight of railroad equipment and high maintenance costs eventually forced the railroad to remove the trestle and fill in the land. In the photo, Engine No. 1 (*Hopewell*) moves across the trestle.

From the collection of Kurt Bell

Deck plate girder bridge over Deer Creek west of Sheffer's.

From the Schminkey collection/Stewartstown Area Historical Society – ca.1920

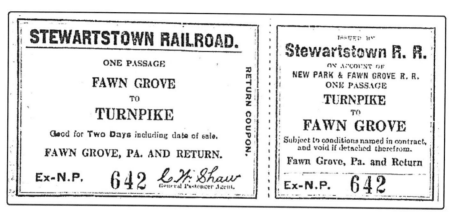

Round-trip passenger ticket from Fawn Grove to Turnpike.

From the collection of the Stewartstown Area Historical Society

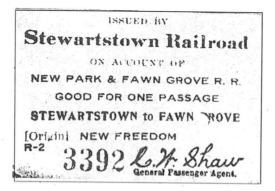

One-way passenger ticket from Stewartstown to Fawn Grove.

From the collection of the Stewartstown Area Historical Society

SHEFFER

One-way passenger ticket from Stewartstown to Sheffer.

From the collection of the Stewartstown Area Historical Society

Sheffer Station (also known as Tolna) was a privately-owned general store and post office. A long siding at Sheffer serviced a warehouse and a nearby mill.

From the collection of Robert H. Shaub/Eric J. Bickleman

Station Stamp for Sheffer, Pa., dated April 14, 1914.

From the collection of the Stewartstown Area Historical Society

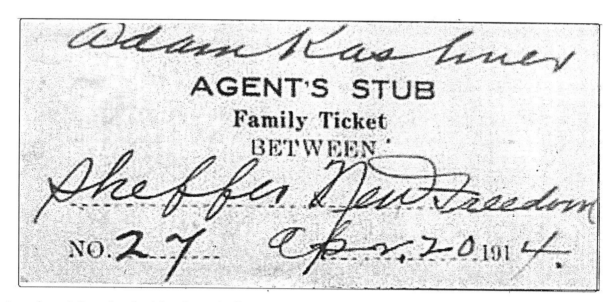

Agent's stub for a family ticket from Sheffer Station to New Freedom dated April 20, 1914.

From the collection of the Stewartstown Area Historical Society

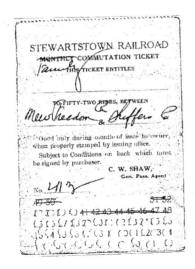 

Stewartstown Monthly Commutation Ticket from New Freedom to Sheffer for the month of November. The ticket was issued on October 28, 1933.

From the collection of the Stewartstown Area Historical Society

Sheffer Daily Sales Report sent to the company treasurer dated April 12, 1912.

From the collection of the Stewartstown Area Historical Society

KEENEY

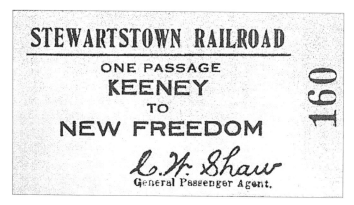

One-way passenger ticket from Keeney to New Freedom.

From the collection of the Stewartstown Area Historical Society

An unidentified S.R.R. engine proceeds from Keeney Station. The stop was named for John Keeney, who is seen (seated) with his family in the photo to the right.

Left: From the collection of the Stewartstown Area Historical Society
Right: From the collection of Eric Bickleman

TURNPIKE

Passenger ticket from Turnpike to Stewartstown.

Courtesy of Greg Halpin.

Engine No.5 drops off a freight car to the Chase Wire Cloth Company at Turnpike Station – ca. 1940.

From the collection of the Stewartstown Area Historical Society

Northwest view of the Turnpike Station.

From the collection of Martin Van Horn

Northward view of the Turnpike Station.

From the collection of Martin Van Horn

Eastward view of the Turnpike Station. The station building was completed on September 1, 1925, and was immediately occupied by an agent. Because of decreased business and traffic, the railroad closed the station in 1969.

From the collection of the Stewartstown Area Historical Society

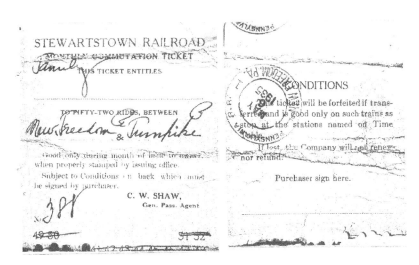

Stewartstown Railroad Monthly Commutation Ticket from New Freedom to Turnpike. The ticket was sold in New Freedom on May 6, 1935.

From the collection of the Stewartstown Area Historical Society

NEW FREEDOM

One-way passenger ticket from New Freedom to Stewartstown.

From the collection of the Stewartstown Area Historical Society

This two-destination first-class ticket issued in Stewartstown allowed the passenger to travel to New Freedom and transfer there to an N.C.R. train to travel north to Glen Rock, Pa.

From the collection of Robert L Williams

Engine No.5, a Baldwin 2-6-0, sits on a siding in New Freedom about 1940.

From the collection of the Stewartstown Area Historical Society

Engine No. 5 sits on a siding in front of the Jacob Mays Building in New Freedom.

From the collection of the Stewartstown Area Historical Society

Station stamps from the Northern Central Railway's New Freedom passenger station.

From the collection of the Stewartstown Area Historical Society

New Freedom Depot, New Freedom, Pa.

Postcard view of the Northern Central Railway's New Freedom combination passenger and freight station that was constructed in 1885.

From the collection of Robert L. Williams – ca.1912

This 1912 postcard shows the construction of the Stewartstown Railroad platforms in New Freedom on the right of the photograph. To the left is the passenger station, which still stands.

From the collection of Robert L. Williams

The Northern Central Railway and the Stewartstown Railroad reached an agreement to construct an enclosed waiting shed for passengers traveling on both railroads. The shed was completed in 1916.

From the collection of Robert L. Williams

Stewartstown Railroad No.7 Gasoline Rail Car sitting in New Freedom.

From the collection of Eric Bickleman

The Missouri Pacific Line issued this baggage claim stub for a train ride from Houston, Texas, to Stewartstown, Pa.

From the collection of the Stewartstown Area Historical Society

BALTIMORE

First-class passenger ticket from Stewartstown to New Freedom and then south to Baltimore, Md.

From the collection of the Stewartstown Area Historical Society

Engine No.5 sits on a siding of the Maryland & Pennsylvania Railroad in Baltimore while awaiting repairs.

From the collection of the Stewartstown Area Historical Society

Stewartstown Railroad Engine No.5 proceeds north from the Mt. Vernon area of Baltimore on the main line of the Northern Central Railway. It is heading to New Freedom.

From the collection of the Stewartstown Area Historical Society – ca.1936

New Freedom Daily Sales Report sent to the company treasurer on April 6, 1918.

From the collection of the Stewartstown Area Historical Society

THE STEWARTSTOWN RAILROAD

-·-

DRAWINGS

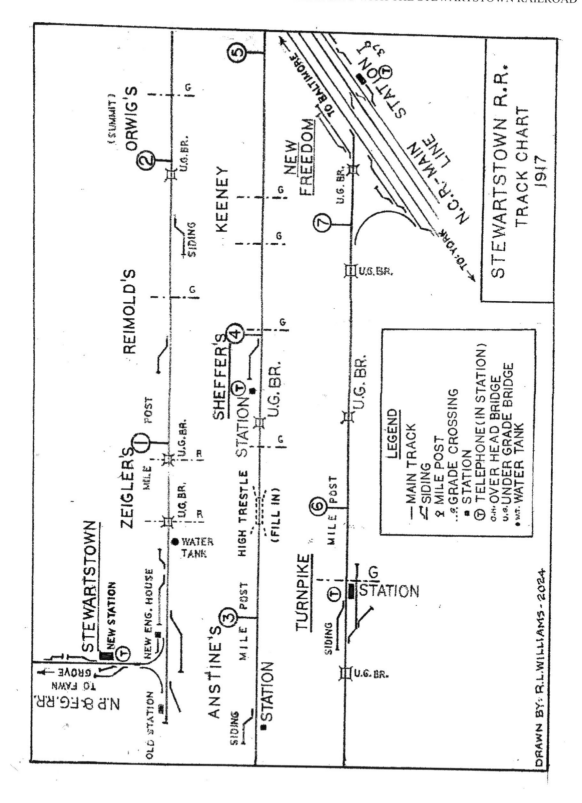

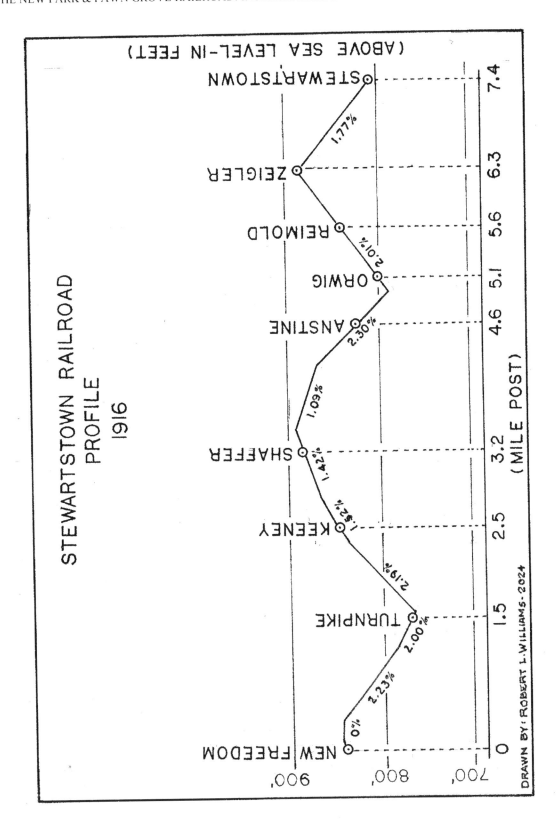

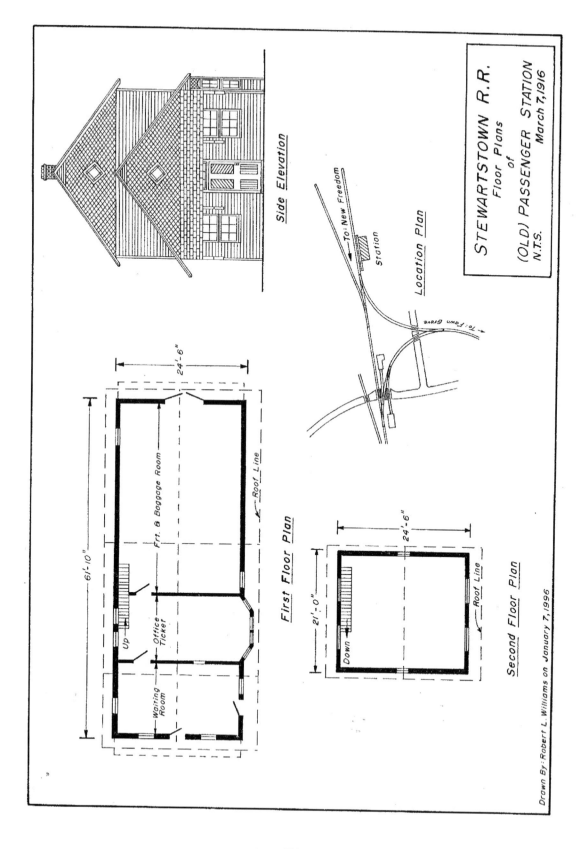

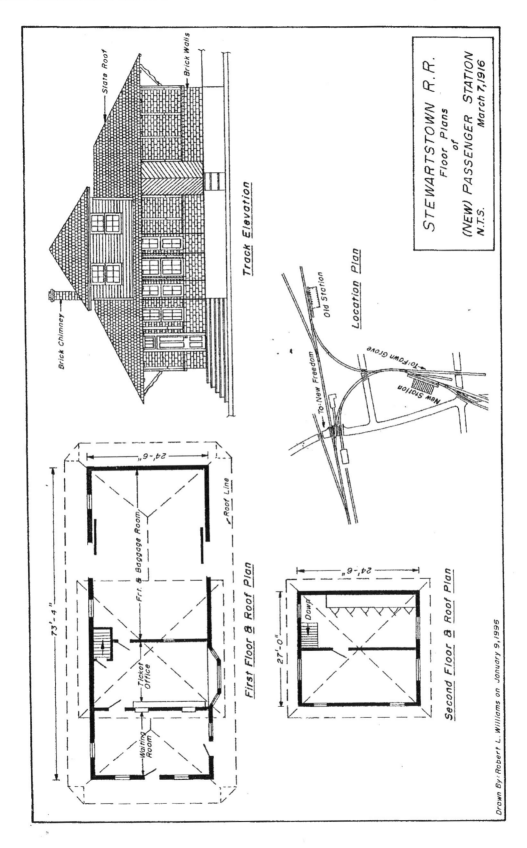

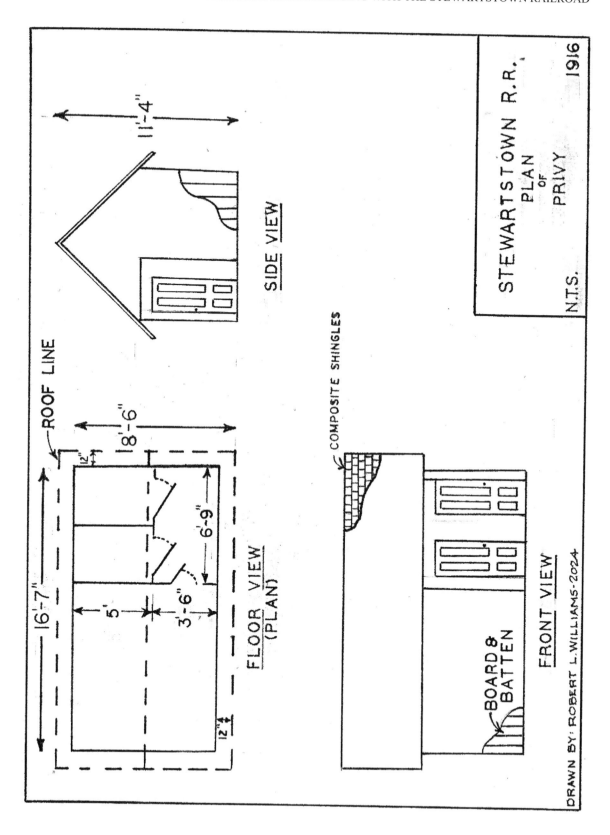

SIDE VIEW

11'-4"

ROOF LINE

8'-6"

12"

6'-9"

3'-6"

5'

16'-7"

12"

FLOOR VIEW
(PLAN)

COMPOSITE SHINGLES

BOARD & BATTEN

FRONT VIEW

STEWARTSTOWN R.R.
PLAN OF PRIVY

1916

N.T.S.

DRAWN BY: ROBERT L. WILLIAMS - 2024

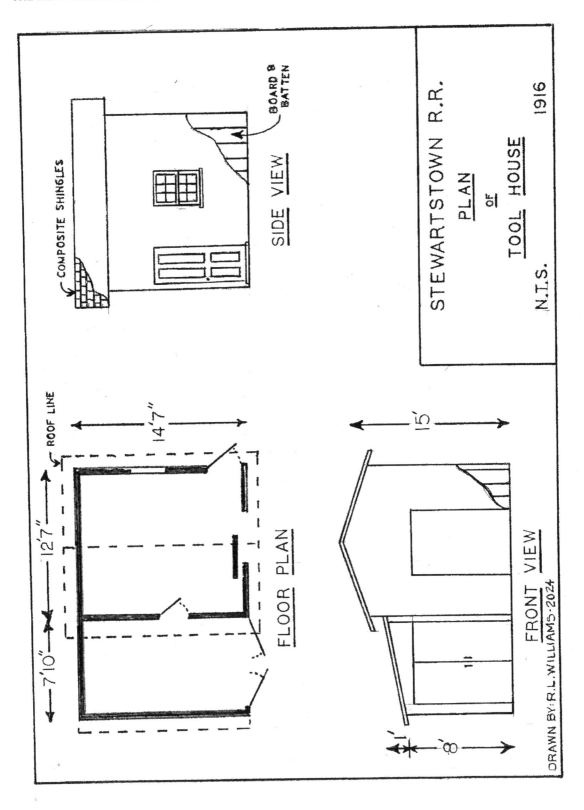

SIDE VIEW

COMPOSITE SHINGLES

BOARD & BATTEN

STEWARTSTOWN R.R.

PLAN

OF

TOOL HOUSE

N.T.S.   1916

ROOF LINE

14'7"

12'7"

7'10"

FLOOR PLAN

15'

FRONT VIEW

8'

1'

DRAWN BY: R.L. WILLIAMS · 2024

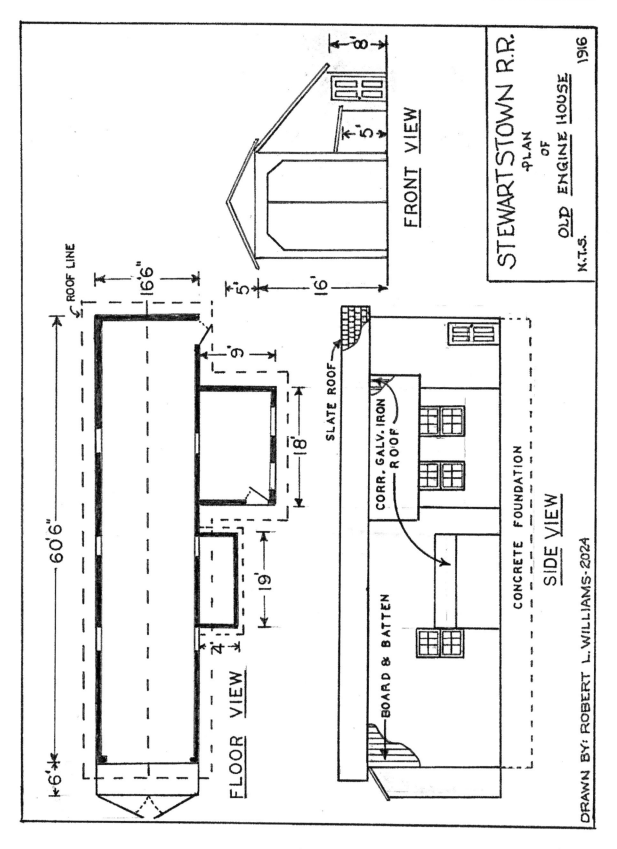

STEWARTSTOWN R.R.
PLAN OF
OLD ENGINE HOUSE
N.T.S.
1916

FRONT VIEW

FLOOR VIEW

SIDE VIEW

ROOF LINE

SLATE ROOF

CORR. GALV. IRON ROOF

CONCRETE FOUNDATION

BOARD & BATTEN

DRAWN BY: ROBERT L. WILLIAMS-2024

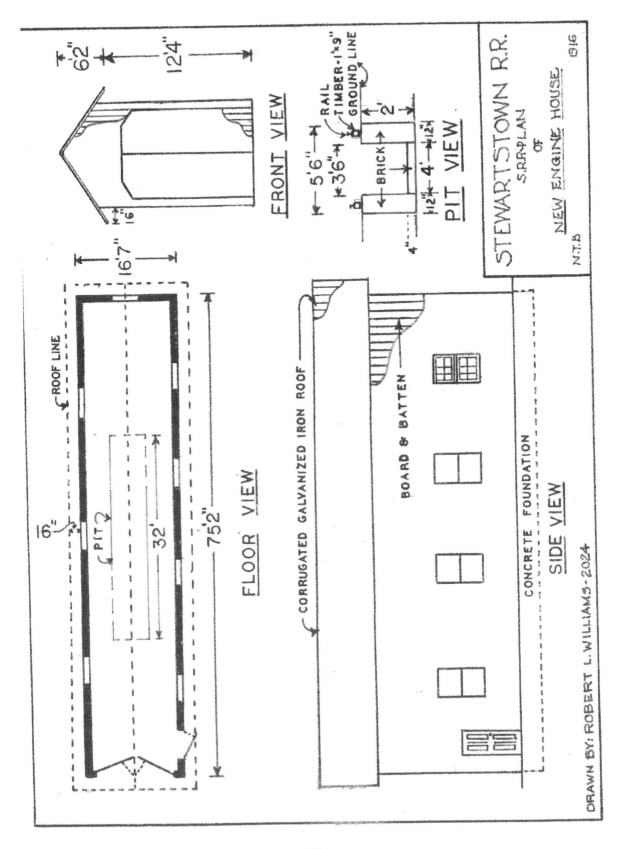

FRONT VIEW

PIT VIEW

FLOOR VIEW

SIDE VIEW

STEWARTSTOWN R.R.

S.R.R PLAN OF

NEW ENGINE HOUSE

1916

N.T.S

DRAWN BY: ROBERT L. WILLIAMS - 2024

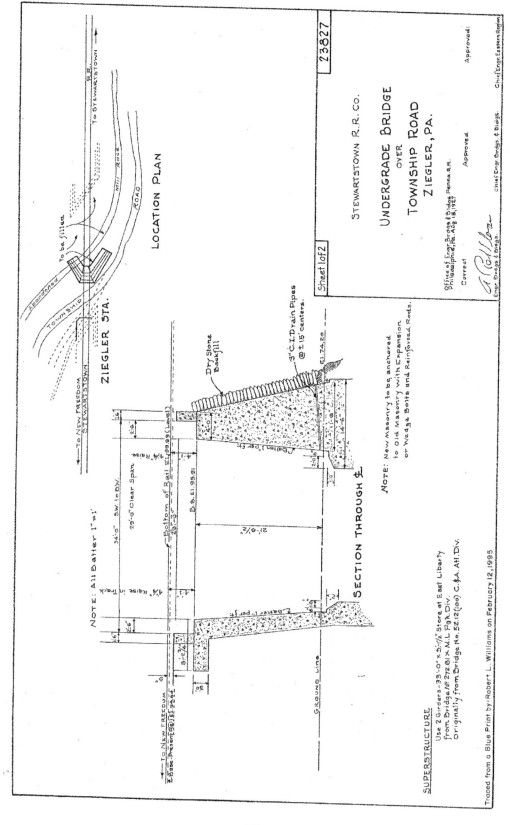

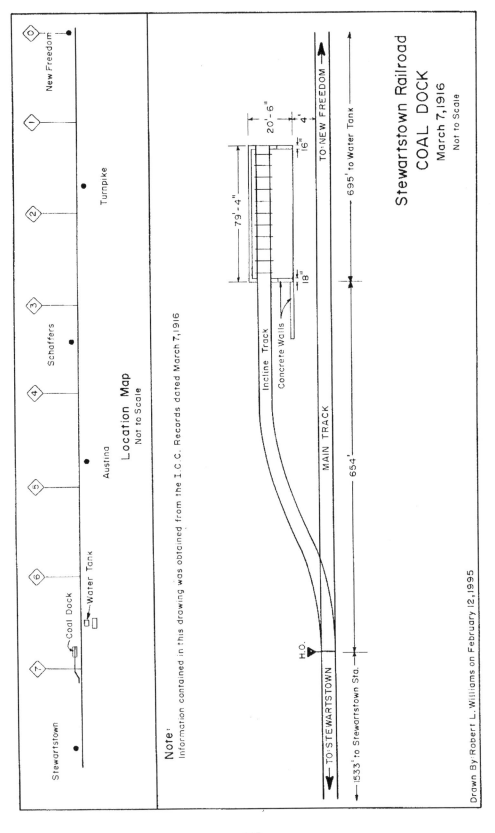

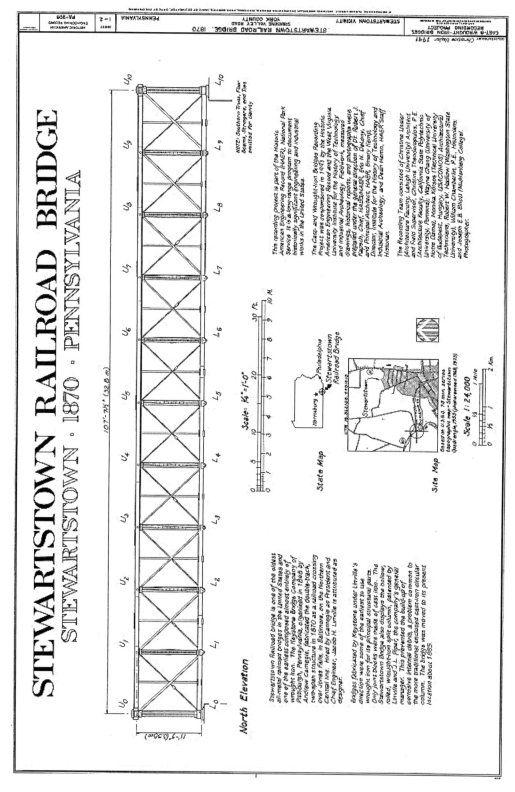

1870 Keystone Bridge Co. plans, 1 of 2. (Library of Congress)

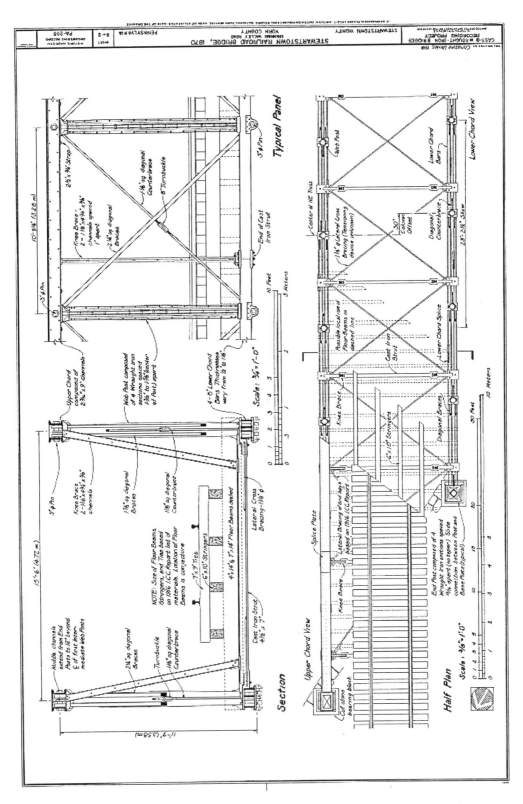

1870 Keystone Bridge plans, 2 of 2. (Library of Congress)

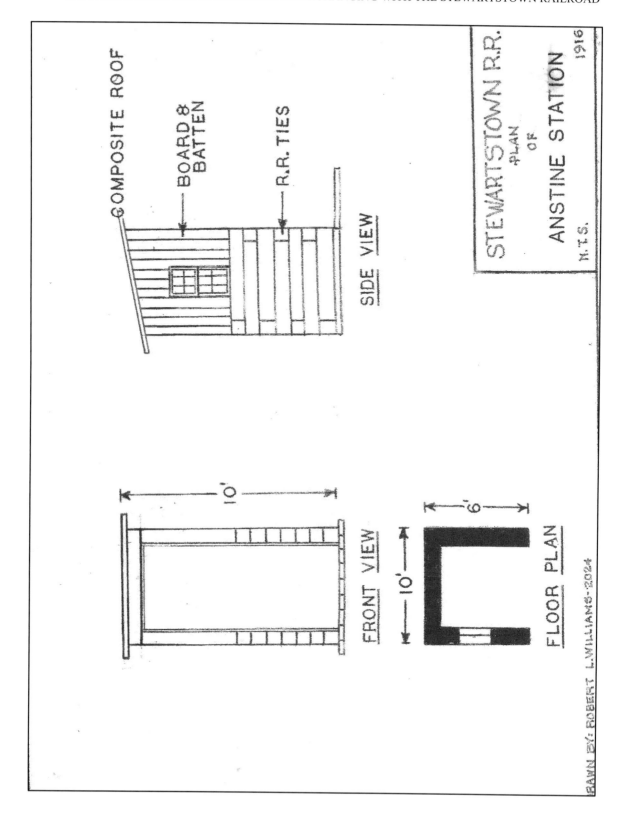

STEWARTSTOWN R.R.
PLAN OF
ANSTINE STATION
1916
N.T.S.

COMPOSITE ROOF
BOARD & BATTEN
R.R. TIES
SIDE VIEW

FRONT VIEW
10'
10'

FLOOR PLAN
6'

DRAWN BY: ROBERT L.WILLIAMS-2024

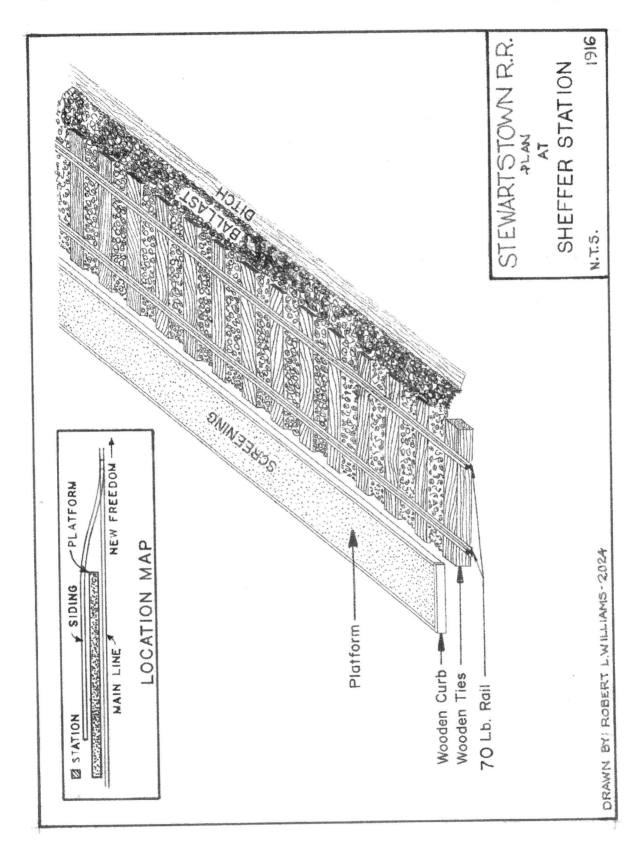

STEWARTSTOWN R.R.
PLAN AT
SHEFFER STATION
1916
N.T.S.

BALLAST DITCH

SCREENING

Platform

Wooden Curb
Wooden Ties
70 Lb. Rail

LOCATION MAP

STATION
SIDING
PLATFORM
MAIN LINE
NEW FREEDOM

DRAWN BY: ROBERT L. WILLIAMS - 2024

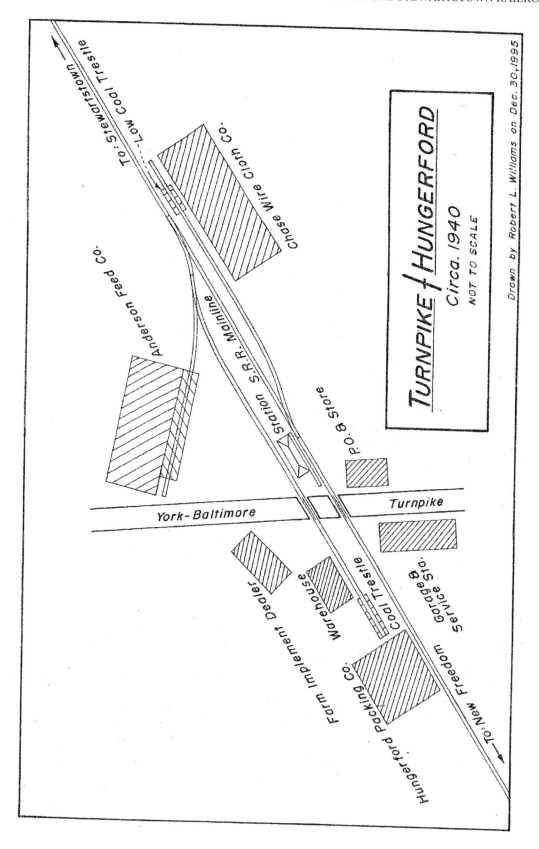

TURNPIKE ✝ HUNGERFORD

Circa 1940

NOT TO SCALE

Drawn by Robert L. Williams on Dec. 30, 1995

To: Stewartstown

Low Coal Trestle

Chase Wire Cloth Co.

Anderson Feed Co.

Station S.R.R. Mainline

P.O. & Store

York - Baltimore

Turnpike

Farm Implement Dealer

Warehouse

Coal Trestle

Garage & Service Sta.

Hungerford Packing Co.

To: New Freedom

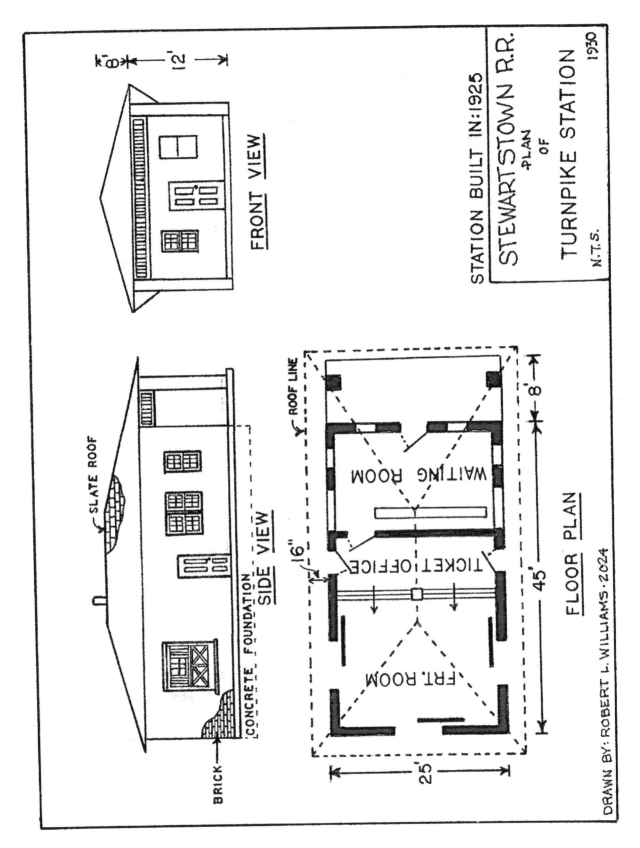

FRONT VIEW

SIDE VIEW

SLATE ROOF

BRICK

CONCRETE FOUNDATION

WAITING ROOM

TICKET OFFICE

FRT. ROOM

ROOF LINE

FLOOR PLAN

STATION BUILT IN: 1925

STEWARTSTOWN R.R.

PLAN

OF

TURNPIKE STATION

1930

N.T.S.

DRAWN BY: ROBERT L. WILLIAMS · 2024

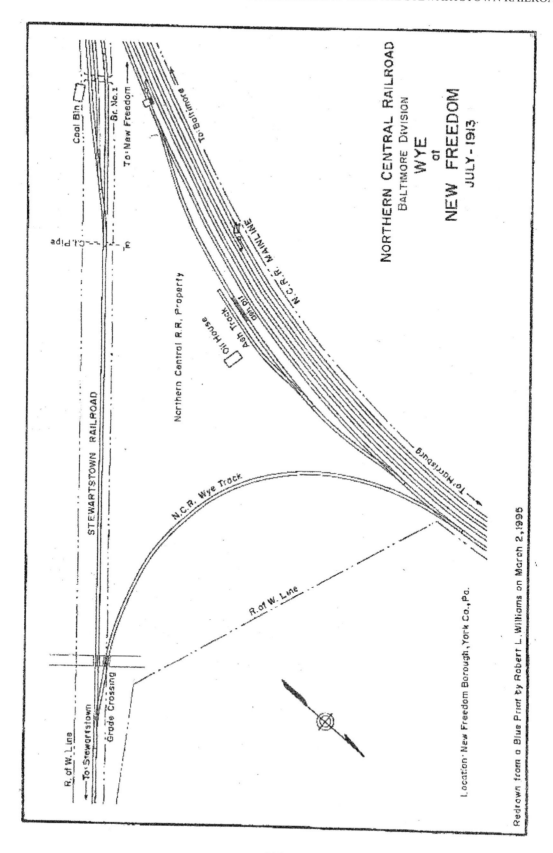

NORTHERN CENTRAL RAILROAD
BALTIMORE DIVISION
WYE
at
NEW FREEDOM
JULY - 1913

Location: New Freedom Borough, York Co., Pa.

Redrawn from a Blue Print by Robert L. Williams on March 2, 1995

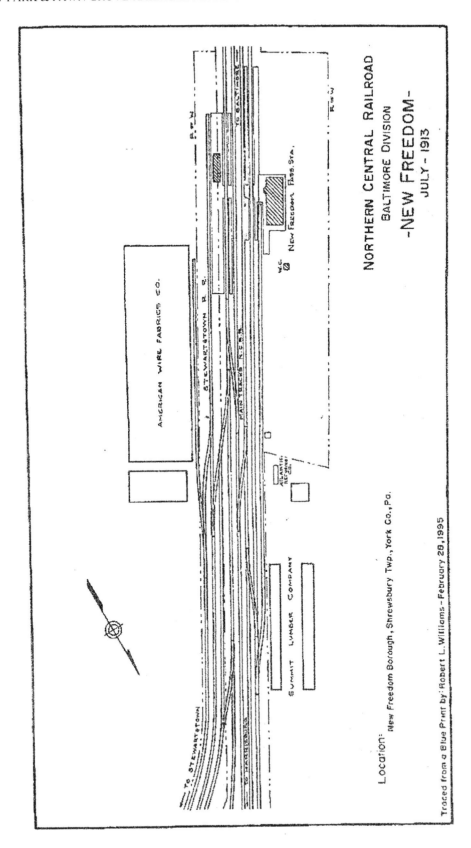

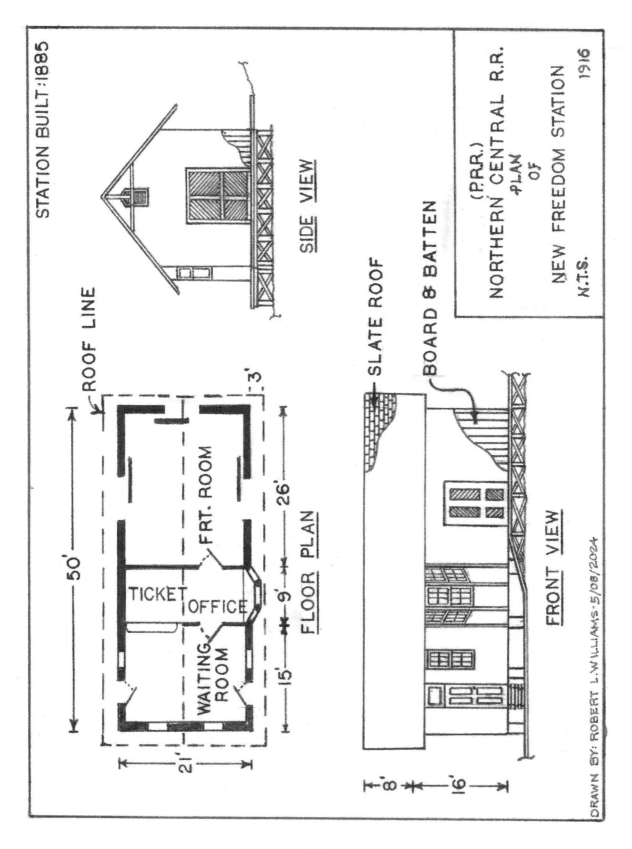

STATION BUILT: 1885

SIDE VIEW

ROOF LINE

FLOOR PLAN

FRT. ROOM

TICKET OFFICE

WAITING ROOM

50'

26'

9'

15'

3'

21'

SLATE ROOF

BOARD & BATTEN

FRONT VIEW

8'

16'

(P.R.R.)
NORTHERN CENTRAL R.R.
PLAN
OF
NEW FREEDOM STATION
N.T.S.
1916

DRAWN BY: ROBERT L. WILLIAMS - 5/08/2024

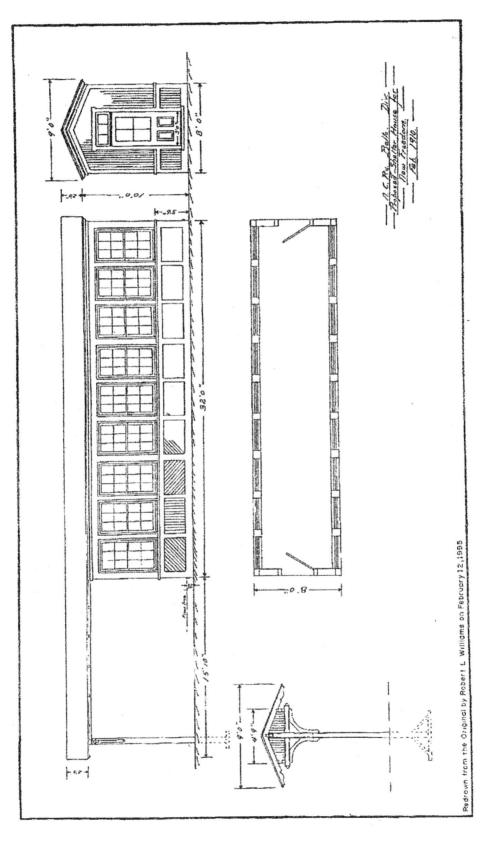

THE STEWARTSTOWN RAILROAD

-- ◆ --

APPENDIXES

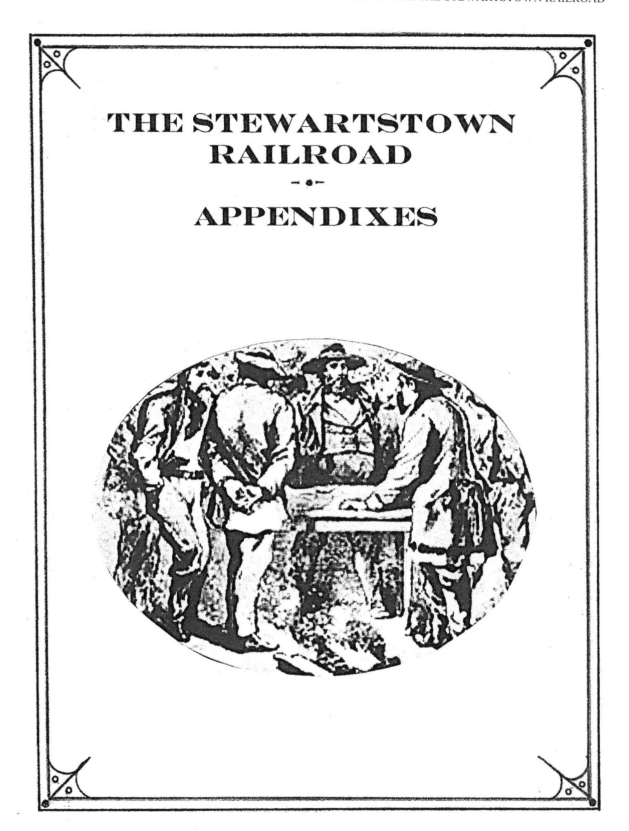

TABLE OF CONTENTS
Appendices

17	Stewartstown Railroad Pass from 1888
	Timetable from May 15, 1889
18	Stewartstown Railroad's new schedule, June 5, 1890
19	Dividend checks issued to individuals for the first six months of 1897 January 25, 1897
	A dividend check issued to John Henry Anderson, Jan. 25, 1897
20	Record of ticket sales sold at New Freedom, February 21, 1898
21	A blank report for mail transported by the railroad, 1900
22	Shipper Freight Receipt, November 10, 1901
23	Stewartstown Railroad Notice to Stockholders, December 30, 1901
24	Bill of Sale for certain assets of the N.P.&F.G.R.R, November 13, 1906
25	S.R.R. Pole Yard Agreement with the American Telephone and Telegraph Company, January 25, 1912
26	S.R.R. Notice of Storage Charges, October 30, 1919
27	Revision of Wages for the Year of 1923
28	J. G. Brill Company specification and costs of a new rail bus with photographs, April 6, 1923
29	Time Account of Trackmen, May 15, 1923
30	Train wreck as reported by the *York Dispatch*, September 20, 1923
31	Requesting Proxy from the Pennsylvania Railroad pertaining to the New Park & Fawn Grove Railroad, June 16, 1925
32	Stewartstown Railroad Timetable, April 26, 1926
33	Pennsylvania Railroad letter pertaining to the construction of the Overhead bridge at Zeigler, November 22, 1927
33b	September 1930 timetable courtesy of William Ward
34	Note from Jacob Orwig granting permission to the S.R.R to cut weeds along the right-of-way on his property, September 11, 1930
35	Specifications and a bill of sale from the Fate-Root-Heath Company for Unit No.6 gasoline engine, December 4, 1939
36	A blank shipping order form for the Stewartstown Furniture Company 1940
37	Stewartstown Railroad Annual Report, September 1, 1909
38	Stewartstown Railroad Stock Certificate, Larry Boyd, 1989

Sources:

All items in the appendices are from the archives of the Stewartstown Area Historical Society except:

     Appendix No. 28 is from the collection of Vincent Skinner.

     Appendix No. 31 is from the collection of Neal DeVoe.

Appendix No.1

STEWARTSTOWN RAILROAD

Price of Stock – May 26,1883

Theo Sykes sub
May 26th 1883
We the Subscribers promise to pay to the
Treasurer of the Stewartstown & New Freedom
RailRoad Company (when organized) the
Sum of Fifty dollars for Each and Every
Share of Stock set opposite our names.
respectively, provided that not more than
Ten dollars per Share Shall be collected within
any Consecutive period of thirty days – Nor
Shall any money be collected on this Subscription
until the whole amount necessary to construct
the road, (as shown by estimates of a reliable

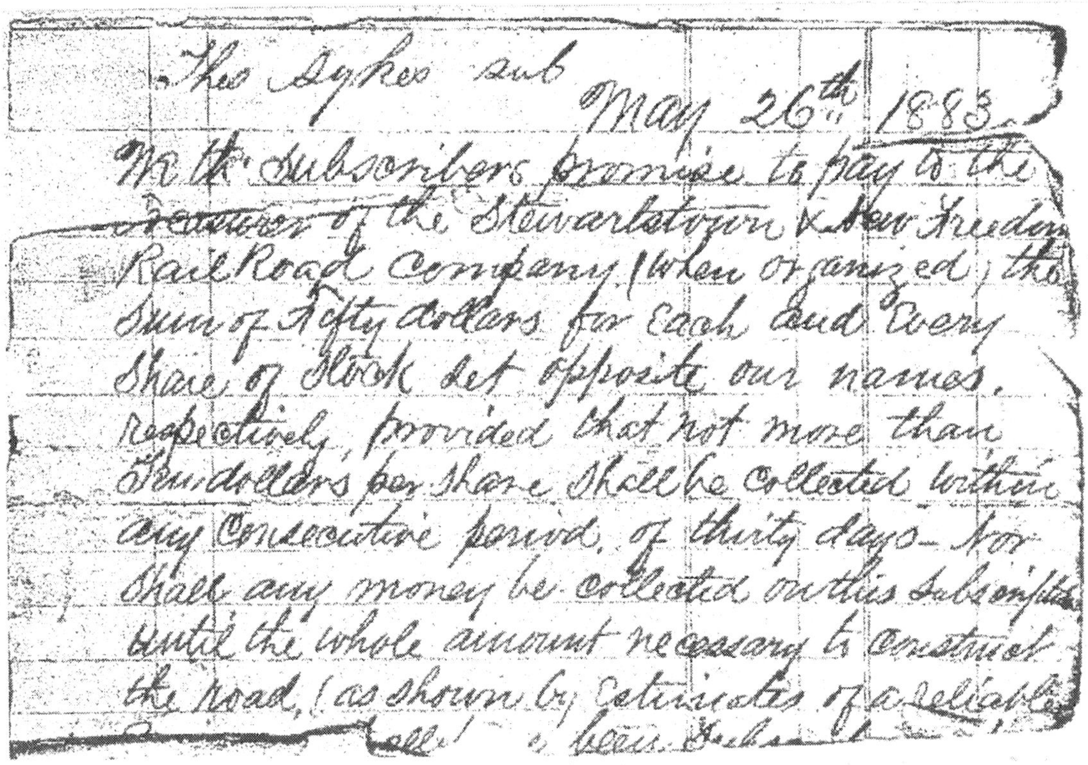

With the subscribers promise to pay to the Treasurer pf the Stewartstown & New Freedom Railroad Company when organized the sum of fifty dollars for each and every share of stock let opposite our names, respectively provided that not more than fifty dollars pert share shall be collected within any consecutive period of thirty days nor shall any money be collected on this subscription until the whole amount necessary to construct the road as shown by estimates of availability

Appendix No.2

OFFICE OF
W. BAHN,
Dealer in
Grain, Flour & Feed,
Hardware, Confectioneries,
Salt, Tobacco, Oils,
Coal & Phosphate,
RAILROAD TIES, &c., &c.,

New Freedom, Pa. Aug 4 1883

James Fulton E
Stewartstown, Pa

Dear Sir.

Owing to a press of business
it is impossible for me to attend Railroad meeting at
your place to-day. I need scarcely say that I wish the enterprise
success but would rather urge
upon all to aid in making
it a success. If all could realize how closely the success of the
Road is allied with their every
interest they would literally con-
tribute to its building, Supt
H. N. Kapp and myself will call
on you at Stewartstown sometime
during the coming week.

Appendix No. 3
STEWARTSTOWN RAILROAD
STOCK HOLDERS - 1884

NAME	NO. OF SHARES	NAME	NO. OF SHARES
Abram Anstine	5	Miss R.A. Duncan	2
Levi Altick	3	James Dorsey	1
Andrew Anderson	23	Jesse J. Downs	2
Jabco Althouse	10	John H. Ebaugh	4
John Almony	6	Adam Ebaugh	4
Jacob Allison	1	A.B. Ebaugh	2
Sylver Alliens	2	W.C. Ebaugh	6
Adam E. Anstine	6	Wm. Ehrhart	2
George Althouse	2	John L. Free	10
J.H. Anderson	2	James W. Fulton	2
John Anderson	2	J.M. Hishel	2
Henry Anstine	6	H. Haston	2
Jos. W. Anderson	50	Thos. B. Fulton	1
Reed W. Anderson	2	William Fulton	2
Anderson&Hammend	6	J.E. Foreman	1
Anderson&Gemmill	4	James Fulton	50
Wm. G. Anderson	4	W.H. Fulton	6
M.J. Arthur	2	Robert Fulton	4
Harvey J. Anderson	3	J.J. Fulton	2
John H. Bayiel	5	J.H. Fulton	2
Jacob Blouse	1	J.K. Folkomer	1
S. Bartenschlager	1	J.D. Fishel	2
John Blasser	1	John F. Fulton	1
W.W. Bell	1	Lizzie Fulton	1
Moses Breneman	3	E.W. Free	11
Jos. W. Butler	3	A.L. Grover	10
Benton J. Bell	2	J.W. Grove	3
Jas. H. Bell	3	J.S. Gemmill	2
Isaiah Bush	2	J.B. Gemmill	3
Catherine Bush	6	H.L. Green	1
Al Bowman	13	Samuel Gantz	2
Chas. Baely	1	W.A. Gilly	1
Geo. A. Barnilz	2	Mary,Ann,LouisGable	6
J.W. Billinger	1	J. Benson Gable	6
A. Bartol	4	John&Rachel Giesey	1
A.M. Berman	2	Jacob of Grove	2
Samuel Boss	1	Jacob Gilbert	1
M.W. Bahn	10	E.S. Gemmill	2
Wm. C. Conwey	1	Ames E. Green	6

Appendix No. 3
STEWARTSTOWN RAILROAD
STOCK HOLDERS - 1884

NAME	NO. OF SHARES	NAME	NO. OF SHARES
William Channel	1	John L. Griffith	1
William Giles	3	Heirs of Kerlinger	6
John Glassie	2	Benj. Keeney	5
Mrs. S.A.E Gessford	2	Henry Koller	3
E. Gilbert	1	Chas. Koller	3
Wm. H. Griffith	2	John L. Keeney	10
John A. Gehb	2	George Keesling	2
John K. Green	2	Geo. Kerlinger	1
J. Gable	1	Dr. H.B. King	3
Wm. Gibson	2	Chas. & Mary King	2
A.H. & Bro. Gore	4	Daniel Leib	8
A.H. Gore	1	Andrew Leib	8
A.S. Gemmill	2	C. Leib	6
Wm. Hammel	12	E.S. Lunoh	1
Jesse Hammel	2	Joseph S. Lanius	2
Wm. L. Hendrix	1	Wm. Leib	1
John Hyson	5	Mrs. Harriet Long	6
R.A. Hess	1	John Henry Leib	2
J.C. Hammond	6	John H. Lanius	2
A.E. Hendrick	1	Edward W. Lanius	2
H.A. Hersey	5	John S. Leib	10
Dise Hashner	3	M.W. Leib	5
John A. Horner	2	Thomas Leib	10
H. Hirshberg	2	Laben Lowe	1
Wm. H. Hartman	2	Allen S. Leib	2
Jas. Hendrix	1	Samuel C. Liggit	2
Luther Hitchcoen	2	J.B. Martin	10
John E. Houston	1	A.C. Miller	2
L.P. Hammond	6	John Marstiller	7
J.S&C.R. Hendrix	1	Henry Marstiller,Jr.	1
Chas. C. Hableston	20	Robert McDonald	5
John M. Hableston	20	Aguilla McDonald	6
John Johnson	10	Grizzele McFatridge	1
C.M. Johnson	4	E.B. McClung	3
J.L. Johnson	2	Wm. J. Mummal	4
J.A. Johnson	4	B.M. Manifold	2
J.C. Johnson	13	Jacob Myers	2
William Johnson	10	Geo. McFatridge	1
Henry Kerlinger	10	V.L. Miller	2
Wm. H. Kerns	4	H.W. McCall	5

Appendix No. 3
STEWARTSTOWN RAILROAD
STOCK HOLDERS - 1884

NAME	NO. OF SHARES	NAME	NO. OF SHARES
Henry Kurtz	3	J.G. McClellan	1
John A. Morris	1	N.Z. Seitz	1
E.M. McDonald	1	J. Shelter Stallman	4
Samuel McClane	1	M.B.&Sons Shahr	4
John E. Miller	2	W.B, Stuck	2
C.J. Noller	1	Sallie M. Spangler	2
J. Wiley Norris	3	F.T. Scott	1
William Norris	1	K.&Bros. Smith	5
A.C. Noremaker	1	Thomas Sykes	2
Henry Owing	2	Jas. Strawbridge	1
John Owing	2	R.&A. Bros. String	1
Joseph Owing	2	John A. Taylor	2
J.B. Oswald	6	Wm. Trout	1
James Poeling	2	Wm. Thomason	1
Jacob Payne	4	A.D. Thomason	2
John Henry Payne	2	Sarah Wilson	3
Cornelus Pall	1	W.H. Winemiller	3
M.E. Price	1	John L. Way	1
C.C. Pall	5	David Wiley	10
John H. Payne	2	H.P Whitcraft	2
Nickolas Ritchey	10	J.C. Wiley	2
E.H. Redding	2	William Wiley	6
Robert Ritchey	1	John Wiley	5
Peter Ruhl	1	George Winezel	1
William Sechrist	10	Jere Waltemyre	1
L. Hardy Sykes	4	Wm. L. Winter	1
Joseph L. Smith	2	C.L. Wright	2
Artimus Shaffer	5	Mrs. Ellen Wilson	1
L.D. Shaw	4	Wm. A. Wilson	1
Harrison Sutton	1	Jacob Waltemyre	6
J.A. Shaw	2	Samuel Waltemyre	8
C.W. Shaw	1	Levi Waltemyre	2
Chas. Schrist	2	A.K. Waltemyre	2
Joseph Smith	6	Wm. G. Wilson	5
John C. Strawbridge	6	D.C. Wiler	1
John C. Stansbury	3	J. Thomas Wilson	2
Mary C. Strawbridge	1	R.A. Wouldbrige&Co.	20
A.M.&F.P.Strawbridge	3	Henry&Bros.Co.Wilson	10
Wm. R. Seregent	2	F.G. Wilson	2

Appendix No. 3
STEWARTSTOWN RAILROAD
STOCK HOLDERS - 1884

NAME	NO. OF SHARES	NAME	NO. OF SHARES
Francis Sechrist	1	Robert Wilson	2
John Sechrist	1	Silas Waltemyre	2
J.V. Winemiller	2	Wm. N. Zeigler	1
J.S. Winemiller	1	Samuel Zellers	2
John Walters	1	E.H. Zeigler	10
Nathen Wiley	1	Peter Zeigler	2
J.A. Whitcraft	5	N.J. Zeigler	2
Chas. K. Yost	2	A.L. Zeigler	1
Jacob Yost	1	Jeremih Zeigler	2
William Zellars	5		

Appendix No.4

STEWARTSTOWN RAILROAD

List of Property Owners who provided the land for the Railroad Right-of-way
1883-1910

NAME	CONSIDERATION
1. Amos Baughman	Donation
2. Charles King	$100.00 - Stock
3. Mary Swartz	$185.00 - Cash
4. H. Noonemaker	$435.00 - Cash
5. C. Swartz	$35.00 - Cash
6. No Record	-----------------------
7. Jno. Habliston	$150.00 - Cash
8. Michael Creamer	$1.00 - Donation
9. Jacob Lanius	$1,645.73. - Condemnation
10. Josiah Grove	$635.00 - Condemnation
11. Mary Myers	No Record
12. John Geesey	$75.00 - Cash
13. Lewis Snerr	$200.00 - Cash
14. Samuel Keeney	$513.89 - Cash
15. John K. Keeney	$200.00 - Stock
16. Henry Sheffer	$200.00 - Cash
17. J.W. Hendrix	$1.00 - Donation
18. Artemus Sheffer	$1.00 - Donation
19. L. C. Bailey	$10.00 - Cash
20. Jno. Waltemyer, Sr.	$65.00 - Cash
21. Levi Waltemyer	$164.00 - Cash
22. Jacob Waltemyer	$1.00 - Donation
23. W.H. Krout	$10.00 - Cash
24. Jacob Owing	$25.00 - Cash
25. Henry Owing	$1.00 - Donation
26. Jas. Waltemyer	$1.00 - Donation
27. Henry Krout	$1.00 - Donation
28. Henry Waltemyer	$20.00 - Cash
29. John Waltemyer	$1.00 - Donation
30. Andrew Kashner	$30.00 - Cash
31. M. Kopp	$50.00 - Cash
32. Silas Waltemyer	$1.00 - Donation
33. Samuel Waltemyer	$1.00 - Donation
34. Henry Anstine	$1.00 - Donation
35. E. H. Zeigler	$1.00 - Donation
36. A. G. Bowman	$1.00 - Donation
37. J. W. Hendrick	$35.00 - Cash
38. John A. Whitcraft	$1.00 - Donation
39. Thomas Sykes	$1.00 - Donation

Appendix No.4
STEWARTSTOWN RAILROAD
Additional List of Owners that provided the Land for the Railroad Right-of-Way
1883-1910

NAME	AMOUNT OF LAND		CONSIDERATION
40. Micheal Creamer	76 Perches	$40.00	Oct. 20,1884
41. Est. of Geo. Griffith	No Record	$33.33	Aug. 1892
42. Wm. Griffith	68 Perches	$300.00	Apr. 12,1892
43. R.M. Richey	7 Perches	$17.50	Dec. 26,1895
44. Thos. Sykes	127 Perches	$300.00	Dec. 31,1884
45. E. W. Free	72 Perches	$300.00	Nov. 22,1886
46. Fred Helb	100 Perches	$78.12	Nov. 29,1892
47. W. H. Althouse	72 Perches	$225.00	Aug. 12,1910
48. J. A. Whitcraft	2 A. 12 Perches	$345.00	Nov. 19,1894
48. J. A. Whitcraft	5 Perches	$105.00	Nov. 19,1894
48. J. A. Whitcraft	7 Perches	$25.00	Aug. 1895
49. J. C. Bowman	----------------------	$325.00	---------------
50. J. C. Bowman	----------------------	$325.00	---------------
51. Conrad Ebauer	--	$20.00	Sept. 1894
52. Conrad Ebauer	--	$80.00	Oct. 1894
53. Silas Waltemyer	--	--	Nov. 1894
54. H. Anstine	--	--	Dec. 1894
55. Eli Zeigler	$30.00 for Land and $70.00 for damages		Dec.1894
56. W.H. Boesser	--	Rent	Feb. 13,1897
57. Silia Waltemyer	--	--	Feb. 1895
58. W.H. Boesser	--	--	July 1897
59. Conrad Ebauer	--	--	Aug. 10,1895
60. J.A. Whitcraft	--	--	Aug. 1895

Land Jacob Lanius, Turnpike, Pa., by condemnation settled thru Court at $1,645.73 plus costs $112.49 Attorney Geise Yeigler & Strawbridge. Added contract with Jacob Lanius approved Nov. 13.1886.

Appendix No.5

Northern Central Railway Company.
Office of the Vice President
Philadelphia, Pa. Sept. 3 1884

James Fulton, Esq.
Stewartstown Pa.

My dear Sir:

I have your letter of Sept. 1st in regard to your proposed road.

I shall be away from Philadelphia for a month and have placed the matter in the hands of Mr. DuBarry, 3rd Vice Prest. Penna R.R.Co. who will forward it as much as possible.

Very respectfully

Vice Prest.

Appendix No.6

The Pennsylvania Railroad Company.

OFFICE OF THE THIRD VICE PRESIDENT.

233 South Fourth Street

Philadelphia, Sept. 9th 1884.

Jas. Fulton Esq.

Stewartstown, Pa.

Dear Sir,

Your favor of 8th inst. has been received. Mr. Thomson asked me to look after this matter during his absence. I took it up last week but was unable to post myself as the Secretary Mr. White was absent from the city. I will now take it up at the earliest moment practicable.

Yours truly,

J. N. Du Barry

3 V. Prest.

Appendix No.7

Stewartstown, York Co. Pa.
Oct. 1 1884

DEAR SIR

PROPOSALS ON ENCLOSED FORM WILL BE RECEIVED
UP TO 12 O'CLOCK AT NOON, OCT. 9th. AND SHOULD
BE MARKED ON ENVELOPE "PROPOSALS",— THE ROAD, SEVEN
MILES IN LENGTH, LEADS FROM STEWARTSTOWN TO
NORTHERN CENTRAL,— CONVEYANCE CAN BE HAD
FROM SHREWSBURY STATION TO THIS PLACE.

FOR FURTHER INFORMATION ADDRESS

JAMES FULTON PRES.

THE NEW PARK & FAWN GROVE RAILROAD: INTERCHANGING WITH THE STEWARTSTOWN RAILROAD

October 9" 1884

President and Board of Directors of the
Stewartstown RailRoad.

Gentlemen:-

We propose to build and complete
your line according to the
plans & specifications and
Quantities given by your engineer
for the round Sum of $62,000.00
The company to furnish the
ties at Thirty (30) Cents a piece
also the white oak timber for
trestleing at $20.00 per Thousand.
The said Bush & Co. to furnish
the engineering at their expense
subject to Col. Stewart's orders
chief engineer of the said Company.

Hoping this may meet
with your approval, We
are   Respectfully Yours

L.L. Bush & Co.

Appendix No.8

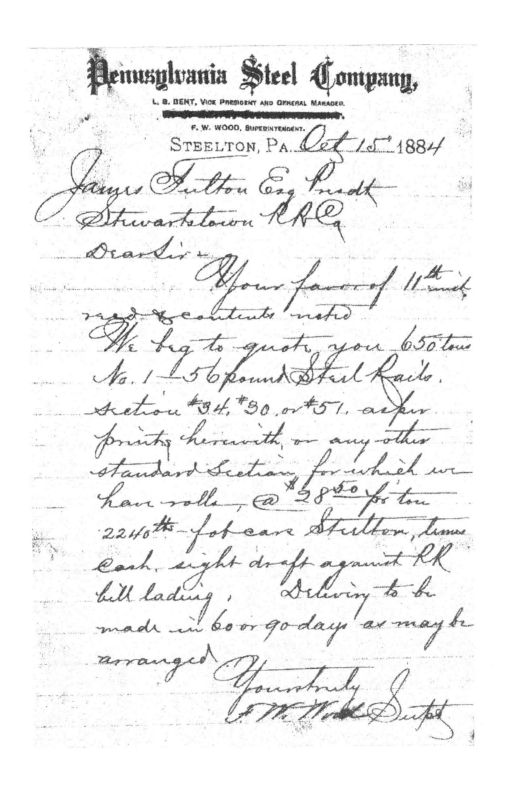

Pennsylvania Steel Company,

L. S. BENT, VICE PRESIDENT AND GENERAL MANAGER.

F. W. WOOD, SUPERINTENDENT.

STEELTON, PA. Oct 15. 1884

James Fulton Esq Presdt
Stewartstown RR Co

Dear Sir –

Your favor of 11th inst
red & contents noted
We beg to quote you 650 tons
No. 1 – 56 pound Steel Rails.
Section #34, #30, or #51, as per
prints herewith, or any other
standard Section for which we
have rolls, @ $28.50 per ton
2240 ℔ – fob cars Steelton, terms
cash, sight draft against RR
bill lading. Delivery to be
made in 60 or 90 days as may be
arranged. Yours truly
F. W. Wood Supt

Appendix No.8

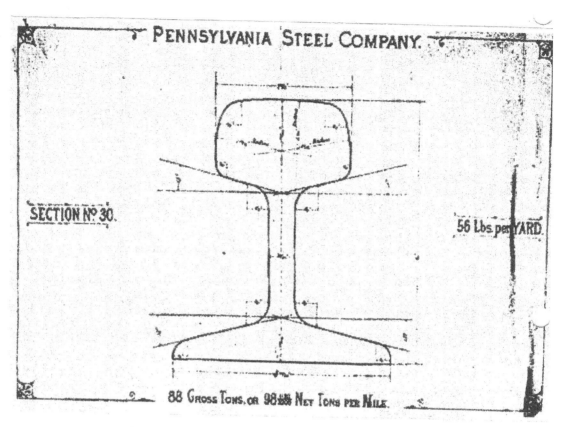

Appendix No.9

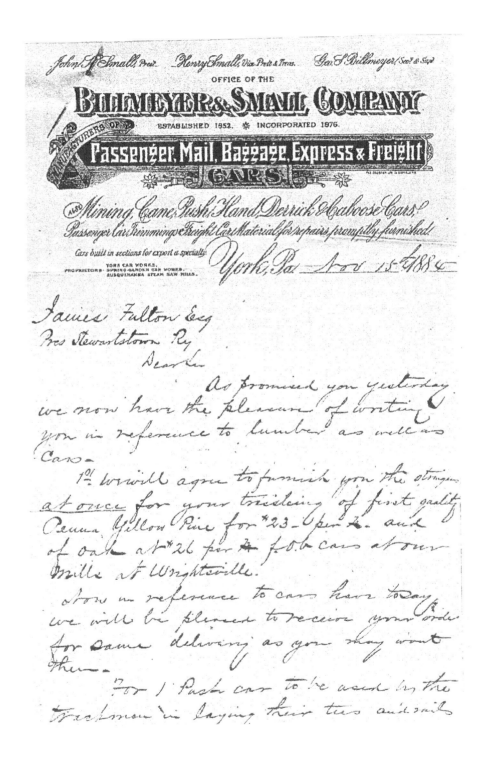

Appendix No.9

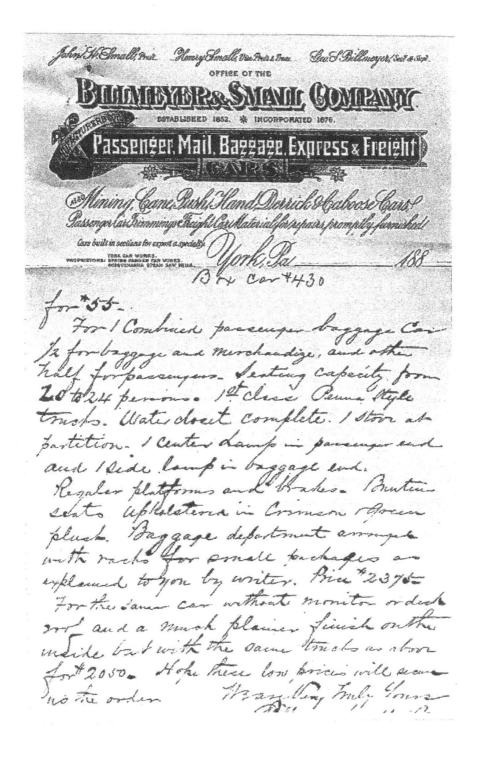

Appendix No.10

Baldwin Locomotive Works

Burnham, Parry, Williams & Co.

Philadelphia, January 19th, 1885.

George Burnham
Charles T. Parry
Edward H. Williams
William P. Henszey
Edward Longstreth
John H. Converse

Mr. James Fulton,

      Prest., Stewartstown Railroad Co.,

        Stewartstown, Pa.

Dear Sir:

    Your valued favor of the 16th inst. is at hand. We note that you require a locomotive to draw a train of four cars each loaded with fifteen tons, up a grade of 118ft. per mile, combined with curves of 573ft. radius.

    It would require a locomotive having about 40,000 lbs. on the driving wheels, and otherwise properly proportioned, to do this work. There is no difficulty whatever in doing the work with a double-ender locomotive. No possible objection can lie against such an engine on the score either of safety or economy. There is, of course, a general prejudice in favor of a locomotive having a separate tender; this is largely on the score of convenience. The separate tender gives so much more room for carrying tools, &c., that where an engine is to be turned at the end of the run, an engine and tender are most popular. If, however, you propose to work the line with a double-ender engine, without turning at the termini, the best form of double-ender would be one as

Appendix No.10

BALDWIN LOCOMOTIVE WORKS.
BURNHAM, PARRY, WILLIAMS & CO.
PHILADELPHIA, PA.

SHEET ....

TO ....

per enclosed photograph of "Park & Ocean" No. 7. This has a truck at each end which will protect the driving tires from excessive wear, and enable the engine to pass short curves without difficulty. We have just built four such locomotives for a road in California, where at last accounts they were working with entire satisfaction.

We enclose proposal and Specification No. 2092 for a similar locomotive. Its weight is somewhat greater than you specify, but in order to provide for all emergencies, and have ample power for your heavy grade, we are inclined to think that it would not be expedient to use a much lighter engine.

If, however, you decide on a lighter engine, we will build you a similar engine with cylinders 14" x 22", 800 gallon tank, and weighing in working order about 58,000 lbs with 46,000 lbs. on the driving wheels for Fifty-two hundred and fifty Dollars ($5250) delivered here.

Hoping to be favored with your commands, we remain.

Very truly yours,

Burnham, Parry & Williams Co.

Appendix No.10

Proposal.

Baldwin Locomotive Works,

Philadelphia, Pa. January 19ᵗʰ, 1885.

We hereby propose and agree to construct for the *Stewartstown Railroad Company*, and deliver same on *track* in *Philadelphia*, One (1) locomotive as per *Specification No. 2092*

Class 8/24¼ C.

Shipment will be made in *forty-five days after order* as nearly as may be, delays by strikes, fires or other unforeseen contingencies excepted.

We will guarantee the locomotive to be built of the best materials of the respective kinds named in the specification, and of the best workmanship. All important parts will be made to gauges, and accurately interchangeable among any number of locomotives of the same class. We will also guarantee the locomotive to be able to draw *145* tons, of 2240 pounds, of cars and lading, up a grade of *118* feet per mile, *combined with curve of 573' radius*, ~~without of the curves of curve~~, cars and track being in good condition.

On arrival of the locomotive at destination our engineer will take charge of putting same in working order, all necessary assistance and supplies being furnished by the company purchasing, and will run same one or more trips on trial. If found in accordance with contract, when the locomotive is ready for service, he will then deliver same to the company and take the company's receipt therefor.

Air brakes, headlights, and other special appliances are not included in price unless specially stated to the contrary in this proposal or accompanying specification.

The price of *the* locomotive constructed and delivered as above, will be *Fifty-four hundred dollars* ($5,400.⁰⁰) and such amount will be due and payable, in Eastern funds, for *said* locomotive when same *has* been delivered and put in working order by our engineer.

This proposal is submitted only for acceptance at this time.

A written acceptance of this proposal will constitute a sufficient contract.

Very Respectfully,

Burnham Parry Williams & Co.

Appendix No.11

~~Northern Central Railway Co.~~

#75 Oak Street, Baltimore, Md., ~~Station,~~

May 23rd 1885

Jas. Fulton Esq,
            President Stewartstown Ry. Co.

Dear Sir,
            Your kind favor of 20th inst.
to hand — & in regard to my application
for a position as Locomotive Engineer on your
Road. — If you please, I
desire my application to be placed before
the Board.

In regard to my qualifications, I have
permission to refer to my former Employers,
the Officers of the Balt. Div. N.C.Ry.

As to my wages, I am willing to Engage
for $2.50 per day.

But if this proposition be not
Satisfactory, pls. advise me at once
and let me know what you are willing
to pay.   Respy. Yours,
                        Jacob Rider

Appendix No.12

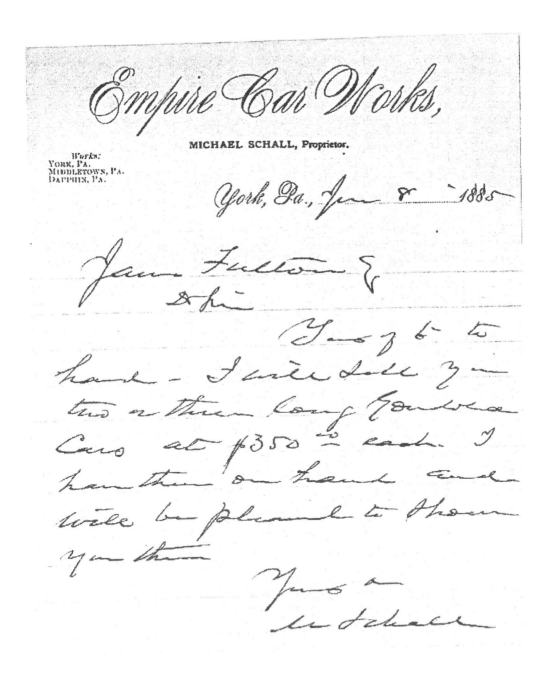

Appendix No.13

Stewartstown RRR Co Jun 19/85

BALDWIN LOCOMOTIVE WORKS.
BURNHAM, PARRY, WILLIAMS & CO., PHILADELPHIA.

No. 2092   GENERAL SPECIFICATION.   Class 8-24¼ C

PLAN — As accompanying photograph of *Park & Ocean*   (Drawing No. 1)

PRINCIPAL DIMENSIONS — Cylinders *15* x *22*   Driving wheels *48* inches outside diameter. Centres *43* inches diameter. Driving axle journals *6½* inches diameter and *8* inches long. Total wheel base of engine *21* feet *7* inches. Driving wheel base *7* feet *0* inches.

GAUGE AND FUEL — Gauge of Track *4* feet *8½* inches. Fuel *soft coal.*

WEIGHT — In working order; total, about *74,000* pounds; on driving wheels about *50,000* pounds.

BOILER — Of best Pennsylvania cold blast charcoal flange iron *⅜* inch thick, or best homogeneous cast steel *9⁄16* inch thick form *straight* with _____ dome placed *about middle of* waist *46* inches diameter at smoke-box end and telescoping back. All horizontal seams, and junction of waist and fire-box double-riveted. Caulking done with round-pointed tools. Boiler tested to 180 pounds per square inch by hot water pressure.

TUBES — Of *charcoal iron 131* in number, *2.⅛* inches diameter, and *10* feet *8* inches long.

FIRE-BOX — *54* inches long and *34½* inches wide inside. Of best homogeneous cast steel; side and back sheets *3⁄16* inch thick; crown sheet *⅜* inch thick; flue sheet *½* inch thick.

STACK AND GRATES — Stack *diamond*   Grates *cast iron*   Smoke-box *ordinary*

FRAMES — Of best hammered iron; main frames forged solid, and front and back lugs forged on front rails for securing cylinders in place. Pedestal caps lugged and bolted to bottom pedestals.

TRUCKS — *Two* wheeled truck with wrought iron frame, bridges and braces, and centre-bearing swivelling bolster. Double plate chilled wheels *28* inches diameter. Axles of best hammered iron; with journals *4½* inches diameter and *7½* inches long.

CYLINDERS — Of close-grained hard iron; each cylinder cast in one piece with half-saddle; placed horizontally or nearly so; right and left-hand horizontal cylinders made to same pattern and interchangeable.

PISTONS — Heads and followers of cast iron, with babbited brass rings and springs, or most approved steam packing. Piston rods of cold rolled iron or steel.

GUIDES AND CROSSHEADS — GUIDES.—Of steel or wrought iron case-hardened. CROSSHEADS.—Cast from close-grained hard iron, with babbited bearings.

VALVE MOTION — Shifting link motion; all parts of best hammered iron well case-hardened.

TIRES — Of best cast steel *2½* inches thick *all*   flanged *5½* inches wide

AXLES — Driving and engine truck axles of best hammered iron, forged from No. 1 scrap.

DRIVING BOXES — Of cast iron, with babbited brass bearings.

CONNECTING & SIDE RODS — Of best hammered iron, forged solid from No. 1 scrap, and furnished with all necessary straps, keys and brasses.

WRISTPINS & SPRINGS — WRISTPINS.—Of best cast steel. SPRINGS.—Driving and truck springs of best cast steel, tempered in oil.

FEEDWATER — Supplied by one brass pump and one injector, or two pumps or two injectors.

CAB & PILOT. — CAB.—Of hard wood put together with joint bolts and corner plates. PILOT.—Of wood, braced with iron.

FINISH — Cylinder casings of *iron painted* cylinder heads of cast iron, polished or painted; steam chest casings of *iron painted* steam chest tops of cast iron; dome casing of *iron painted* ; _____ ; running board nosings of angle iron; wheel cover nosings of *brass* . Boiler jacketed with best planished iron, secured by brass or iron bands.

FURNITURE — Engine furnished with sand-box, bracket and shelf for head-lamp, bell, whistle, heater, blower, and safety-valves, steam gauge, cab lamp, gauge cocks, oil cans, tallow pot, two jack-screws and levers, one pinch-bar, a complete set of wrenches to fit all bolts and nuts on engine, one monkey-wrench, hammer, chisels, cab-seat, poker, scraper, and slice bar.

GAUGES — All principal parts of engine accurately fitted to gauges and templates, and thoroughly interchangeable.

TANK — *900* gallons capacity, carried on *boiler*   Tender frame

Trucks

Chilled wheels _____ inches diameter. Springs, best cast steel, tempered in oil. Axles of best hammered iron. Journals _____ inches diameter and _____ inches long.

Appendix No.13

The Baldwin Locomotive Works sent this photograph of the New York & Sea Beach Railroad engine along with the general specifications to the Stewartstown Railroad for review.

From the collection of the Stewartstown Area Historical Society

Appendix No.14

Northern Central Railway Company.

New Freedom Station, *July 27, 1885*

James Hilton Esq
President
S. C. R. R. Co

Dear Sir,

Capn Frank Kuhn telephones me to notify you he will be here tomorrow morning via 8.36 am Train. He expects you to provide for him in some way to carry him to the Stewartstown. I would like to go to the meeting and will do so if possible. Need I send any for Provision of our subscribers here? Is there anything as issue that they might be needed?

Yours truly,
M. W. Bailey

APPENDIX No.15
STEWARTSTOWN RAILROAD
REQUEST FOR TICKETS FOR THE GRAND OPENING – AUGUST 31,1885

CARD NUMBER	NAME
283	WILLIAM HAMMER-BALTIMORE
284	M. HALL-BALTIMORE
285	C. THOMAS-BALTIMORE
286	R. HALL-BALTIMORE
287	WM. M. McDONALD-BALTIMORE
288	J. WILEY-BALTIMORE
289	MRS. KARSIN-SPRING GROVE
290	JAS. T. BAYLIES-#330 N. EDEN
291	MRS. JAS T. BAYLIES-#330 N. EDEN
292	AUGUST ECK-JEFFERSON ST.
293	MRS AUGUST ECK-JEFFERSON ST.
294	MRS. EMMA MUSSEE-FRONT ST.

Stewartstown, Pa. Aug. 31. 1885.

Mr. Wm. Hammer

DEAR SIR

Please find enclosed *12* complimentary tickets and card orders, to opening of STEWARTSTOWN R. R. be kind enough to insert on ticket, the name of friends, [to whom you present them] and also name and address on slip below to correspond with number of card order. Detach slip and return to me promptly; also return by September 10th all card orders not used.

YOURS TRULY

Charles T. Wright,
CHAIRMAN EX. COM.

Card no. 283, William Hammer. Balto,
" 284 M Hall "
" 285 C Thompson "
" 286 R Hall "
" 287 Wm McDonald "
288 J Wiley "
289 mrs Karsin Spring &c
290 Jay T Baylies, 330 N. Eden
291 mrs Jas T Baylies " Jefferson
292 August Eck "
293 mrs " " Front St
294 mrs Emma Mussee

Appendix No.16

STEWARTSTOWN RAILROAD

FORMAL OPENING OF THE NEW ROAD

A Large Gathering and Interesting Ceremonies – A Hospitable People – History of the Successful Undertaking – Speeches and Incidents

----

As reported on September 18,1885 by The York Daily

Over four thousand strangers gather at Stewartstown yesterday to attend the formal opening of the new Stewartstown railroad. Early in the morning the northern and southern bound trains on the Northern Central railroad brought hundreds of persons to New Freedom who had heard of the wonderful origin and completion of this superb piece of railroad, and were curious to see not only the road itself, but the clear-headed and indefatigable people who originated, engineered and completed its construction.

THE STEWARTSTOWN RAILROAD

At New Freedom, a pleasant little town just north of the Maryland line, the road joints the Northern Central railroad, at which place preparations are new being made for the erection of a most commodions and comfortable union depot. The curious visitors took the trains in waiting, to have their first ride on, and observation of, the Stewartstown railroad. Leaving New Freedom by a regular but slightly up grade, the well equipped and heavily loaded trains, drawn by a first class engine which was managed by Jacob Gitt, an engineer who evidently understood both hi business and his duty thoroughly, proceeded smoothly along through a rolling country noted for its fertility and unexcelled qualities of production, past several station houses to Stewartstown, its terminus, and the place in and around which reside its able and indefatigable originators and managers. The road is laid with the best white oak ties and steel rails, and is trestled, bridged and graded in the best and most substantial modern style, and is equipped with rolling stock equal to the larger and more costly thoroughfares of the country; and the most remarkable feature about it is that its whole cost was not more than eight thousand dollars per mile. It opens up in direct communication with the markets of the country a country unexcelled in agricultural productiveness, and places in immediate communication with the world a people who will compare favorably in point of intelligence with those of any rural district in the United States. The very feat of constructing such a railroad through a rolling country and equipping it in the manner that the Stewartstown railroad is, at the cost of only $50,000.00, paid for when completed, without either mortgage or bond, evidences the mental clearness, the thoughtful foresight, and honest and careful management as just such people have who live in and about this pleasant little village of

STEWARTSTOWN.

Appendix No.16

Stewartstown has a population of about four hundred inhabitants and bears striking evidence of the thrift, neatness and intelligence of its inhabitants. It has an academy at which a majority of its present inhabitants received their preliminary education, and the influence of which has been felt throughout all the surrounding country and which very probably is the cause of the intelligent management of the superb farming done in this neighborhood. This academy is still doing it good work under the able direction of Prof. Wright, it esteemed and intellectual principal. The inhabitants, many of whom came from that substantial class of people known as the Scotch-Irish, with a sprinkling of sturdy German and honorable Welshmen among them, form a community which combine almost all the hereditary traits of progressive humanity, wit, energy, enterprise, deliberation, and honor. Quite recently Mr. Robert Richey has started up a planning mill in the town, and with the advantage of the new railroad we may well expect more industries and a consequent improvement and enlargement of Stewartstown. Just southeast of the town and adjoining the Presbyterian church is situated the pleasant grove of Mr. Nicholas Richey, in which was held the

FORMAL OPENING OF THE ROAD.

After alighting from the train which bore us from New Freedom, the visitors were escorted to this grove by the Shrewsbury cornet and Logansville bands, and there were found hundreds of others who had congregated from the surrounding country, north and south of the Mason and Dixon's line. Vehicles and conveyances of various kinds and styles greeted the visions on all sides, and one swarming crowd surrounded the speakers' stand and filled the seats that had been prepared for their accommodation. Everything was systematized and prefect order prevailed, through the direction of Col. Fulton and his lieutenants, and the gentlemanly management of the Morrison G.A.R. Post, of Stewartstown, who were on duty throughout the day. Soon a call to order was made by Col. Fulton, the president of the railroad, from the stand, and Col Levi Maish, of York, being nominated was unanimously chosen President of the meeting. The Colonel responded with a good speech and proceeded to gracefully wield the duties of his position. The following officers were than chosen:
Vice Presidents-John S. Leib, Wm. H. Stevenson, Henry Wilcox, C.W. Slagle, all of Baltimore; Michael Schall, York; Jos S. Gitt, New Oxford; John Johnson, Hopewell township; L.Y. Diller, East Berlin. Secretaries – N.Z. Seitz, Glen Rock; Thomas J. Hunt, Towsontown, Md.

THE ADDRESS OF WELCOME

After this the president introduced Jos. R. Strawbridge, Esq, junior counsel of the company, who delivered the address of welcome, he spoke of the difficulties of railway construction and of the peculiar difficulties which had been encounter in bring the Stewartstown road to a successful completion.
He also gave a brief history of the road, which will no doubt be of interest to many. He said: "Previous to the location and construction of the York and Peach bottom road, the building of a railroad from the Susquehanna River at Peach bottom to some point on the Northern Central railroad was agitated the citizens of Shrewsbury, Hopewell, Fawn. Peach bottom and Lower Chanceford townships. Large and enthusiastic meetings were held all along the proposed line and much interest in the new enterprise was awakened.

Appendix No.16

You are welcomed by a people whose resources and energies, long struggling for proper development and direction, are at last connected with the marts of trade, the humming life and activity of the world of business, and the educating and refining influences of metropolitan social conditions. And, finally, you are welcomed by a people whose gratitude for your appreciation for their hospitality, they promise, will be abundantly manifested in time to come by an intellectual and conscientious application of their awakened business and social talents to the new and salient opportunities with which a kind Providence endowed them.

OTHER ADDRESSES

Mr. Strawbridge's speech was an example of conciseness and attractive oratory highly commended by all who listened to it. The gentleman who had been selected to respond to the address of welcome not being present, the meeting was adjourned for dinner, until 2 o'clock p.m. Repairing to the elaborately spread and bountifully supplied tables, which were furnished and waited upon by many ladies from the surrounding country, we found the same systematic arrangement to avoid confusion which pervaded the whole exercises throughout the day, and which did so much to render them the complete success that they were. After filling ourselves almost too full for utterance and watching the surrounding crowd do the same, we sauntered around and mingled with the good nature crowd, talking "railroad" until the afternoon exercises. Promptly at 2 o'clock the president introduced H.C. Niles, Esq. of York, who, he stated, had been prevailed upon, in the absence of expected speakers, to respond to the address of welcome. Mr. Niles stated that under the peculiar circumstances which surround him on this occasion, he could not be expected to acquit himself as he would desire. That when spoken to and requested to respond to the able address of welcome which he had heard his Brother Strawbridge deliver, his heart sank within him. Mr. Niles spoke for about a half an hour, commending and eulogizing the enterprise and the energy of building of the Stewartstown railroad, truly characterizing it as the greatest piece of railroad work ever done, and applying its production to the influence and direct effect of the intelligent creators. His speech was attentively listened to and was indeed a happy impromptu. Other able and interesting speeches were then delivered by John F. Thomas of York, Judge Ebaugh of Stewartstown, whose humor and pointed sense was felt and enjoyed by the attentive audience, and Prof. S.G. Boyd, of York, James Fulton, the honored president of the road, being called upon responded in a most interesting speech, giving a condensed history of the road and the many trials incident to its completion, and such valuable data as only one connected with the enterprise as he has been, could give. His speech was full and interesting and was warmly applauded at its close. Joseph Gitt, of New Oxford, Adams County, and the original surveyor of the road, was then pressed upon the stand, and compelled to relate his experience with the road and survey. Rev. B.F. Stevens, one of the originators of the project, and who was referred to in the able address of welcome, then spoke, and was followed by Prof. Wright, of Stewartstown. Thus closed the successful opening exercises of a most successful enterprise—and indeed Col. Fulton and the other friends and managers of this admirable undertaking cannot but be congratulated on their liberal spirit of enterprise, which has so culminated in a decided and growing benefit to all their country round about.

Appendix No.16

Mr. Shoaf, a Lancaster engineer, made a survey from a point on the Northern Central, near Hanover Junction, as far east as Stewartstown; but the grade proving to heavy, a farther survey was abandoned and with it any further attempt to construct a road between the two points named.

On a stormy day in the winter of 1871-72, Mr. Thomas Sykes, an enterprising citizen of Stewartstown as well as a skilled mechanic, with his mason's level traced a railroad line over the hills from New Freedom to Stewartstown and claimed that the building of a railroad between the points named was not impracticable. In the same winter, in February, Mr. James Fulton, the energetic and indefatigable president of the Stewartstown railroad, on the strength of Mr. Sykes' opinion, procured a leveling instrument from the Northern Central Company, and assisted by the late Col. Fulton, made a trail survey which satisfied him that the road was feasible.

Not much, however, was done in the way of an organized effort to build the road until early in 1883. At the instance of Rev. B.F. Stevens, the anniversary of Washington's Birthday, February 22, 1883, was observed by a dinner at Stewartstown hotel. Fifty or sixty leading citizens participated. After the dinner among other toasts, one referring to a prospective railroad from New Freedom to Stewartstown, was responded to by Thomas Leib, Esq., an official of the Northern Central Company.

After his response one of the party proposed to suspend for a time the regular toasts and by the appointment of a committee set in motion on the community an attempt to build the road. This proposal was heartily agreed to and the committee appointed.

The proposed road was talked about in public and private. Meetings were held, and early in the summer of the same year an organization was affected, a survey and estimate of cost made, and subscriptions of stock taken.

It was part of the agreement with the subscribers for stock that not a dollar was to be paid until all the stock necessary by the estimate to build the road had been taken. As this obviated the necessity of mortgaging the road, confidence in the management was inspired, and the subscriptions were liberal and the payment prompt.

The grading of the road as begun in the fall of 84. Track laying was commenced at New Freedom on the 2nd day of June of this year and on the 2nd day of the present month the last rail was laid and the last spike driven at Stewartstown.

Mr. Strawbridge, after speaking at some length of the great benefits to be derived by the community from the road, said: "The people who have done this thing are convinced that God help those who help themselves, and they rejoice today in the work of their own hands. Conscious of a baptism elevated progress they meet you with open hearts and a cordial greeting. They feel and know that the day of their deliverance from the absurd condition of living civilization of the 18th century in the blazing noon of the 19th is at hand. They delight in the joys of conscious strength and welcome you all with feelings of self-congratulation, yet self-congratulation that is divorced from all selfishness. You are welcomed by a people filled with new ideas and awakened to new purposes: a people stirred by new hopes and quickened by the enchantment of an elevating, material achievement. You are welcome to the presence of a community whose most lovely dream has become a tangible existence and whose most cherished ambition has been fully realized.

Appendix No.16

No more powerful agent of commercial enhancement has ever been noted in the history of the world than the railroads. They are the true propagators of intelligence and developers of commercial resource. Improvement and financial benefit invariably follow in their wake, and happy must be the consequences of a railroad originated and completed under plans so remarkably independent, novel and successful as this one. We say to the people of Stewartstown and their railroad *esto perpetua*.

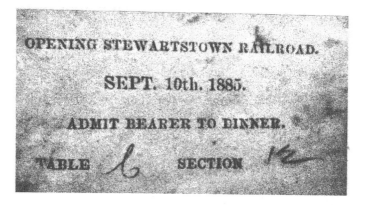

A Ticket for the Grand Opening Celebration of the Stewartstown Railroad
From the collection of Robert Williams

Stewartstown Railroad Engine No.1 - "Hopewell" sitting in New Freedom, Pa. – ca.1890.
From the collection of the Stewartstown Area Historical Society

Appendix No.17

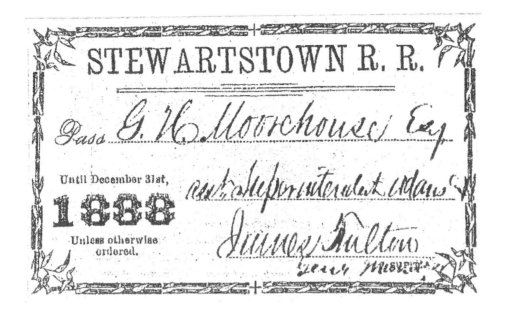

TIME TABLE

STEWARTSTOWN RAILROAD.

NEW SCHEDULE - To Take Effect May 15th, 1889.

STATIONS.	TRAINS GOING WEST.			TRAINS GOING EAST		
	No. 1.	No. 3.	No. 5.	No. 2.	No. 4.	No 6
	A. M.	A.M.	P M.	A. M.	P. M.	P M
STEWARTSTOWN, ... Leave	5 30	11 30	5 00	Ar. 7.00	2 05	6 45
ZIEGLER, ... "	5.33	....	5.03	6 57	....	6.42
REIMOLD, ... "	5 35	....	5.05	6.55		6 40
ORWIG, ... "	5 37	11 36	5 07	6.53	1 50	6.38
ANSTINE, ... "	5.39	.....	5.09	6 51	....	6 35
DEER BROOK... ..... "	5.41	....	5 11	6.48	....	6 32
SHEFFER, ... "	5 45	11.44	5.15	6 44	1 50	6.28
KEENEY ... . "	5 49	....	5.18	6 42	....	6 26
TURNPIKE, ... "	5 52	11 50	5 22	6 39	1 45	6.23
HABLISTON, ... "			....	....	....	....
NEW FREEDOM. ..... Arrive	5 58	11.56	5 28	Lv. 6.33	1.39	6.17

These trains connect for all points South at New Freedom with the York Accommodation, 6.30 a. m.; Washington Passenger 4.37 p. m.; Day Express, 6.32 p. m., and for points North with News Express, 6.12 a. m; Fast Line, 12.03 p. m; Harrisburg Passenger, 6 13 p m. Tickets sold and baggage checked to and from all points between Baltimore and Harrisburg. Trains do not stop at stations where time is omitted on the above table. Train No 7 will carry Express Goods for points North or South on the Northern Central. Train No. 3 will carry Express Goods for points South only. Train No. 5 will carry Express Goods for points North only.

JAMES FULTON, General Manager.   JOHN H GEMMILL, Superintendent.

Appendix No.18

Stewartstown Railroad.

NEW SCHEDULE
To take effect June 5th, 1890.

Trains leave	No1 A.M.	No3 A.M.	No5 P.M.		No2 A.M.	No4 P.M.	No6 P.M.	
Stewartstown,	5.30	12. 5	4.32	Trains moving West	7.00	2.15	6.15	Trains moving East
Ziegler,	5.33	....	4.35		6.57	.....	6.10	
Rennold,	5.35	....	4.37		6.55	.....	6.08	
Orwig,	5.37	12.21	4.39		6.53	2.08	6.06	
Austine,	5.39	....	4.41		6.51	.....	6.03	
Deer Brook,	5.41	....	4.43		6.48	.....	6.00	
Shoffer,	5.45	12.29	4.47		6.41	1.58	5.56	
Keeney,	5.48	....	4.50		6.42	.....	5.54	
Turnpike,	5.52	12.35	4.54		6.39	1.53	5.51	
Hahnston,	......	....	......		......	.....	.....	
New Freedom,	5.58	12.41	5.00		6.33	1.47	5.45	

These trains connect for all points South at New Freedom with the Accommodation, 6.40 A. M. Fast Line, 6.10 A M., arriving in Baltimore at 7.2 A M.; Way Passenger, 1.45 P. M. Day Express, 5 2 P. M., and for points North with News Express, 6 1 A. M, Fast Line, 1.04 P. M., Harrisburg Passenger 5,15 P. M. Tickets sold and baggage checked to all points between Baltimore and Harrisburg. Train No 6 connects with Cincinnati and St. Louis Express. leaving Union Station, Baltimore, at 4.32 P. M., and runs to New Freedom without stopping.

June 5, 1890.   John B Gemmill, Supt.

Appendix No.19

STEWARTSTOWN RAILROAD – INDIVIUALS RECEIVING DIVIDEND CHECKS FOR JANUARY 25,1897

(Note: July 24, 1897 Dividend payments for each individual not listed)

Levi Attig - $2.00
Silves Althouse - $2.00
Jno. H. Anderson - $2.00
John Anderson - $2.00
Jos. W. Anderson - $66.00
Reed W. Anderson - $2.00
J. Harvey Anderson – $3.00
W.W. Bell - $5.00
Isaiah Bush - $2.00
A.G. Bowman - $20.00
Geo. A. Barnitz - $22.00
Jno. W. Bittinger - $1.00
A.M. Bartol – $4.00
M.W. Bahn - $10.00
A.M. Borman - $2.00
National Bank of Baltimore - $50.00
A.K. Diehl - $1.00
Jess I. Downs - $2.00
W.H. Emig - $6.00
Dr. W. C. Ebaugh - $9.00
Ella N. Ebaugh - $1.00
Adam Ebaugh - $4.00
J.J. Fulton - $2.00
Dr. E.W. Free - $24.00
Thos. B. Fulton – 1.00
Jno. M. Fishel - $2.00
H. Freeston - $2.00
W.H. Fulton - $7.00
J.H. Folckemmer - $1.00
Estate of James Fulton - $111.00
Joseph Freeland - $4.00
John Fulton - $1.00
Mary J. Fulton of R. - $4.00
Annie M. Fulton - $2.00
Lida Leib - $2.00
Mary J. Fulton of J. - $2.00
James Fulton & Sons - $53.00
James Fulton & Sons Vo. - $13.00
Caleb Freeland - $4.00
Anna Gable - $1.0
Israel Gable - $7.00

S.A.E. Gessford - $2.00Jno. K. Grover - $2.00
W.J. Gemmill - $10.00
A.T. Grove - $5.00
Sallie G. Hendrix - $2.00
Jess Hammer - $2.00
Wm. Hammer - $11.00
R.J. Hess - $3.00
H. Dise Co. – $3.00
W. Hollauder & Co. - $2.00
Estate of Chas. C. Habliston - $20.00
Est. of Henry K. Houston - $190.00
Annie M. Huber - $4.00
Maria Johnson - $2.00
John Johnson - $10.00
C.M. Johnson - $4.00
Jos. A. Johnson - $4.00
W.B. King - $3.00
J.R.W. Keesey - $1.00
Estate of Albert Kraft - $2.00
Horace Keesey - $3.00
Elizabeth Kraft - $3.00
Henry Kerlinger - $10.00
Henry Kurtz - $4.00
Benj. Keeny - $6.00
Jno. Y. Keeny - $24.00
W.C. Koller - $2.00
Estate of Andrew Leib - $8.00
Christian Leib - $6.00
Joseph Lanius - $2.00
Harriet R. Long - $6.00
Jno. H. Leib - $3.00
Catherine A. Leib - $90.00
Samuel C. Liggit - $2.00
Z.K. Loucks - $10.00
Jno. H. Lanius - $2.00
E.W. Lanius - $2,00
J.R. Martin - $12.00
E.B. McClung - $3.00
V. T. Miller - $2.00
H.W. McCall - $3.00

Appendix No.19

STEWARTSTOWN RAILROAD – INDIVIUALS RECEIVING DIVIDEND CHECKS FOR JANUARY 25,1897

(Note: July 24, 1897 Dividend payments for each individual not listed)

M. Gotwalt - $1.00
Jno. A. Morrison - $1.00
Lizzie Meise - $5.00
J. Wiley Norris - $3.00
Charles Newman - $10.00
Albert M. Owen - $1.00
J.B. Oswald - $2.00
C.W. Coe - $4.00
J.W. Payne - $4.00
Peter Rubl - $1.00
Raymond Campbell - $4.00
Susie E. Rhodes - $20.00
Jno. R. Sechrist - $1.00
W.T. Bay Stewart - $200.00
Wm. Sechrist - $6.00
L.H. Sykes - $4.00
Artemas Sheffer - $5.00
Joseph Smith - $6.00
Wm. R. Sergeant - $2.00
Wm. Sechrist - $1.00
H. Shetter - $4.00
M.B. Spahr - $6.00
J.H. Smith - $5.00
Thomas Sykes - $4.00
Chas. W. Slagle - $2.00
Kate R. Slagle - $2.00
J.W. Slagle - $2.00
C. Virginia Schall - $14.00
Wesley B. Snyder - $3.00
C.W. Shaw - $3.00
Estate of Dr. J.A. Taylor - $2.00

Wm. Trout - $1.00
Asa J. Vansant - $6.00
Estate of Sarah J. Wilson - $3.00
Wm. H. Winemiller - $3.00
Jno. C. Wiley - $3.00
Catherine B. Welsh - $2.00
Mary E. Wiley - $5.00
Addie Wilson - $2.00
Wm. S. Wilson - $5.00
Francis G. Wilson - $6.00
Henry Wilcox & Bro. – $10.00
F.P. Whitcraft - $25.00
Robert Wilson - $2.00
J.V. Winemiller - $4.00
Sarah H. C. Welhelm - $9.00
Isabel S. W. Wilhelm - $10.00
Elizabeth B. Wilhelm - $14.00
J. Thos. Wilson - $5.00
A.K. Waltmyer. - $2.00
Jacob Yost - $1.00
Chas. K. Yost - $2.00
Wm. N. Zeigler - $1.00
Wm. Zellers - $5.00

TOTAL DIVIDEND PAYOUT FOR 1897;
JAN. 25,1897 - $1,400.00
JULY 24,1897 - $1,394.00
TOTAL - $2,794.00

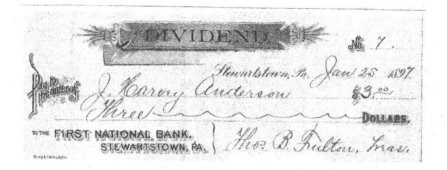

Appendix No.20

STEWARTSTOWN RAILROAD COMPANY.

No. 18

Reports of Tickets Sold at _New Freedom_ Station, for _2. 21._ 1898

DESTINATION.	PROGRESSIVE NOS. Commencing	PROGRESSIVE NOS. Closing	NUMBER WHOLE TICKETS.	WHOLE TO BLANK TICKETS.	EXCURSION TICKETS.	HALF TICKETS.	TOTAL NO. OF TICKETS ISSUED.	RATE.	AMOUNT. Dollars	Cents
Stewartstown Reg.	1274									
Stewartstown Ex.										
Ziegler's	12									
Reinold.										
Orwigs.	50									
Anstine.										
Sheffers.										
Keeneys.	570									
Turnpike Reg.										
" Excursion.										
New Freedom Reg.										
" Excursion.										
" Spcl. Excursion.										
Baltimore.	23									
Excursion Baltimore.										
York.	3866	3868	2				2	36		72
Excursion York.										
Ex. Blank.										
Blank.										

Stewart Ux

On W. Dahn &

Appendix No.21

Report of Side, Terminal and Transfer Service Performed

in connection with

Transportation of Mails by Railroads

Route No. 102740 S

I, _____, an officer of the
Stewartstown Railroad Company, conversant with the cost of performance of side, terminal and transfer service in connection with the transportation of mails by this Company, hereby certify that to the best of my knowledge and belief all such service required of this Company on Route No. 102740 S has been performed, and that no changes affecting the annual rate of compensation for this class of service under the rulings of the Post Office Department in regard thereto, other than those specifically reported to the Department, have occurred during the

quarter ended _____ 19___ , except as follows:

[Seal]   (Signature) _____
                                                                                      AUDITOR

SWORN and subscribed before me, a

this ___ day of _____ 19___

(Signature) _____

RAILWAY MAIL SERVICE CERTIFICATE

The foregoing statement is correct according to the records of this office, except as follows:

_____

Superintendent _____ Division R. M. S.

Appendix No.22

OFFICE OF

STEWARTSTOWN RAILROAD CO.

Stewartstown, Pa. Dec. 30, 1901.

To the Stockholders of the Stewartstown R. R. Co.

Your Board of Directors wish to say that on account of extraordinary heavy expense incurred by August floods, the purchase of a new Combination Car and remodeling of the Locomotive, they have decided to pass the January dividend, and in future dividends will be paid annually on July 1st, instead of semi-annually as heretofore.

The management wish to state further that they have spent considerable money during the year strengthening bridges and laying heavier ties necessary to accommodate heavier equipment.

A. G. BOWMAN,

Sec'y.

Appendix No.24

Appendix 20

Stewartstown Railroad Company.

ACCOUNTING DEPARTMENT.

C. W. Shaw, Auditor, Gen'l Freight and Pass. Agt.

OFFICE OF THE AUDITOR OF PASSENGER AND FREIGHT.

Stewartstown, Pa., Nov 13. 1906 190

PROPOSITION

1st That we sell the N.P.&.F.G.RCo, Engine No 3 at the purchase price plus rhe interest on the investment from the date of purchase to the time when full settlement has been made,

2nd That we sell the N.P.&.F.G.R.Co. 9/16 of coach no,3 for $1125.00 that all future repairs and renewals on coach or coaches used on joint traffic shall be divided on same basis or as 9is to 7,

Settlement for past serviceof pperation shall be charged at the rate of $2.50 per day this charge to cover the charge for use of coaches cost of management, less charge of auditor whose cost of service shall be based on percentage of business done, The above to cover cost of agencies,

4th

That the charge for the agent at NEW Freedom shall be divided 1/3 to the N.P.&.F.G.R. and 2/3 to the S.R.R.

N P & F G R R shall keep [illegible] up one leg of the Y viz the one leading from Eng House to [illegible] Corner +

Charge for use of [illegible] on either line 40c per [illegible]

Appendix No.25

FORM U.S.A.

SUBJECT: Rental of Pole Yard - Stewartstown, Pa.

AMERICAN TELEPHONE AND TELEGRAPH COMPANY.

ROOMS 400-402 TELEGRAPH BLDG.,

HARRISBURG, PA.

January 25, 1912.

1980-579

Mr. Thomas Fulton, Treasurer,

    Stewartstown Railroad Co.,

    Stewartstown, Pa.

Dear Sir:-

    Referring you to conversation with our Mr. Jamison on January 24th, this is to advise that we have cancelled check #4262 of January 2nd, amounting to $5.00, which has become lost, and enclose herewith check #1717 amounting to $5.00, along with another voucher, to cover the pole yard rental for the year 1912.

    Please receipt and return voucher at once, in the enclosed/stamped envelope.

        Yours truly,

        J. L. McKay,

        District Plant Chief.

        By

        Chief Clerk.

JBU/RLG

Enclosures.

Appendix No.26

NOTICE!

STEWARTSTOWN RAILROAD COMPANY

Storage Charges

On all Freight that must be housed, remaining on hand more than three working days, the following rates of storage will be made, and such charges will become a part of the regular freight charges:

Remaining on hand over three, up to ten days,   5 cents per 100 lbs

Remaining on hand over ten, up to twenty days, 10 cents per 100 lbs

Remaining on hand over twenty, up to forty days, 20 cents per 100 lbs

With 20 cents per 100 lbs for each successive 20 days or fraction thereof.

The minimum charge shall be 15 cents.

Time will be computed from 7 A. M. following arrival of shipment.

Perishable Goods held at risk of consignee.

Effective October 30, 1919

C. W. SHAW, Gen. Manager

Appendix No.27

STEWARTSTOWN RAILROAD

REPORT SUBMITTED TO THE EXECUTIVE COMMITTEE ON REVISION OF WAGES FOR 1923

POSITION	PRESENT WAGE-1922	AMT. RECOMMENDED
President	$200.00 a year	No Salary
General Manager	$500.00 a year	$600.00 a year
Superintendent	$300.00 a year	$300.00 a year
Agent-Stewartstown	$120.00 a month	$130.00 a month
Agent-Turnpike	45.00 a month	$55.00 a month
Agent-Sheffer	$15.00 a month	$15.00 a month
Agent-New Freedom	$225.00 a month	$225.00 a month
Agent-New Park	$40.00 a month	$45.00 a month
Agent-Fawn Grove	$40.00 a month	$45.00 a month
Freight Engineer	$3.45 a day	$3.60 a day
Freight Fireman	$3.25 a day	$3.45 a day
Freight Brakeman	$3.15 a day	$3.30 a day
Freight Conductor	$3.45 a day	$3.60 a day
Auditor	$125.00 a month	$135.00 a month
Treasure	$30.00 a month	$30.00 a month
G.B. Smenkie	$110.00	$110.00
Charles Paxton	$80.00	$80.00
Trackmen	$0.35 per hour	$0.40 per hour
Bus Conductor	$3.25 a day	$3.25 a day
Bus Motorman	$3.45 a day	$3.45 a day

Note:

In addition to Conductor and Motorman wages, they are to divide the Express Messenger service.

General Manger, Agent at Stewartstown and Auditor's wages are retroactive to Jan. 1,1923 New Schedule on the balance starts Jan. 1,1924

Appendix No.28

THE J.G. BRILL COMPANY

PHILADELPHIA, PA., U.S.A.

April 6, 1923.

Mr. G. W. Shaw, Gen. Mgr.,
Stewartstown Railroad Co.,
Stewartstown, Penna.

Dear Sir:-

As promised you last week, I am sending you herewith an exterior and two interior photographs of your gasoline rail car. While these no doubt will be too late for any newspaper publicity, they can be kept around the office or placed in your files.

very truly yours,

THE J. G. BRILL COMPANY

By

Special Work Dept.

CS.

Appendix No.28

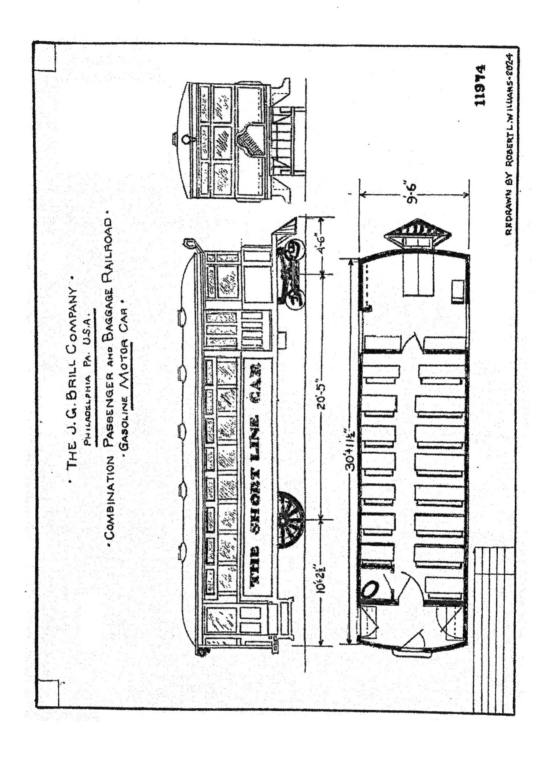

Appendix No.28

Rail Bus No.7 sitting in New Freedom, Pa.

From the collection of the Stewartstown Area Historical Society-ca. 1924

Appendix No. 28

Interior view looking toward the engineer room.
From the collection of Vincent Skinner

Interior view looking toward the baggage room.
From the collection of Vincent Skinner

Appendix No. 28

Front view of Rail Bus No.7 and its train crew at New Freedom, Pa.

From the collection of the Stewartstown Area Historical Society

Back view of Rail Bus No.7 with a passenger posing at the windows.

From the collection of the Stewartstown Area Historical Society

Appendix No. 28

Stewartstown R. R. Company
— N P & F G Div —

TIME ACCOUNT OF TRACKMEN

For half-month of _May 1_ to _May 15_ 192 3

Names	Hrs.	Cts.	$	Cts.
C. M. Paxton			40	00
Sam'l Emore	139½	35	48	83
H. Roseberry	112	35	39	20
Eli Freeman	108½	35	37	98
M. Knopp	113½	35	39	73
W. Akens	118½	35	41	48
W. Stermer	112½	35	39	38
J. Mays	92½	35	32	38
A. Kupp	92½	35	32	38
M. Grabin	118½	35	41	48
F. McLane	66	35	23	10
Geo Gibney	118½	35	41	48
Alex Roseberry	118½	35	41	48
R. Knopp	113½	35	39	73
J. Barton	20	35	7	00
			$ 545,63	

Date _May 18_ 1923

Thos. B. Fulton Supt.

Appendix No. 29
STEWARTSTOWN RAILROAD
TRAIN WRECK
(As report by the York Dispatch on September 20,1923)

"The accident happened about 4:15 o'clock at Zeigler station about a mile from Stewartstown. The car in which the injured were riding was a combination baggage and passenger open coach, the section for passengers at the time being on the rear. The car was at the end of the train.

At Zeigler station the car in some manner become uncoupled from the rest of the train. Conductor McElwain was on the car and brought it to a stop. The engine then backed for the purpose of recoupling the car, but when contact was about to be made the loose car was bumped so hard that it was given a rapid start down the grade. The conductor at the time was off the car for the purpose of making the coupling and was unable to go aboard again in time to stop the car.

The freight train was following the passenger and at the time was moving at a rapid speed. The runaway coach gained momentum and those aboard did not know what to do to stop it. Before the freight train engineer, Lewis Roseberry of Fawn Grove, could bring it to a stop he saw that a crash was inevitable and is said to have put on the brakes and jumped to save his life. He was slightly injured when he struck the ground at the side of the track;

The freight engine plowed through the passenger coach as far as partition separating the baggage section. This is about two-third the length of the car. The woman passengers who were so severely scalded and burned were thrown against the hot boiler of the engine and were unable to escape the steam coming from broken pipes. The crash jammed the whistle of the freight engine causing a long blast which attracted the attention of people in the neighborhood so that help came quickly to the injured."

The injured included Mrs. Reeling, Mrs. Anderson, Mrs. Diehl, Rose Rigdon and a traveling salesman who jumped through a window. Heaton and McElwain on the mixed were unhurt. Roseberry was injured slightly when he jumped from No.4 but fireman Herman Few, conductor William Duncan and brakeman Glen Brown escaped injury, Damage to the engine amounted to $800.00 and to the coach, $2,300.00."

INJURIES AS REPORTED BY THE NEW CASTLE HERALD, NEW CASTLE, PENNSYLVANIA-SEPTEMBER 20,1923

"Mrs. Elizabeth Anderson – Owing, York County, Pa.- cut on forehead and both wrists broken.
Miss Rose Rigdon, Stewartstown. Pa. – both hands badly burned and scalded that flesh came off. Severe scalds on chest and arms.
Mrs. Jemima Rehling, New Freedom, Pa. – scalds of both legs, and cuts and bruises.
Mrs. Samuel Diehl, Shrewsbury, Pa. – scalds both hands and injury to left hip caused by jumping from the train.
Samuel Young, Hopewell, Pa. – right leg broken
A Traveling Salesman said to be of New York, name and address not known, cut by glass when jumping through window."

Appendix No.29b

Both images are courtesy of Kurt Bell

Appendix No.29c

Both images are courtesy of Kurt Bell

Appendix No.29

Appendix No.30

Pennsylvania Railroad System

General Office Broad Street Station

J. County,
  Vice President in charge of Accounting.
J. Adams,
  Asst to Vice President in charge of Accounting.

Philadelphia June 16th, 1925.

Mr. H. E. Anstine,
      Secretary, Stewartstown R.R.Co.,
      Stewartstown, Pa.

Dear Sir:

I have your letter of the 15th instant requesting the Pennsylvania R.R.Co. to forward its proxy for use at the special meeting of the stockholders of the Stewartstown R.R.Co. to be held on Tuesday next, the 23rd instant, in favor of proposed leasing of the New Park and Fawn Grove Railroad.

Will you kindly advise me the terms of the proposed lease and such other facts as may be pertinent to the matter? My recollection is that in 1922 this Company furnished its proxy in favor of the purchase by the Stewartstown R.R.Co. of the New Park and Fawn Grove Railroad, and, I assume that said purchase was never consummated and that the lease will be resorted to in lieu thereof. Kindly advise why the purchase has not been carried out.

Yours truly,

Vice President - Accounting and
    Corporate Work.

Appendix No.31

STEWARTSTOWN RAILROAD
TIME TABLE

Connecting with the Pennsylvania Railroad at New Freedom, Pa.

Daily, except Sunday—In Effect April 26, 1926

Motor Bus No. 7	Freight No. 5	Motor Bus No. 3	Freight No. 1	STATIONS	Freight No. 2	Motor Bus No. 4	Freight No. 6	Motor Bus No. 8
P. M.	A. M.	A. M.	A. M.		A. M.	A. M.	P. M.	P. M.
3 25	10 15	7 00		Lve FAWN GROVE Arr	9 55	10 47		7 12
3 28		7 04		......KISINER......		10 44		7 06
3 30	10 30	7 12		....NEW PARK.....	9 40	10 36		7 03
3 40		7 17		...STRAWBRIDGE...		10 32		7 00
3 45	10 45	7 20		......WILEY......	9 25	10 28		6 55
3 49		7 24		.....GEMMILL.....		10 24		6 53
3 51		7 26		....MAPLE HILL....		10 21		6 50
3 53		7 29		....ANDERSON.....		10 18		6 48
3 57		7 32		....MANIFOLD.....		10 16		6 45
4 00	P. M. 12 20	7 37	6 45	.STEWARTSTOWN..	8 50	10 12	2 17	6 40
4 03	12 22	7 39		.......ZEIGLER...		10 09	2 14	6 37
4 07	12 24	7 42		.....REIMOLD.....		10 06	2 11	6 34
4 09	12 27	7 45		......ORWIG......		10 03	2 08	6 31
4 12	12 30	7 48		.....ANSTINE.....		10 01	2 06	6 29
4 16	12 34	7 52	7 05	.....SHEFFER......	8 30	9 56	2 01	6 24
4 19	12 37	7 55		......KEENEY......		9 52	1 57	6 20
4 23	12 42	8 00	7 20	....TURNPIKE.....	8 20	9 49	1 54	6 17
4 28	12 47	8 07	7 30	.. NEW FREEDOM ..	8 10	9 42	1 47	6 10
				—P. R. R.—				
5 22	1 30	9 50		........YORK.........		8 56	1 02	5 11
6 13	3 20	9 15		....BALTIMORE		7 20	P. M. 12 00	4 27
P. M.	P. M.	A. M.		Arrive Leave		A. M.	A. M.	UNION P. M.

Trains stop at way stations only when signaled or on notice to conductor. Tickets sold and Baggage checked to all points on P. R. R. between Baltimore and Harrisburg. All trains carry Mail, Express, Baggage.

Passengers wishing to leave Fawn Grove and intermediate points between morning and evening passenger trains can do so by using the freight train leaving Fawn Grove 10:15, New Park 10:30, Wiley 10:45.

P. R. R. Train due at New Freedom at 1:30 stops at Glen Rock and Smyser. This is a change, as formerly no stop was made between New Freedom and York.

C. W. SHAW,
      General Manager

THOS. B. FULTON,
            Supt.

Appendix No.32

The Pennsylvania Railroad
Eastern Region
Baltimore Division
Baltimore, Md.

November 22, 1927.

G. M. SMITH,
GENERAL AGENT & SUPERINTENDENT

Mr. C. W. Shaw,
    General Manager,
        Stewartstown Railroad Co.,
            Stewartstown, Pennsylvania.

Dear Sir:

      Referring to letters written in connection with changing plans, covering the construction of an overhead bridge on line of public road at Siegler, Pa.:

      I am sending you, herewith, six prints for your use in connection with filing plans with the Public Service Commission of the State of Pennsylvania.

            Yours truly,

            Division Engineer.

encl.

Appendix No.32

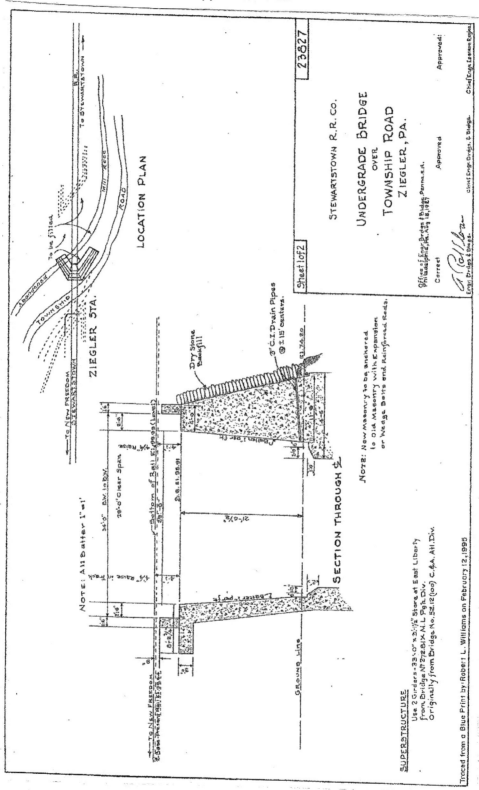

Appendix No.33

Sept 1, 1930.

Stewartstown Railroad Co.,
Stewartstown,Pa.

Gentlemen:-

Permission is hereby granted for you to mow the weeds on my property along the Railroad right of way so they may be raked together and burned thereby lessening the danger of fire spreading to fields and woodland.

Yours truly,

Jacob Orwig
Signature.

Appendix No.33b

STEWARTSTOWN RAILROAD
TIME TABLE

Connecting with the Pennsylvania Railroad at New Freedom, Pa.

Daily, except Sunday—In Effect Sept. 28, 1930

	Going West--Read down			STATIONS	Going East--Read up			
Motor Bus No. 7	Freight No. 5	Motor Bus No. 3	Freight No. 1		Freight No. 2	Motor Bus No. 4	Freight No. 6	Motor Bus No. 8
P. M.	A. M.	A. M.	A. M.		A. M.	A. M.	P. M.	P. M.
3 05	10 00	6 53		Lve FAWN GROVE Arr	9 40	10 50		7 12
3 08		6 57		KISINER		10 47		7 06
3 10	10 15	7 05		NEW PARK	9 25	10 39		7 03
3 20		7 10		STRAWBRIDGE		10 35		7 00
3 25	10 30	7 13		WILEY	9 10	10 31		6 55
3 29		7 17		GEMMILL		10 27		6 53
3 31		7 19		MAPLE HILL		10 24		6 50
3 33		7 22		ANDERSON		10 21		6 48
3 37		7 25		MANIFOLD		10 19		6 45
3 40	P.M. 12 30	7 30	6 45	STEWARTSTOWN	8 35	10 15	2 20	6 40
3 43	12 32	7 32		ZEIGLER		10 12	2 17	6 37
3 47	12 34	7 35		REIMOLD		10 09	2 14	6 34
3 49	12 37	7 38		ORWIG		10 07	2 11	6 31
3 52	12 40	7 41		ANSTINE		10 04	2 09	6 29
3 56	12 44	7 45	7 05	SHEFFER	8 15	9 59	2 04	6 24
3 59	12 47	7 48		KEENEY		9 55	2 00	6 20
4 03	12 52	7 53	7 20	TURNPIKE	8 05	9 52	1 57	6 17
4 05	12 57	8 00	7 30	NEW FREEDOM	7 55	9 45	1 50	6 10
				P. R. R.				
5 08	3 28	10 00		YORK		8 44	1 00 P. M.	4 57
5 35		9 05		BALTIMORE		7 35		4 52
P. M.	P. M.	A. M.		Arrive Leave		A. M.		UNION P. M.

Trains stop at way stations only when signaled or on notice to conductor. Tickets sold and Baggage checked to all points on P. R. R. between Baltimore and Harrisburg. All trains carry Mail, Express and Baggage.

Passengers wishing to leave Fawn Grove and intermediate points between morning and evening passenger trains can do so by using the freight train leaving Fawn Grove 10:00, New Park 10:15, Wiley 10:30.

Railway Express Agency, Inc., operates over this line.

C. W. SHAW,
General Manager

THOS. B. FULTON,
Supt.

September 1930 timetable courtesy of William Ward

Appendix No.34

Specification for Locomotive Unit No. 6

Operated by _The Stewartstown Railroad_ Company

Built by _Fate-Root-Heath Co._ at _Plymouth Ohio_ Date _December 19th_, 19_29_
Builder's number _3984_ Propelled by _Gasoline Engine_
Gauge of wheels _56½"_
Kind and number of current collectors _None_
Trolley wire or third rail voltage _None_
Number, make, and type of motors _None_ Voltage _None_
Make and type of control equipment _Fate-Root-Heath Co._ Control circuit voltage _None_
Make and type of internal combustion engine _Le Roi RXIS 6 cyl. Gasoline engine_
Kind of air brake _Westinghouse Straight & Automatic A.M.E._
(Give make, type, and schedule number)
Number, make, and type of air compressor _One Le Roi built in single cyl. direct driven_
Main air reservoir pressure _110#_ Train line pressure _70#_
Make and type of lightning arrester _None_
Does unit carry steam boiler? _No_
Total weight, working order _50,000_ pounds, weight on driving wheels _50,000_ pounds,
weight on trucks _None_ pounds.
Maximum tractive effort _20,192# @ 2.6 M.P.H._

1'-6" High   33"dia. Wheels
"-7" Wide   56½" ga.
13½" W.B.   34½" rail to ℄ of coupler
7'-0" length over bumpers
:1'-0" coupled length

Approved _Harry J. Johnson_
Title _First Chief Engr._

Appendix No.34b

"Little Mo" is approaching Five Forks Road between Anstine and Reimold on the Stewartstown RR, photo by Jim Shaw, K.R. Bell Collection

Appendix No.35

[2] THIS SHIPPING ORDER

(Uniform Domestic Straight Bill of Lading, adopted by carriers in Official, Southern, Western and Illinois Classification territories March 15, 1922, as amended August 1, 1930, and June 15, 1941.)

THE STEWARTSTOWN RAILROAD COMPANY

RECEIVE, subject to the classifications and tariffs in effect on the date of the issue of this Shipping Order,

At Stewartstown, Pa., _____ 194__ From Stewartstown Furniture Company,

Shipper's No. _____
Agent's No. _____

Consigned to _____

(Mail or street address of consignee—For purposes of notification only.)

Destination _____ State of _____ County of _____

Route _____

Delivering Carrier _____ Car Initial _____ Car No. _____

No. Pkgs.	DESCRIPTION OF ARTICLES MARKS AND EXCEPTIONS	WEIGHT	RATE		No. Pkgs.	DESCRIPTION OF ARTICLES MARKS AND EXCEPTIONS	WEIGHT	RATE
	Wd. Crt. Carton DRESSERS					Wd. Crt. Carton CHAIRS, SU.		
	Wd. Crt. Carton DRESSER TOILETS					Wd. Crt. Carton BED ENDS		
	Wd. Crt. Carton CHIFFONIERS					Wd. Crt. Carton BED RAILS		
	Wd. Crt. Carton CHIFFONIERE TOILETS					Wd. Crt. Carton DESKS		
	Wd. Crt. Carton CHIFFOROBETTES					Wd. Crt. Carton TABLES, SU. WD.		
	Wd. Crt. Carton DRESSORS					Wd. Crt. Carton BOOKCASES, SU.		
	Wd. Crt. Carton VANITIES					Wd. Crt. Carton STOOLS, SU. WOEN		
	Wd. Crt. Carton VANITY TOILETS					Wd. Crt. Carton SIDE STANDS,AL.WOEN		

Subject to Section 7 of Conditions, if this shipment is to be delivered to the consignee without recourse on the consignor, the consignor shall sign the following statement:

The carrier shall not make delivery of this shipment without payment of freight and all other lawful charges.

_____ (Signature of consignor.)

If charges are to be prepaid, write or stamp here, "To be Prepaid."

Received $_____ to apply in prepayment of the charges on the property described hereon.

Agent or Cashier.

Per _____ (The signature here acknowledges only the amount prepaid.)

Charges Advanced:

$_____

SHIPPER LOAD AND COUNT — R. R. CO. NOT RESPONSIBLE NO. ARTICLES

**If the shipment moves between two ports by a carrier by water, the bill of lading shall state whether it is "carrier's or shipper's weight."

Note—Where the rate is dependent on value, shippers are required to state specifically in writing the agreed or declared value of the property.

The agreed or declared value of the property is hereby specifically stated by the shipper to be not exceeding _____ per _____

Stewartstown Furniture Company, Shipper, Per _____

Agent _____

Per _____

Permanent postoffice address of shipper _____

THE FIBRE BOXES used for this shipment conform to the specifications set forth in the box maker's certificate thereon, and all other requirements of Rule 41 of the Consolidated Freight Classification.

Twenty=Fourth Annual Report

of the

Stewartstown Railroad Co.

Stewartstown, Pa., September 1st, 1909.

To The Stockholders of the Stewartstown Railroad Co.

Your Directors respectfully submit the following Report of the Operation of the Company for the year ending June 30, 1909.

RECEIPTS.		EXPENDITURES.	
Freight	$ 17,392 61	Repairs of Roadway	$2,794 60
Passengers	5,483 26	Rails and spikes	468 41
U. S. Mail	407 18	New Ties	1,344 50
Adams Express	524 55	Repairs on buildings	181 31
Miscellaneous	1,216 15	Other expense on track	127 90
		Repairs on locomotive	2,843 43
Total	$25,023 75	Repairs on cars	76 66
Operating Expenses	17,112 29	Repairs on tools, etc	27 82
		Other expense on equipment	26 71
Net earnings	7,911 46	Engineer and Fireman	1,372 16
Balance cash on hand, June 30, 1908	8,126 48	Coal for locomotive	2,380 75
		Oil and waste	230 11
Total	16,037 94	Conductor and Brakesman	1,036 88
From which was paid 5 per cent dividend	3,500 00	Station agents	1,664 35
		Station Supplies	331 98
Balance cash on hand	$12,537 94	Per Diem charges	686 97
		Loss and damage	142 48
		Other expense	520 78
		Salary officers	821 95
		General expense	34 50
			$17,112 29

GENERAL BALANCE SHEET.

Cost of road and buildings	$96,168 35	Stock issued	$70,000 00
Cost of equipment	16,588 49	Profit and Loss	56,648 93
Cost of real estate	353 16		
Material on hand	1,000 00		
Cash on hand	12,537 94		
	$126,648 93		126,648 93

CLASSIFICATION OF FREIGHT.

	TONS.		TONS.
Grain	2,615	Oil	70
Flour	55	Sugar	78
Feed	540	Iron and machinery	799
Hay	4,859	Fertilizers	5189
Fruit and Vegetables	3,177	Brick and Lime	3209
Live Stock	234	Merchandise	3046
Anthracite coal	1,858		
Bituminous coal	3,885	Total tons freight	33,252
Lumber	3,158		
Tobacco	480	Total number passengers	39,219

We again commend the efficiency of the employees in conducting the business of the Company another year without accident or injury to passengers or damage to property.

C. W. SHAW, AUDITOR.   **J. W. ANDERSON, PRESIDENT.**

ABOUT THE AUTHORS

Robert L. Williams was a project engineer for the Maryland State Highway Administration before retiring. The native of Washington, DC, graduated from Towson State University with a degree in Civil/Environmental Engineering. As a resident of Lutherville, Maryland, Williams' enthusiasm and love for railroad history started by taking a walk down Seminary Avenue and discovering a charming train station under renovation by the owner.

While working for Amtrak, Mr. Williams had the opportunity to retrieve and save the Pennsylvania Railroad (Baltimore Division) archives that were stored at Penn Station in Baltimore City from being lost forever by digging in the dumpster. Since then, Williams has co-authored six books on various railroad histories, written numerous articles, and produced maps and drawings for publication, Williams is also noted as a railroad historian and has given many lectures on the history of the Northern Central Railway and the Pennsylvania Railroad.

He is the author or co-author of several previous books, including *The Green Spring Branch*; *The Northern Central Railway (Images of Rail series)*; *The Baltimore & Potomac Railroad: A Pictorial History*; *This Trying Hour: The Philadelphia, Wilmington & Baltimore Railroad in the Civil War*; *The Northern Central Railway and Heritage Rail Trail Guidebook: Mason-Dixon Sites*; and *The Western Maryland Railroad and Its Civil War Legacy* (the latter three books with Scott L. Mingus, Sr.). He has also penned two books for the Maryland & Pennsylvania Railroad Historical Society.

Scott L. Mingus is a retired scientist and executive in the global specialty paper industry. The Ohio native graduated from Miami University in 1978 with a B.S. in paper science and engineering. He was part of the research team that developed the first commercially successful self-adhesive U.S. postage stamps, and he was a pioneer in the early development of bar code labels. He has written more than 35 Civil War and Underground Railroad books and numerous articles for *Gettysburg Magazine* and other historical journals. He has appeared on C-SPAN, C-SPAN3, PBS, PCN, and other TV networks. Mingus writes the Cannonball blog on the Civil War history of York County, PA, where he and his wife Debi live. He also has written six scenario books for miniature wargaming and was elected to the hobby's prestigious Legion of Honor.

Mingus received lifetime achievement awards from the York County History Center and the Camp Curtin Historical Society for his many contributions to local Civil War history. His biography of William "Extra Billy" Smith won two major awards for Confederate military history and was nominated for several others. The Gettysburg Civil War Round Table presented Mingus and co-author Eric Wittenberg with the 2023 Bachelder-Coddington Award for the best new book on the Gettysburg Campaign, *If We Are Striking for Pennsylvania*.

Made in the USA
Columbia, SC
17 December 2024

49780478R00200